THE HAWKINS DYNASTY

I. Sir John Hawkins. The 'Chatham' Portrait, now at the
National Maritime Museum

The Hawkins Dynasty

∽∽∽

THREE GENERATIONS OF A TUDOR FAMILY

BY

MICHAEL LEWIS

C.B.E., Litt.D., F.S.A., F.R.Hist.S.
Late Professor of History, R.N. College, Greenwich
President of the Society for Nautical Research

London
GEORGE ALLEN AND UNWIN LTD
RUSKIN HOUSE   MUSEUM STREET

FIRST PUBLISHED IN 1969

© *George Allen & Unwin Ltd 1969*
SBN 04 923051 4

PRINTED IN GREAT BRITAIN
in 11 *on* 12 *pt Bell*
BY W & J MACKAY & CO LTD, CHATHAM

ACKNOWLEDGMENTS

For permission to include the following illustrations I am indebted to:

The Trustees and the Director of the British, Museum, for part of the Defence Map of Plymouth in the Cotton MSS.

The Trustees and the Director of the National Maritime Museum, for the Frontispiece—the 'Chatham' portrait of Sir John Hawkins.

The Mayor and Corporation of Plymouth for the portraits of Sir John Hawkins and Sir Francis Drake in their possession.

Also, as ever, I am bound most gratefully to acknowledge the generous help given to me, in reading the MSS. and in criticizing it, by my dear friend Mr Richard Ollard of Messrs Collins, and my son, Dr M. J. T. Lewis of Hull University. These two have fallen into the habit of coming to my assistance, and I cannot adequately express how much I have come to rely upon their judgment as well as upon their kindness in once more giving so freely of their time and the benefit of their erudition.

I also owe a real debt of gratitude to Mr Crispin Gill, of the *Western Morning News*, for his great kindness in showing me over the locality of Plymouth.

CONTENTS

∽∿∽

ILLUSTRATIONS

∽∾∽

Introductory

PLYMOUTH is a fair city, lying in a lovely setting of green slopes
and blue seas: and its burgesses have civic pride in their city,
because it has a great past. It is true that Time—and brutal
War—have levelled much of the city, so that new squares, new
streets now take the place of the old ones. Yet civic pride lives
on, and the great days of old are not forgotten.

Or are they? One sometimes wonders! In the time of the first
Elizabeth, when the Town became the foremost port of the West
Country, there were two names which were great not only in
Devon but in all England too. They were 'Drake' and 'Hawkins'
—the names of England's incomparable seamen, and the glory
and pride of Plymouth.

What now? The newcomer to the city will find memorials to
Sir Francis Drake a-plenty. His island lies just off shore to the
south, H.M.S. *Drake* is still the name of the Royal Naval
Barracks; on the Hoe stands a full-size and exciting statue of
him; and up and down the streets are humbler signs of him in the
shape of inns and public houses.

But what of Hawkins? Where is 'Hawkins Square', or even
'Hawkins Street'? Where stands his statue, or even a bust of
him? Where is there so much as a lowly pub named after him?
The newcomer will not find them—not even a 'Hawkins Mews'
or a humble 'Hawkins Arms'. In local landmarks, it would seem,
the name is utterly forgotten, as though it never were: in Plymouth too of all places, where once the family, for three consecu-
tive generations, was the best-known and the wealthiest in the
town, supplying it with all sorts of officials, from Mayor downwards, filling its wharves with shipping and its warehouses with
merchandise from all the Seven Seas, representing it in Parliament and in the counsels of the great.

Why not, then, somewhere in the city, a statue (or at least a bust) to the great Sir John, and perhaps some tangible memorial to her 'Complete Seaman', Sir Richard; or to her Armada-year Mayor, William, not to mention something to commemorate the first merchant who took his own ship, the *Paul*, to trade in Brazil, or the first Englishman to represent his Sovereign at the court of the Great Mogul?

If this book does nothing else, perhaps it may help to remedy this apparently ungrateful omission, so that no longer may the name of one of her outstanding families be utterly lost to the city of Plymouth.

CHAPTER I

The Hawkins Family

∾∾∾

In their day they spelt their name 'Hawkyns', all of them. But here we use the spelling 'Hawkins' because, now, it would be almost an affectation to do otherwise.

The Plymouth Hawkinses were almost certainly no relation to the 'older' family of that name residing at Nash Court in the County of Kent, though Burke, in *Landed Gentry*, derives them from that line. For, when the Plymouth people became names to conjure with, there were not wanting 'fans' who were bent on linking up a new and rising family with an old and long-established one. But we can ignore them, since the historical Hawkinses of Plymouth, as opposed to hypothetical or fictitious ones, really emerge only at one generation above the first of the 'Big Five' that this book is about. The earliest one's name was John, a fairly well-to-do man who, in the course of his life, came south to Plymouth from Tavistock, a town some few miles to the north. This John of Tavistock was probably a merchant, enjoying the 'freedom' of Plymouth; and, again probably, before he died he was a burgess of that town.

One suspects also, though one cannot prove it, that as a person he was already 'on the rise'. He had married, for instance, rather above himself, which is often a pointer to an improvement in social status. He himself was obviously of merchant standing—a member, one might almost say, of the most important class in fifteenth-century England: shrewd businessmen who were already appearing as leaders in the new towns that were springing up all over the country, and at a time when the towns were already growing in importance *vis-à-vis* the more rural areas. His wife, however, was Joan, daughter and coheiress of one William Amadas of Launceston, who had been Serjeant-at-Law

in the court of the King of England (probably Edward IV): not
an outstandingly great post, of course, but one which (in addition to the Arms he bore) marked him out as 'county'. But the
social gulf between husband and wife, though real enough at that
time, would not perhaps be very great or very startling, especially if he were fairly well-to-do and Amadas—like so many
country gentlemen—rather hard-up. For already the astute, up-
and-coming burgesses of the new towns were not unwilling to
invest some of their newly-won profits upon the fingers, the
backs and the necks of their brides, whose parents had graciously
permitted the espousals in order to 'tide them over until good
times appeared again'. For here England differed markedly from
the Continent. Unlike Frenchmen or Spaniards of their day, the
islanders could always rise or fall in the social scale, though they
did so a good deal less often then than they do today. And what
advanced the new townsman was moral worth and commercial
ability, combined with ambition and—once money really began
to talk as it did under the Tudors—affluence. Such were, in all
probability, some of the qualities possessed by John of Tavistock,
and by all his descendants after him.

But John is not our target. *Our* task is to look at the five great
Hawkinses who followed him—the true 'Hawkins Dynasty', of
which John's son William was the first. As to christian names,
there is ample room for confusion, if only because no less than
three of them were christened William. There *has* been confusion too!

Here the five of them are designated as follows:

(1) William the Eldest, here called WILLIAM I.
(2) His elder son, here called WILLIAM II.
(3) His younger son, the most illustrious of them all, JOHN.
(4) John's only son (called by his contemporaries The Compleat Seaman)—RICHARD.
(5) William II's eldest son, distinguished here as WILLIAM
III.

The order in which the names are set down here is that in
which they were born, and it is the order in which they will be
treated here. The story is mainly a Tudor one, because William I
came into the world very soon after the first Tudor seized the
throne, and his major impact upon events fell in the reign of

Plymouth in the early
1540s. From the defence
map in Cotton MSS. Aug. I.
i. 38, at the British Museum

(1) (1a)

III. Old Plymouth: (1) No. 32 New Street; front and back views

(2) Site of Hawkins Wharf

æ 74   An Dñi 1596.

IV. Portrait of an old man (? William Hawkins II). From the
Lord Mayor's Parlour, Plymouth

ÆTATIS SVÆ LVIII
Ano Dni 1591

V. Sir John Hawkins. From a portrait now in the possession of
the City of Plymouth at Buckland Abbey

Henry VIII: William II and his brother Sir John are both purely
Tudor figures too, both born in Henry VIII's reign, and both of
them dead before Queen Elizabeth died. The main events of
Richard's life also took place in Elizabeth's reign, though he
survived into the anti-climax of the first Stuart's time. William
III was also an Elizabethan seaman though the most important
events of his career happened under James I.

In genealogical form they look like this, the five main ones
shown in capitals, the rest in small letters:

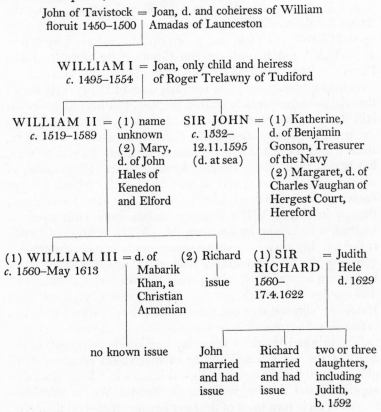

John of Tavistock = Joan, d. and coheiress of William
floruit 1450–1500 | Amadas of Launceston

WILLIAM I = Joan, only child and heiress
c. 1495–1554 | of Roger Trelawny of Tudiford

WILLIAM II = (1) name   SIR JOHN = (1) Katherine,
c. 1519–1589 | unknown   c. 1532– | d. of Benjamin
(2) Mary,   12.11.1595   Gonson, Treasurer
d. of John   (d. at sea)   of the Navy
Hales of   (2) Margaret, d. of
Kenedon   Charles Vaughan of
and Elford   Hergest Court,
Hereford

(1) WILLIAM III = d. of   (2) Richard   (1) SIR = Judith
c. 1560–May 1613 | Mabarik | RICHARD | Hele
Khan, a   issue   1560–   d. 1629
Christian   17.4.1622
Armenian

no known issue   John   Richard   two or three
married   married   daughters,
and had   and had   including
issue   issue   Judith,
b. 1592

a. THE HOME-TOWN

In the early days when John the Elder first came from Tavistock,
the home-town of the Hawkinses was not much like the Plymouth

of his grandsons William II and Sir John—and, of course, still less like the Plymouth of the mid-twentieth century. Up to a few years before John the Elder's birth it had not been a borough at all, but a very small township and an even smaller port. But in 1439–40 it had been incorporated by an act of Parliament in Henry VI's reign when it achieved the status of a mayor and corporation of its own.

The Mayor and Commonalty were 'to hold the Borough of the King by 40 shillings paid yearly into the Exchequer', and were committed to 'building stone walls and defences about the Town for defence'. The Mayor was to be 'chosen every year upon St Lambert's Day, and sworn on Michaelmas Day before 11 o'clock:' and the Mayor and Commonalty were 'to make Burgesses (or Freemen) to help them govern the Town'.

A map probably drawn in the early days of Henry VIII shows that the town has already started to grow. But the old nucleus is still there. It lies round Sutton Pool: indeed, in *very* early days the town itself was often called Sutton. Stonehouse was there, though still separated from Plymouth by fields. So was Saltash, but it was then called, simply, Aysshe. Mount Edgecombe, of course, was there too, and so was St Nicholas Island, not yet known as Drake's Island. Lastly the Hoe (or How) was there, though in Henry VIII's time no houses were built upon it. Instead, it had along its southern side the line of original fortifications, facing seawards, with a square castle at their eastern end guarding the narrow entrance from the Cattwater to the inner harbour of Sutton Pool, with a chain thrown across the channel. The earliest Plymouth (or Sutton) in those days, says Miss Hawkins, 'climbed up from Sutton Pool, in appearance and size, rather like Dartmouth is now'.[1]

The original Hawkins home lay in Kinterbury Street, in the heart of the old town. The line of that street remained until quite recently, although its original houses had long since disappeared; and the Luftwaffe in the Second World War destroyed in their turn most of the later houses erected on their site, together with most of the street itself. So Plymouth now possesses few if any of those princely mansions in one of which the great family once resided. A better chance of reconstructing

[1] *Plymouth Armada Heroes*, p. 1.

them now, perhaps, would be to visit an old seaport town like King's Lynn, where a number of the gracious residences of the old burgesses still survive. These are roomy places, with very real comforts, and they give a good idea how the more solid citizens lived.

In Plymouth, it is true, there survive, particularly in the area between Sutton Pool and where Kinterbury Street once ran, several Tudor residences, notably in one of the oldest thorough-fares in the town—now characteristically called New Street. But there is no certain evidence that any of the Hawkinses ever dwelt in any of them. Indeed the chances are that they did not, since they were probably occupied by a rather lowlier class of burgess —say the Hawkins captains. The 'dynasty', having made their money and established their position in the town at least as early as the time of William I, would live in the more commodious and stately mansions which had been erected in the 'fashionable' quarter further up the hill.

On the other hand, though the name has not survived, the site of the Hawkins Wharf can still be deduced with considerable accuracy. It lay in the very innermost recesses of Sutton Pool, where an arm of the harbour turned through a right angle to the left, giving a maximum of shelter to all shipping. Parts of the warehouses which still stand in that area may contain original Tudor masonry, and so may actually be survivors of John Hawkins's installations. In those days, before the slope between Kinterbury Street and Sutton Pool had been built over, the owners of the original houses in that street would have had an uninterrupted view down to the Hawkins Wharf on the Pool.

Later, the family spread outwards from its earliest home. By the will of Sir John, proved in 1596, he leaves what seems a goodly heritage, though by then, probably, the original Kinterbury house had passed to the elder brother William and his heirs. His total property in the town, however, is still very extensive. It is described in three separate articles:

(1) To my son (Richard) . . . the moiety of the house with the appur-tenances and the garden, stables, cellars, the pallace, wharf and forge-house upon the saide wharf in Plymouth that he now occupieth.
(2) To my nephew (also Richard, eldest son of William II's second wife) . . . the moiety of the dwelling house with the appurtenances

19

in Plymouth . . . and the moiety of the garden, the tower house to it, the shop, the brue house (brew-house), the backe house (bake-house), the sellers upon the wharfe before the house, the moietie of the Crane; and my parte of the gardeine and Orcharde in the Howe Lane;[1] and my moitie of the stable.

(3) All the rest of my lands in Plymouth I bequeath to my son Richard Hawkins and his heirs male.

The first and second appear to be complete, rounded-off estates. Perhaps the second was the original property now returned to William II's family. The first is probably the estate assembled by Sir John himself, and so left to his son. The third (which somehow sounds extensive) might consist of almost anything.

One name—that of William III, William II's first-born of all —is nearly ignored. He receives none of his uncle's lands, and only one share of the one-fifth part of Sir John's 'ventures outstanding at the time of my death', which share he has in common with all his brothers, half-brothers, sisters and half-sisters. But right at the end, among the bequests, he *is* mentioned at last by name:

> To every child which William Hawkins, the eldest son of my said brother, shall have living at the time of my decease, £100.

It would be interesting to know why this William III received such austere treatment, not only from Sir John, from whom perhaps he might not expect very much, but also from his own father, William II. The latter's will is a much briefer affair than John's. Nor is it of much use if we would assess the total Hawkins properties in Plymouth, because he does not specify them at all. He simply leaves 'all my lands to my wife Marie for life', with the remainder to Richard, the eldest son of the second family. William III, however, is not entirely forgotten: he has a comparatively beggarly annuity of ' £40 a year out of my lands in Plymouth'. It looks as though the second wife had made William II rather forgetful of the claims of his first family: William III and two girls. It was, perhaps a case of 'out of sight out of mind', because William III had left the paternal roof several years before the Will was made; and, when it *was* drawn

---

[1] Probably the lane leading out on to the Hoe, to which the town was now extending: but there was a 'Howe Street' more in the heart of the town.

up, he was a grown man in his late twenties: but his half-brother
Richard was still a child of only ten. William III's own sisters
too had already married and left home.

The Hawkins fortunes suffered several serious blows during
the 1590s, for Richard was captured by the Spaniards in 1594,
and Sir John died at sea in 1595. William II was already dead
(1589), leaving, save for William III, only quite young children: and even William III had somehow left the Hawkins fold.
So, until 1602 when Richard returned to England, there were no
adults of the family in the town. Then, some years later, Richard
himself gave up residing there and bought an estate at Slapton,
some sixteen miles to the east. At that time, probably, he disposed of most of his Plymouth property. But he did not sever *all*
connection with the place: for in his will, dated 1622, he left to
Judith his wife,

> all my other said lands, tenements, cottages and hereditaments, with
> th' app'tences lyinge and being in or about Plymouth in the County
> of Devon.

It was clearly a mere shadow of what the family had held in its
great days. The prolonged absence of both John and Richard had
played havoc with the estates, not to mention the fact that
Richard and William III had both ceased to be true 'merchants'
—the former having become in effect a fighting servant of the
Crown and the latter almost a diplomatic one.

Richard's widow Judith passed on the remains of his Plymouth
holdings to their son, a younger John. But he sold them in
1637–8, when his branch of the family ceased to hold any land
there.

This last John, by the way, had also been born in the old town
in 1604, in the parish of St Andrew's, before Sir Richard left for
Slapton. He was buried, when *his* time came in 1678, at Slapton,
not Plymouth. What happened to William II's Plymouth patrimony does not appear. Mary Hawkins carries down his line for
two more generations, but then infers that the Hawkins name
died out there, though the female line continued under the
names of Newton and Calmady.

Being unwilling to join the Plymouth Hawkinses to any
known 'landed' families, into what Tudor class are we to put

them? The answer is a comparatively simple one. They needed no bolstering up by deriving them from any 'old' family. They have made their own grade. They belonged to what was, in a very real sense, the newest and most significant class in six-teenth-century England, as that country emerged on to the modern stage. They were the denizens of the 'new towns', and for the most part the aristocracy of them.

There had been, however, wealthy merchants dwelling in London and elsewhere for many centuries before the sixteenth. Therefore there was nothing startlingly new about just being a merchant. They were also, often, shipowners; and again there was nothing particularly new about being a merchant who owned ships, because for a very long time many of them had been accustomed to acquire their stocks of merchandise, or part of them, from overseas. There were also, of course, seamen in England, as there had been for ages untold. But up till now the merchants, though often shipowners, had seldom if ever gone to sea themselves.

Here then was a really new thing about the Hawkinses and their contemporaries. They began, *for the first time*, to take their own ships to sea, and so to become at one and the same time merchants and seamen. And this *was* new—to combine the trade of merchant with that of seaman, hitherto an entirely different one. Moreover this great novelty was rapidly transforming the whole country.

Naturally it paid handsome dividends, if only because it is axiomatic that no one looks after one's own business quite so well as one does oneself! Yet it took some doing, not only because the handling of ships was an entirely different proposi-tion, with a totally different technique, from handling goods for sale; but also because it chanced that, in the world as it then existed, the profession of seaman was socially a good deal lower than the profession of buying and selling goods—because, of course, in those rough days, shiphandling was a good deal less comfortable, a good deal more unpleasant than the handling of commodities for sale.

Again, this new race of sea-going merchants were true mer-chants. Their *raison d'être* was to collect their wares and then to sell them. This must always be remembered. There was in them very little of the exploring urge—only enough to impel them to find new markets—little that was in its origin either scientific or geographic. Some altruists—Columbus himself was the outstanding example—did exist in that same age, and as pioneers they helped greatly to transform it. But there was little that was starry-eyed about the shipowning merchants who took their own ships to sea, and whose motives were, in the first place, essentially down to earth. Yet they were good merchants too, with the talent and imagination to secure a good turnover for their money. What is more, they were endowed with other gifts besides the ability simply to make money. Many of them—and all the best of them—looked well beyond their own selfish interests, and worked for the good of the community to which they belonged. In a word, they possessed patriotism, both local and country-wide. And, in England anyway, this was the class of man who, more than any other, made England great and powerful.

The whole Hawkins clan belonged to this class in varying degrees. The first three of them were all skilled merchants, making their own fortune and that of their families. But they were more than this: all loved intensely their own home town and their own home shire. But also—and it was this that made them outstanding in their own age—all had a very real love of their country, and a very real loyalty to that country's head, whoever it might be. All had, in fact, that call to service—service to their town, their county, their Monarch and *England*.

All these Hawkinses—to whom now we must add the last two who were no longer strictly merchants—conform to a common type. Yet in detail they were essentially dissimilar. Thus William I, one of the very earliest English merchant shipowners to take his own ship to sea, was probably evenly composed of 'merchant' and 'seaman'. His eldest son, William II, though he did use the sea, was probably predominantly 'merchant', with a very strong bias towards his home town. The younger son, Sir John, was again both 'merchant' and 'seaman', perhaps about equally, but also (being by a wide margin the greatest of the whole clan) a particularly loyal servant to his Sovereign, and a big public figure in the England of his day, serving Queen Elizabeth in all sorts of capacities—as, for example, administrator and civil servant, as sea-captain, admiral, general and counsellor. Next, Richard was, perhaps, mainly sea-man, and (his house's fortunes already established) less a mer-chant than a sailor, though he too served his Queen—and later (when allowed) his King—as a sea-captain and most effective sea-leader. The last of the five—William III—seems never to have made a fortune of any kind, not being strictly a merchant at all. Yet he too served the Crown faithfully at sea, becoming in the end, and possibly even by chance, one of England's first 'accredited agents' (if one may be forgiven the anachronism), and so one of the forerunners of the British Empire.

The earliest Hawkins was, in his young days and in his day-to-day life, a distinctly rough diamond, without many of the refine-ments which gradually came with a gradually-growing civiliza-tion. He would not be at all 'well-read'; nor would he have had much aptitude, or even chance, for reading. As a boy he doubtless received rather a crude education in a Plymouth school or monas-tery, but it would not probably have provided him with more than a rudimentary knowledge of the 'three R's'. As he could certainly write, he could certainly read too, but it is doubtful whether he could speak, or understand, that be-all and end-all of Tudor education—Latin. On the other hand, in order to be a successful business man, he must have mastered the common rules of arithmetic and cyphering; and also the elements of geo-metry, in order to make him a competent navigator.

His house, to start with, would be rough and ready, with strictly utilitarian furniture and household utensils, solid but of plain oak. But even during his life, and certainly in that of his sons and grandsons, much of the roughness and simplicity would disappear. Slowly education and culture were seeping into every-day life, especially where the wheels were being greased by the presence of comparative wealth, as doubtless was the case in the Hawkins home. Thus unquestionably William II and John would be more conformable to the fashion of their day than William I, better dressed, better educated, better spoken. And Sir Richard and William III would doubtless, in all these superficial respects, be superior to William II and Sir John.

How fascinating to be vouchsafed a glimpse of them as they

were in real life! This of course may never be, though a fairly
modern attempt to catch a likeness of two of them is made in
that pleasant piece of fiction *Westward Ho!* Charles Kingsley,
often successful as a novelist in presenting impressionist sketches
of his subjects, tries his hand on Sir John and Sir Richard.

The scene, we recall, is on Plymouth Hoe, where the naval
worthies of England are awaiting the appearance of the Spanish
Armada.

> A burly grizzled elder, in greasy sea-stained garments contrasting
> oddly with the huge gold chain about the neck, waddles up, as if he
> had been born and had lived ever since in a gale of wind at sea. The
> upper half of his sharp, dogged visage seems of brick-red leather, the
> lower of badger's fur; and he claps Drake on the back and, with a
> broad Devon twang, shouts, 'Be you a-coming to drink your wine,
> Francis Drake, or be you not?'

Certainly a man stands out. The only pity is that it is essentially
the wrong man! For this purports to be John; and John was
patently not like this at all. Had it been meant for William the
Elder it might have been nearer the truth (if still grossly exaggerated), because it was William I, and not John who had
founded the family fortunes; who brought the money into the
family, being himself what we used to call a self-made man.
Moreover it is sad, but it is probably true, that to many folk
Kingsley's description—or caricature—remains the image of the
man that exists in their minds.

They are wrong, of course; very badly out indeed, because
John was of the second (if not the third) generation of wealth,
of prosperity and, beyond all doubt, of *savoir faire* born of
consorting with the great and the gentle. The age, for all its
gradual emancipation from the toils of 'class', was still class-
conscious to a degree which would seem unbelievable to the
mid-twentieth century. So, though very very far removed from
the tarry-breeked individual of Kingsley's imagination, John was
not even yet accepted as a 'gentleman', as Howard of Effingham
was accepted, or even Grenville or Raleigh. But this, probably,
was more a matter of social convention than of ungentle 'broadness' in the outer man. Take that 'greasy sea-stained garment'.
It will not do. When John Hawkins went to sea, we learn, he was
known to take *fifty* changes of raiment with him; to dine in state

in his own cabin off silver and even gold plate, and to the accompaniment of his own choice orchestra. Or take that broad Devon twang. Well, we must own, sadly, that we shall never hear any Tudor Hawkins talking 'in the flesh'; and it would be rash to assert that no Devonshire dialect ever slipped from John's lips, especially when he was excited. It almost certainly did: for 'local' pronunciations were still due to hold their own for some centuries, even up to the coming of the BBC and the so-called Oxford accent. Even the much more cultured Raleigh is said to have retained throughout his life the broad Devon 'burr', though probably not the characteristics of Devon grammar, syntax and phrasing. But this cannot allow us to suppose that John, less gentle and less 'literary' than Raleigh though he was, could have moved for half his lifetime in polite, even in court, circles and still retained such broadness, even if he ever had it. No, John Hawkins certainly dressed, wrote and (save perhaps for mere accent) spoke like an Elizabethan gentleman, even if many of the gentry were not prepared to admit him to perfect and equal intimacy.

It follows from this that, if the Hawkins family is running true to form, William I will be a good deal less sophisticated than John; less readily accepted in polite circles: but that Richard will be the opposite—more acceptable, more sophisticated. And so it obviously is. William I is the provincial burgher who has made good; a great man in his own town, but scarcely even upon visiting terms with the 'aristocracy'. John, a 'figure' in any company, can hold his own anywhere, even in the outward trappings of gentility. But Richard, of the third generation, is clearly much more the man about town—London Town too: yes, and about court. He is accepted as gentle, even in those fastidious times, and by that still class-conscious caste, the nobility and gentry. For Sir Richard was unquestionably a well-educated, cultured person, compared even with his father. A single illustration will serve to show how the wind was blowing. When, on his travels, Richard had occasion to communicate with the Spaniards, knowing no Spanish he did his communicating in Latin. It is very doubtful whether John could have done this, and virtually certain that William could not.

But now let us see how Kingsley deals with the third generation. (Sir John is fulminating against the degenerate croakers who still exist in the England of the Armada Year.)

'Marry come up, what says Scripture?—"He that is fearful and faint-hearted among you, let him go and—" What? Son Dick there! Tha'rt pious and read'st thy Bible. What's that text? A mighty fine one it is too."

' "He that is fearful among you," quoth the Complete Seaman, "let him go back." '

And then he takes up his father's quarrel with a certain Captain Merryweather, who is the cause of Sir John's outburst, and who has challenged the older man to fight.

'Captain Merryweather, as my Father's command, as well as his years, forbid him answering your challenge, I shall repute it an honour to entertain his quarrel myself—place, time and weapons being at your choice.'

'Well spoken, son Dick,' [cried Sir John], 'and like a true courtier too! Ah, thou hast the palabras [correct jargon], and the knee, and the cap, and the quip, and the inuendo, and the true town fashion of it all—no old tarrybreeks of a sea-dog, like thy dad!'

This certainly catches a better likeness of the son than the former portrait did of the sire: for doubtless Richard's manners were, by comparison, court-like. Yet once more Kingsley goes sadly wrong: for, later, he makes Sir John say, on finding that Richard has gone off with the Lord Admiral,

'On his punctilios too, I suppose, the young slash-breeks. He's half a Don, that fellow, with his fine scholarship and his fine manners and his fine clothes. He'll get a taking down before he dies, unless he minds!'

There are at least two things wrong here. First—the former fault—fifty-suit Sir John would never have called himself an 'old tarry-breeks': and secondly he would not have criticized his boy for overdressing. Indeed it is fairly certain that he would not have criticized his son at all, in public and to any third person. For a great feature of all the clan was their love of, and loyalty to, one another. There are endless examples of this. When, after his third voyage in 1568–9 John failed to return home, and it began to look as though he were lost, William II wrote a touching letter to Cecil, the Queen's minister, in which he refers to

> my brother's absence which, unto me, is more grefe than any other
> thing in this world, whom—I trust—God will likewise preserve and
> send well home safely.

and Sir John's pride in his son Richard, his distress at his capture
and his efforts to secure his release tell the same story of an
affection only to be equalled by that son's filial love and respect
for his father; which, as we shall see when the time comes, stands
out in almost every page of his book.

Kingsley's cardinal blunder lies in picturing Sir John so very
wrong. But now there is a secondary blunder too, because he
insinuates that Richard is effeminate and smug, when there is no
proof whatever that he was either. His first introduction to him
is in the words:

> That short prim man in a huge yellow ruff, with sharp chin, minute
> imperial and self-satisfied smile is Richard Hawkins, the Complete
> Seaman.

This is hardly fair comment either, because the only known likeness of Richard (and that not certainly he) shows neither sharp
chin, minute imperial nor self-satisfied smile. Yet there seems to
be this of truth in Kingsley's description: it may well be that
William I might have been a little shocked by the personal attire
of his grandson, 'young slashed-breeks', just as a Victorian
grandmama might be a little shocked at the mini-skirts of her
granddaughter. But John's generation would certainly not have
turned a hair.

On the never-to-be-forgotten day on the Hoe, in Kingsley's
account, there is yet another Hawkins. But the novelist admits to
knowing very little about him, and so gives a very brief view of
him. This is Richard's 'Good Uncle William' and our William
II, John's elder brother, who stands talking to his nephew—and
does not even wear the gold mayoral chain to which he is surely
entitled seeing that it was he, and not brother John, who was
Plymouth's Mayor in 1588. He also makes John speak of 'My
old father' (William I); but he was not on the Hoe that day, nor
had been there these thirty-four years, having departed this life
in 1554. Only about William III he has nothing to say—of him
he probably knew nothing.

The growth in the standards of English culture and civilization accelerated considerably during the later years of Elizabeth's long and eventful reign, when the merchant element, playing an ever-increasing part in the struggle against Spain, grew considerably, not only in wealth but also in self-respect, and in general know-how. Three illustrations, in their nature rather apart from one another, may serve to pin-point the degree and diversity of that progress.

b. COUNTING AND ACCOUNTING

In William I's day a few theorists were scholars to this extent—that they normally used the modern 'arabic' notation of figures. But the less scholarly (of whom William would almost certainly be one) were still at the mercy of that dismal bar to arithmetical accuracy—that fruitful time-waster—the medieval pseudo-Roman cyphers. So, no doubt, the everyday little addition and subtraction sums in his account books would be wrong almost as often as they were right. And can we altogether blame him? How many of us, even now, would feel altogether happy when faced with long rows of figures to add, of whose form the following is a specimen?

$$\text{iij}^{\text{m}}\text{DCCIIjIIjxxvii} + \text{MCCQIIIjL} + \text{VVIIjXIXL}$$

Sir John and his brother may still have used this notation. Their near-contemporary William Cecil, Lord Burghley, certainly did, right up to the end of his life. But in this respect he was rather notoriously old-fashioned, so that the brothers may well have come over to the infinitely simpler arabics which we use today—a vast revolution alike in accuracy, logical thought, and sheer labour saved.

Richard, of the later generation, would almost certainly have used the new method of notation, probably from the first.

c. READING-MATTER AND THE THEATRE

It has been said earlier that the eldest William Hawkins had not much time for reading and, even if he had, had not very much to read: for what there was might very well be above his intellectual level. 'Popular' literature in any modern sense was only just beginning to appear. The nearest thing to it at that time was probably the 'romance', a long-established form originating in France, and in the latter half of the fifteenth century translated into English. One of the earlier books of this kind, as well as one of the best, was the *Morte D'Arthur* of Sir Thomas Mallory, written in 1470 and printed by Caxton in the very year that Henry VII seized the crown.

Somehow, however, there seems but little that was romantic about William. He was a much more hard-boiled type, and one cannot readily see him with a copy of Mallory in his hand. What then was there for him to read?

There were, first, the detached and rather controversial writings of current religious pamphleteers. Some of these William may have possessed; and even have read, or tried to read, especially those concerned with the new doctrinal views coming out of Wittenberg and afterwards from Geneva, the early homes of the Reformed Faith. For, like most of his fellow-townsmen in Plymouth and elsewhere, William and all his clan were greatly influenced by the teaching of Humanism, and soon of Protestantism too. He may even have possessed some of the philosophical works of that great Englishman Sir Thomas More, and he would almost certainly have followed, with painful interest, if not with grave misgivings, his clash with King Henry which brought him to the block in 1535. William I certainly knew, and corresponded with, the King's minister Thomas Cromwell, who was so closely mixed up with More's tragic end. Such events he could not help but follow, yet not so much by reading of them as by hearing the gossip, often indignant, of those around him. In fact he did *not* probably read them himself, because—one can almost hear him saying it—he 'had not much time for reading'.

Poetry, one feels rather more sure, was even less in his line, though he *might* have read the works of Geoffrey Chaucer, or Gower, or Lydgate—among the earliest printed books to emerge from Caxton's press. And the mention of Caxton reminds one of another thing—of the phenomenal spreading of knowledge as printed books took the place of the old manuscripts. In William's youth the printed book was an extreme rarity, almost a curiosity, but by his sons' time it was becoming reasonably common, and by his grandson's almost the norm.

Where William may have become acquainted with a rudimentary form of 'literature', was in the early drama: and here he would have had his introduction to it, not through reading so much as through direct seeing. Performances on the stage may well have appeared, even in his younger days, in the crowded streets of Plymouth, where itinerant companies of strolling players acted from their mobile carts the old Miracle Plays or the rather later Moralities. He may too, when he journeyed to London—as we know he did as a member of Parliament—have witnessed some of the Interludes—crude comedies composed by the King's Jester, John Heywood. He may well have watched, and guffawed at *The Four P's* or *Johan Tyb, his Wife and Sir John the Priest*, first played in 1533. They would surely be well within his cultural capacity.

All this, however, amounts to just nothing at all when compared with what his grandson Richard must have read, or seen on the stages of the Globe or the Swan. He was almost certainly living in his father's house, and in close touch with the Court, when, in 1590, the first books of Edmund Spenser's *Fairie Queen* came out; and doubtless he was waiting with what patience he could muster for the subsequent books, though he cannot have read them until 1602, when he returned from his captivity. And he must have seen acted most of the great plays of the Elizabethan and the Jacobean eras—the dramatic works of Marlow and Kyd, of Greene, Beaumont and Fletcher, and 'rare' Ben Jonson: and, of course, all those of his near-contemporary the actor Will Shakespeare himself. (He was four years younger than Richard, and died six years before him.)

In town too, when at court or later as an M.P., he may very likely have dropped in at the Mermaid Tavern, and actually hobnobbed with the bearers of these illustrious names. Indeed he had every chance of receiving a most liberal education, and probably seized it with both hands, since for so long he lived at the heart of the new culture, then at the height of its flowering; when—as Wordsworth wrote of another and entirely different climacteric of History—

> Bliss was it in that dawn to be alive,
> But to be young was very Heaven!

d. SHIPS AND SHIPBUILDING

It was also during the period between 1530, when William I made his first note-worthy voyage to South America, and 1593, when Richard made his, that a great revolution took place in the art of constructing wooden ships: and in this case, as will appear later, it was William's son and Richard's father who played a vital part in the process.

The *Paul*, William's ship of 1530, would be a merchantman of some 250 tons burthen, very much in the tradition of the medieval 'cogge'—clumsy, though singularly solid craft of the type known to later writers as a 'round ship'. This must not, of course, be taken quite literally. It does not mean that such a vessel was really circular. But its length was in the neighbourhood of twice its beam. Though in its pot-belly there was ample space for a great deal of cargo, it was inevitably unhandy, very leewardly in the sailing and difficult (compared with later types) to steer: not built really, in fact, to compete with the wide open spaces of the oceans, but intended rather for coast-wise work, through the Channel or along the shores of Spain and the Mediterranean.

Experimenting mainly with the Royal Ships, it was Sir John who improved this type by, as it were, pulling it out lengthwise until its dimensions were three lengths, or a little more, to one breadth and providing it with a vastly improved sail-plan so that it would sail several points nearer to the wind. His efforts were directed mainly, of course, to the fighting ships of the Navy Royal—the warships of their day. But as he, and his son Richard, built their own private ships which they intended to use primarily for trade, taking them to sea themselves, they could not but be aware that they would have to fight their way to their destinations just as though they *were* full ships of war. Therefore they armed them for fighting too, though retaining in them as much as possible of the characteristic roominess necessary for the carriage of merchandise.

Such then was the *Daintie*, laid down by father and son at the close of Armada Year, with the express intention or cruising far from home, off the New World or even of circumnavigating the

globe. She was a very new and up-to-date long-distance merchantman: not all that larger in sheer tonnage than the *Paul*,
being only of some 350 tons, but designed—relatively—long in
proportion to her beam: a ship such as only experienced users
like the Hawkinses *could* design. She was meant from the start
for the triple purpose of trading, sailing and fighting in distant
seas. In fact between the *Paul* and the *Daintie* there were *vast*
differences. The *Paul* was almost a survival from the Middle
Ages: the *Daintie* was, to all intents and purposes, a merchant
sailing ship of the modern world, not thereafter to be basically
altered until the coming in the nineteenth century of the Steam
and Iron Age.

What then were these Hawkinses really like as a family? Ap-
preciations of various members of it begin to appear quite
early on. But for an estimate of the whole clan one must perhaps wait until the last of them has completed his course. One
has in fact to wait for the verdict of that amiable cleric, the Vicar
of Totnes and Berry Pomeroy, the Reverend John Prince, whose
Worthies of Devon, published in 1701, called them

> Gentlemen of worshipful extraction for several descents, but made
> more worshipful by their deeds. For three generations they were the
> master spirits of Plymouth in its most illustrious days; its leading
> merchants, its bravest sailors, serving oft and well in the civic chair
> and in the House of Commons. For three generation too they were
> in the van of English seamanship, founders of England's commerce in
> South and West and East: stout to fight, of quenchless spirit in
> adventure—a family of merchants, statesmen and heroes, to whom
> our Country affords no parallel.

John Prince, of course, was a Devon man through and through.
So one may expect—what one certainly gets—a very full-
throated eulogy. Yet, by and large, subsequent investigators
have done little or nothing to upset his estimate of their work.
Perhaps if anything, indeed, they have enhanced it, especially
where Sir John is concerned. Doubtless the Hawkinses loomed
a little larger in Prince's pages than they do in those of authors
who paint the larger canvas of the whole of Tudor England—in
the relative diversity, say, of a great work like the *Dictionary of
National Biography*—and suspicious, carping souls may boggle

a little at Prince's very last words: 'Merchants, statesmen and Heroes to whom our Country affords no parallel.' It is the utter finality of that little word 'no' which is a little daunting. All right, then. Let us substitute for 'no' the word 'few'—'few parallels'—and very few carpers will remain.

CHAPTER II

William Hawkins I

✍

THE eldest of this family, then, whose career is to be treated in these pages was Mr Hawkins of Plymouth, born some time in the 1490s and dead by 1554. There are two aspects of this man to be discussed, though the two are closely interwoven throughout. It will be convenient here, however, to consider them separately.

There was first the local magnate, the first Hawkins of Plymouth to establish himself incontestably as the founder of his dynasty in his own west-country town. And there is secondly the man whose influence upon his times extended far beyond Plymouth to the whole field of English history. This latter person is, of course, much the more important of the two; but first we must follow the 'local magnate', establishing himself as a big figure in his own home town.

a. BURGESS, FACTION-LEADER AND MAYOR

It is best to admit at once that *this* William Hawkins remains obstinately in the shadows. Was he tall or short, thickset or thin, dark or fair? Who shall say now? All we can hope to do is to let his actions—the few of them we can still come by—speak for themselves. It is not even clear from the local records at what exact moment in time we can lay hands on him and say for certain, 'This is the father of William II and Sir John.' There are too many of this by no means uncommon name who appear even in the town records, let alone elsewhere in England.

There is first a man certainly bearing this name who, in 1497–8, was doing business as a Plymouth merchant. He may have been a relative, but surely he is too early in time to be our man himself, who in those years could hardly have reached his tenth year. Then there is another Hawkins, recorded in 1513 as being the Master of Henry VIII's *Great Galley*. But again, for so responsible a post, this was probably an older man than the one we are looking for, who even then was only in the region of twenty. Nor is there any evidence at all that, at so early a date, our man was in the confidence of the King. Later still, in 1531, there is evidence of a man of this name who was a baker in practice in Plymouth; and lastly, in 1533, there was yet another who was a bailiff in Weymouth. These last two, however, are *most* unlikely to be our William I if only because, well before their dates—in 1523, to be exact—we find one who was almost certainly our man. This was the William Hawkins who, in that year, was serving as Collector of the Subsidy for Devon, and who, in the following year, was made Receiver or Treasurer to the Plymouth Corporation. After that, there are enough references to him to make it reasonably certain that we have found the Hawkins we seek.

It may be assumed, then, that by 1524–5 William I has become what we should probably now call Borough Treasurer of Plymouth—a really responsible post in the hierarchy of the town: and even then he would only have been a bare thirty years old.

Very soon after that, however, his name figures in a cause tried in the Court of Common Pleas at Westminster: and here he appears in a much less responsible light. 'William Hawkins, Merchant, James Horsewell, Gentleman, Peter Grisling, Merchant' and three other men are charged with 'beating and wounding John Jurdon of Plymouth in such a manner as to endanger his life'.[1] The other two whose names are mentioned above are well-known figures in contemporary Plymouth, the first featuring throughout as a stout ally of Hawkins, the second to become later his bitterest enemy.

This—the first hint which can be found of William's *personal* characteristics—seems somehow prophetic of much which follows. It seems to show him as rather a violent man; anyway, one not afraid when he thought it necessary to take the law into his own hands. And such, according to twentieth-century standards, he almost certainly was. So doubtless were almost all his

[1] *Plymouth Calendar*, p. 43.

contemporaries. They were tough lads, these Tudor Plymothians, and they liked their leaders to be tough!

What was the result of the proceedings we do not know. Yet clearly Hawkins did not lose the confidence of the townsfolk by this display of toughness because in the same year he was told off to organize the defences of the town in repelling a French raid. On that occasion he sold 196 pounds of powder to the Corporation, and a little later two brass guns. Were these warlike commodities his own? Very likely. Already he probably had merchant ships of his own, almost certainly well-armed ones too.

Later, on many occasions he was to fall foul of Peter Grisling. This worthy was a 'searcher'—that is, roughly speaking, a customs officer. And, although the facts are never allowed to come right out into the open, perhaps we may hazard a guess as to one cause of the feud. How does one get on the wrong side of customs officers? By smuggling. And who, in that somewhat lawless age, will be prepared to affirm that Hawkins was altogether guiltless of *that* offence?

Yet there was certainly another, and more long-lasting bone of contention between Hawkins and Grisling: one that savoured much more of 'local politics'. Grisling, though a Plymouth man, had migrated to the near-by (but rival) township of Saltash, and from there was obviously trying to set his new place of residence up in competition with the older town. In 1535 he brought a suit against Plymouth before the Privy Council. That body did its best to settle the dispute amicably; but then Grisling announced that he was returning to Plymouth, and at once tried to persuade Hawkins, who had already once been Mayor, to get him on to its Council. But Hawkins refused to do it. Then Grisling, furious, returned to Saltash, and next year succeeded in getting one Bull elected to the mayoral chair in Plymouth. Still conspiring, Grisling and Bull now secured an order from the Privy Council banishing Horsewell from the town for a year. But Hawkins and his friends refused to take it lying down and, calling a Corporation meeting, they pushed in Horsewell as Town Clerk, openly ignoring the Privy Council's order. All parties were now summoned once more to London, and the Minister (Thomas Cromwell) debarred Hawkins and Co. from the Corporation.

So the fight swayed to and fro, especially when, in 1537, Grisling was elected Mayor of Saltash and from that vantage-point claimed for Saltash certain ancient dues over the whole harbour, and the right to hold a half-yearly court which subjected Plymouth to its rival. Faction raged hot and fists flew, for the stake now was the paramountcy of Saltash or Plymouth. At length, choosing his moment shrewdly, Hawkins appealed to the all-powerful Star Chamber, Cromwell's own court; and though its findings are unknown in detail, there can be no doubt that Hawkins prevailed, winning the ear of Cromwell for the rest of that Minister's life. Clearly as an exponent of one-upmanship there were no flies on William!

Thereafter it all went Hawkins's way. He had been Mayor once, in 1532–3, but now, in 1538–9, he was chosen again. Moreover at the General Election of 1539 he and Horsewell went up to Westminster as members for the Borough of Plymouth. They were now the blue-eyed boys not only of Cromwell but even of the King himself. And in securing Court favour, Hawkins had also won the quarrel over the supremacy of Saltash and his own town. Thereafter Plymouth was never again in danger from its neighbour.

There can be little doubt that, in giving his whole-hearted support to Hawkins, Cromwell was only rewarding faithful service from William to himself. For Cromwell stood above all for Protestantism: and so, already, did Hawkins, though he was not then doctrinally Protestant.

It remains a possibility, though there is no direct evidence for it, that in this struggle for the ear of the great ones in London, so decisively won by William, there may have been traces of 'petticoat' influence. It still remains something of a mystery how, in the first place, Hawkins secured the favour, not so much of Cromwell—that is to be explained by their common religious views—as of Henry himself. How, it may be asked, did the Monarch first become acquainted with the rising young Plymothian? Well, it is at least possible that it was William's mother, or rather perhaps his maternal grandfather who had something to do with it. For, it will be recalled, William Amadas of Launceston was (or had been) one of Henry VIII's sergeants-at-arms—officers of the Crown's Chancery Court. And even though these posts carried but little weight at Court, it might have been sufficient at least to bring the young man to the knowledge of the King, so that, in a very minor way, Henry may have regarded himself as a kind of patron to Hawkins, or at least may have, in this way, got to know Hawkins's name when he heard it.

The mention of William's relations by marriage serves to remind us of his own wife. Socially she was a distinct advance on his mother. She was Joan, daughter and coheiress of Roger, himself the son of Sir John Trelawny, of an old and respected county family of Cornwall. One odd thing about this up-grading alliance is the fact that William must have married her when he was quite a young man, not more than twenty-eight years old and probably several years younger than that: and not later than 1518, because his elder son (William II) was born in 1519. By that date he can have had no great fortune, unless he inherited from his father, John of Tavistock, more than is usually supposed. Nothing is known of the lady, or her influence upon her husband. Much the most important thing that we know she did was to give birth to her younger son, afterwards the great Sir John. It must not be forgotten, however, that the records are even more obstinately silent about his wife than they are about William himself, to whom we must now return.

By this time he was, with Horsewell, the most important man in the town. In 1538 the small religious House of the Grey Friars was dissolved, and to Hawkins, now Mayor Elect, the guardianship of the property was left. He was given the disposal of the monastery's valuables—74 ounces of silver plate—which he sold to the Council for £12 9s 2d. Later, the Council decided to re-sell it in London, and Hawkins was left to do the bargaining. He sold it there for £41 13s 5d! There is here no suspicion of sharp practice. It only shows up William I as efficient in his primary business, which was, of course, selling goods for more than he had paid for them. On this occasion the money was put to good account. It bought arms and powder for the defence of the town, threatened, at the time, with invasion by the French.

Not that, even now, all was plain sailing. Far from it. When, in the middle 1540s, England and France went to war, Hawkins became more and more involved in the business of Channel privateering, which was in fact one of the bigger weapons in the armoury of Henry in his waging of the war. Moreover, this peculiar institution of Private War continued until the end of the century, playing an even more important part in the financing of Elizabeth's war with Spain. (In that struggle, indeed, it has been said, rightly, that England was 'waging war by means of joint stock company', making the private and patriotic efforts of her merchants and her seamen the main front of the struggle. Yet, though rather more often than not disguised, rather thinly, in legal dress, the whole institution of privateering lent itself all too readily to lawlessness, if only because the dividing line between privateering and rank piracy, though it always existed, was often nebulous in the extreme and very hard to define. There can be no doubt that William overstepped the mark several times, being heavily fined once and once seeing the inside of a gaol, though he soon bought his way out of that.

Yet if William was a rough diamond and by no means perfect, he was far from being a rogue. Such little matters as those just described would emphatically not, in Henry's later days, cast any real slur on the character of a respectable merchant, if only because sea-trade and privateering, as well as war itself, had for so long, and in so many ways, become almost identical terms. Anyway, he never seriously lost face with the Government; and when Cromwell fell he did not fall with him. Evidently the King knew all about him, and liked what he knew.

So, well before the end of Henry's life—and of his own too, since he outlived the Great King by some seven years, departing only in the second year of Queen Mary's troubled reign—he had begun to emerge as something more than a big local figure. Already he was Henry's unofficial adviser for all West of England affairs, and perhaps his personal friend as well. And not only was he the King's trusted counsellor, but now he had many other irons in the fire. He was deeply involved in privateering in the Channel and elsewhere, and a leading figure in the western port. He was also by now a very wealthy man, one of the largest property-owners in the town, with a considerable fleet of his own and extensive wharfage and warehouses on Sutton Pool. He had even tried to borrow money from the

Crown, though it is doubtful whether he succeeded here. (See below, p. 47.) But this part of his story belongs to his second and even wider-ranging set of interests: interests so wide as to make him something of a national figure in his own right. It is to these then that we must now turn.

b. MERCHANT, SEAMEN AND PIONEER

It is here that, almost for the first time, William I comes out of comparative obscurity, to show up both as a pioneer and as a personality. Hitherto we have been assembling from various sources of English history such assorted and isolated pieces of evidence as we could find, for lack of anything more substantial. But now, for a moment, he appears on the front of the stage as a real live figure, and that in the pages of another very great Englishman, serving his country in a very different capacity. For Richard Hakluyt, in his *Principal Navigations* has an account of his adventures which no other authority contains.

It is true that, in one respect, this passage about William I differs from most of Hakluyt's other work. As a rule he uses completely first-hand accounts, written (or sometimes told) either by the voyaging leader himself or else by one of those who took the trip with him. This time, however, his story is not so contemporary: for he does not pretend that it is written either by William I or by any of his companions. Indeed the inference, coming out strongly towards the end, is that the narrative is based upon evidence which is good enough, but which is not contemporary. It is certainly the next best thing though, because his informant was almost certainly William's younger son, Sir John.

The voyages described, Hakluyt says, took place in 1530, 1531 and 1532, and Sir John was only born, probably, in the last-named year. He cannot therefore have gone on any of them himself. So the information in Hakluyt can only be what the father told the son about them. In one sense this is disappointing—one would have liked William's own account. Yet in another way it has an interest all its own. For it does tell a thing which otherwise we should have no means of knowing—Sir John's opinion of his own father. As we should expect from so close-knit and loving a family, this opinion is very high indeed.

The passage is here quoted in full, as the only account in detail of William I in action, and as a striking illustration of what the middle generation of Hawkinses thought of the first.[1]

A brief relation of two sundry voyages made by the Worshipful M. William Hawkins of Plimmouth, father to Sir John Hawkins, Knight, late Treasurer of Her Majesties Navie, in the yeere 1530 and 1532.

Olde M. Hawkins of Plimmouth, a man for his wisdome, valure, experience and skill in sea causes much esteemed, and beloved of K. Henry the 8, and being one of the principall sea-captaines in the West parts of England in his time, not contented with the short voyages commonly then made onely to the knowne coasts of Europe, armed out a tall and goodly shippe of his owne of burthen 250 tonnes, called the *Paul of Plimmouth*, wherewith he made three long and famous voyages unto the coast of Brasil, a thing in those dayes very rare, especially to our Nation. In the course of which voyages he touched at the river of Sestos[2] upon the coast Guinea, where hee traffiqued with the Negros, and tooke of them Elephants teeth, and other commodities which that place yieldeth: and so arriving on the coast of Brasil, he used there such discretion, and behaved himself so wisely with those savage people, that he grew into great familiarity and friendship with them. Insomuch that in his second voyage, one of the savage kings of the Countrey of Brasil was contented to take ship with him, and to be transported hither into England: whereunto M. Hawkins agreed, leaving behinde in the Countery as a pledge for his safetie and returne againe, one Martin Cockeram of Plimmouth. This Brasilian king being arrived, was brought up to London and presented to K. Henry the 8, lying as then at White-hall: at the sight of whom the King and all the Nobilitie did not a litle marvaile, and not without cause: for in his cheekes were holes made according to their savage maner,

---

[1] *Principal Navigations* (Everyman's Edition, vol. VIII, p. 18). Hakluyt's title as given here comes from his second, and enlarged, edition of 1600. The subjoined text is identical in both editions. The title is not strictly accurate; nor does it enshrine quite all that the great geographer knew of the expeditions. For though he speaks of 'two sundry voyages', he obviously knew that Hawkins had made three.

[2] Lat. $5\frac{1}{2}°$ N., now in Liberia.

and therein small bones were planted, standing an inch out from the said holes, which in his owne countrey was reputed for a great braverie. He had also another hole in his nether lip, wherein was set a precious stone about the bignes of a pease: All his apparel, behaviour, and gesture, were very strange to the beholders.

Having remained here almost the space of a whole year, and the king with his sight fully satisfied, M. Haukins according to his promise and appointment, purposed to convey him again into his countrey: but it fell out in the way, that by change of aire and alteration of diet, the said savage king died at sea, which was feared would turn to the losse of the life of Martin Cockeram his pledge. Neverthelesse, the Savages being fully perswaded of the honest dealing of our men with their prince, restored againe the said pledge, without any harme to him, or any man of the company: which pledge of theirs they brought home againe into England, with their ship fraighted, and furnished with the commodities of the countrey. Which Martin Cockeram, by the witness of Sir John Hawkins, being an officer in the towne of Plimmouth, was living within these few years.

From this, surely, we learn a great deal. Here, first, is the pioneer: the man who forsakes the old, well-beaten track and starts something *new*. He was not, of course, the first *man* to make such voyages. The Portuguese had been at it for many years—not far off fifty. And as early as 1504 the French had begun to break into the Portuguese monopoly. In that year, it is known, a certain de Gonneville had sailed from Honfleur to the Brazilian coast in his ship *Espoir*, and other Frenchmen followed, often engaging in hostilities with Portugal. They traded in gold and ivory from the Guinea Coast, and brought back Brasil Wood and pepper from the New World. But they made no permanent settlements in those early days either in Africa or America. Their importance at this time lay in the fact that, almost certainly, they provided quite experienced pilots for Hawkins. And he had to have them, because he received no assistance at all from the Portuguese. For there seems to be no doubt that he was the first Englishman to enter the trade, and he was certainly the first Devonian to do so.

Next, it seems that he was the first Englishman to use that 'triangular run' which became with those who followed him, and especially with his own son John, the standard way to the New World and back. Course was shaped first for the West African coast, partly because the wind made it a good natural route to the Americas, partly in order to pick up a cargo suitable for the next leg of the triangle. (His principal trading commodity, we notice, was ivory: and here we may feel he was somewhat ahead of his more famous son, who also dealt in ivory; but black ivory—slaves. Though we should not blame John unduly for doing what all his contemporaries did, as a matter of course and without a thought for the ethics of it, we may still feel that white ivory was, by a very great deal, the cleaner and nicer commodity.) Thence he ran westwards on the second leg, using the steady easterly Trades and so reaching South America, where he traded his African goods for the local ones. Then, by returning considerably further north, he was able to avail himself of the predominant sou'-westerlies of the North Atlantic. Here he showed real flair for navigation. It should be added, however, that the novelty of his journey lay in being the first Englishman to visit Africa *en route* for the Western Continent, not in using the more northerly way back to Europe. That dates right back to Columbus' first voyage.

Next comes Hakluyt's most striking contribution to our knowledge of William I. Where his information came from he does not disclose directly. But his words seem to make it clear that he had it from Sir John himself. He might possibly, one supposes, have had it from Martin Cockeram, who, he says, was still alive. But by Hakluyt's time that old salt was very old indeed, and beyond giving so clear an account of anything.[1]

It is abundantly clear that the main thing which Hakluyt— and by inference Sir John—wants to bring out about Old William is that he was a scrupulously honest man who believed in straight dealing with everybody; not only with his own compatriots but even with those benighted heathen from the other side of the world. Here is a quality so unusual in his contem-

---

[1] It will be recalled that Kingsley has his vignette of Cockeram too, and a very good pen-portrait it is, much better, one feels, than that of either of the Hawkinses. For he pictures an immemorially ancient man with nothing left but slightly confused memories and a senile craving for sugar.

poraries as to place him far ahead, not only of them but also of all his successors for many years to come. We have only to consider how the Spaniards and the Portuguese treated *their* natives; or even, once the slave-ramp had begun, how the English treated theirs. Indeed it is almost true to say that, to all white men *but* old William, the native was such a 'savage' as not really to be human at all, or at best of a different, and lower, order of humanity: so much so, in fact, that the European, whatever his nation, though he might often be honest enough in his dealings with his own colour and kind, felt no obligation to extend his honesty to the savage.

Yet here was William the Eldest, the first (or almost the first) to trade with savages, treating them exactly as though they were men: not using his superior civilization to get the better of them; not cheating them as a matter of course; but, when he said he would do a thing, cheerfully doing it, even when it was not particularly to his advantage. It is true that by such fair-dealing he obviously prospered as a 'tradesman', because the savages themselves trusted him, loved him and acted fairly by him. But this in no way alters the fact that so amiable a quality was altogether exceptional in his day—and, it must be added with regret, it has never become anything like so common as it should have become.

Englishmen are notorious self-depreciators, unwilling to lay claim to qualities to which they are really entitled. They hate self-praise. So perhaps they will not like to be reminded that the Anglo-Saxon peoples are luckier than other countries in producing men who possess these estimable qualities. We are richer than most in our Livingstones, our Nicholsons, our Lawrences and many others of their breed; of any of whom, as of old William, Hakluyt might have written, 'He used there'—in whatever land he found himself—'such discretion, and behaved himself so wisely with those people that he grew into great familiarity and friendship with them.'

In passing we may observe that his son John inherited something of this great virtue; only, like almost all his contemporaries, he was too prone to confine it to men of his own colour. He was, says Maynarde, a writer not over-inclined to judge others kindly, 'merciful and apt to forgive, and faithful to his word'. Here the father was much more to be admired than the son, in that—all things considered surprisingly—he extended his humanity to all races.

In all this, no doubt, something must be allowed for Sir John's abiding affection for his old father. Yet he was speaking from first-hand knowledge, because he was already a grown man in 1554 when that father died, and he must have had as good knowledge of him as anyone—at least anyone still living in 1589, when Hakluyt's first edition appeared. So we are surely entitled to add this evidence to the other fragmentary pieces assembled here.

It is reasonably certain, then, that old Mr Hawkins made three voyages to Africa and Brazil in his own ship the *Paul* in 1530, 1531 and 1532: and that, though to the last principally a 'merchant', he conducted all three himself, thereby qualifying as a fine seaman and navigator also. Moreover it is morally certain that his ships—his own property—made some more voyages too, though it is by no means certain that he himself went with them: in fact he probably did not, for by the middle 1530s he had become too involved in affairs nearer home. That as late as 1536 he is still personally interested in overseas trade is clear from a surviving letter addressed to Thomas Cromwell in that year. It is the only known one from him, and as such it may be reproduced here in full.[1] It is interesting as showing how a man like Hawkins hoped for support and recognition from the Government of the day. Compared with surviving letters from the pens of Sir John and Richard, it certainly seems, as is only to be expected, rather unpolished, though by no means illiterate.

> Most honourable and my singular good lord,
> So it is that I durst not put myself in press to sue unto your good lordship for any help or succour to be obtained at your hands in my poor affairs, until such time I had first put my ship and goods in adventure to search for the commodities of unknown countries, and seen the return thereof in safety; as, I thank God, hath metely well happened unto me, albeit by four parts not so well as I suppose it should if one of my pilots had not miscarried by the way. Wherefore, my singular good lord, I now, being somewhat bold by the reason aforesaid but chiefly for the great hope and trust I have in your accustomed goodness, I most humbly beseech your good lordship to be mean for me to

[1] In State Papers, Henry VIII, Section 113, folio 180.

the Kings highness, to have of His Grace's love four pieces of brass ordnance and a last of powder, upon such good sureties to restore the same at a day. And furthermore, that it may please His Grace, upon the surety of an hundred pound lands, to lend me £2,000 for the space of seven years towards the setting forth of three or four ships. And I doubt me not but in the mean time to do such feats of merchandise that it shall be to the King's great advantage in His Grace's custom, and to your good lordship's honour for your help and furtherance herein. And nevertheless after my power, I shall presently deserve your pains taken in this behalf, and continue your daily bedeman and servant to my little power,

Your most bounden orator,
William Hawkyns of Plymouth.

That Henry VIII did not respond is pretty clear, because, had he done so, some evidence of the loan must have shown up among the records. But though we must assume that Hawkins received no direct help from the Crown at that time, it does show that he expected it: and it also shows that he had had a voyage—much more recent than his original ventures of 1530–2—which had 'miscarried' under another leader. Moreover, the Customs ledgers of Plymouth[1] also show that he carried on on his own, almost certainly with some paid underling in command. For as late as 1540 it is certain that the *Paul* made a voyage—destination not disclosed—and returned in the following October with 'one hundredweight of elephants' teeth and 92 tunnes of Brasil Wood'. Such commodities tell their own tale. They can only have come from yet another 'triangular run'.

It would be interesting to know whereabouts, on the long coast of Portuguese South America, William made his landfall in 1530–2, and whence came the barbarian king whose facial decorations so tickled Henry and his court. But it is hardly possible to find out now. It was only in 1500 that the Porguguese discovered the huge eastern thrust of the New Lands, instantly naming the area Brazil, from the very valuable dyewoods, highly prized in Europe and there known as Brasil Wood: and, for many years after that, their settlements on this coast were few and far between, because Portugal was distinctly slow in taking over the new country. They moved faster in Africa, and founded their earliest trading-stations there some years before they got round to South America—very soon, in

[1] Exchequer Records, E. 122 ii6/13 (Plymouth Customs Register).

fact, after Bartholomew Diaz' epoch-making voyage in 1486, and especially da Gama's even more exciting trip of 1498 which carried him right round the Cape to India. This is why Hakluyt, getting his information from William's son John, is able to pin-point William's landing at Sestos. For, even as early as 1530, Englishmen skirting the African coast could not move far with-out bumping into the settlements of a monopolistic and very hostile Portugal, which had already moved far into the great Gulf of Benin. But there can be little doubt that, in new-found Brazil, Hawkins made no contact at all with the Portuguese, and so, probably, could not have pinpointed his landfalls even if he would. At any rate, even if he did know where they were, he failed to pass on his information to his son; or alternatively—and perhaps more likely—that son proved unwilling to pass the information on to Hakluyt, so that, now, the localities must remain unknown to us. From the furore which the barbarian king created in London, however, it is fairly safe to suppose that Henry and his court were now obtaining their very first glimpse of the native inhabitants of South America.

After Hawkins's last venture, in or about 1540, it seems that trading with Brazil was given up for at least ten years: not so much on account of Portugal's hostility, but rather because, as we have seen, Henry went to war with France in 1545, and now needed the resources of his sea-going peoples to engage in the privateering war in the Channel—a war at once highly profit-able to the merchants themselves and also to Henry, whose notions of maritime war did not go very far beyond embarras-sing his enemy's trade with the private warships both of himself and of his merchant subjects.

No wonder that Henry always found a soft spot in his heart for one of the principal, if not *the* principal, instruments of his maritime policy!

Old William was elected as Member for Plymouth, in the first Parliament of Queen Mary. He died during the winter of 1553–4; whether in Town or at home it is not known. If it was in Town—and if he was buried there—it is an odd circumstance that the bones of none of the great Plymouth family rest in Plymouth itself.

A final assessment of the old man may now be attempted. Despite the paucity of the evidence, William I emerges as a shrewd business man, with a good and successful eye to the main chance. Living in a day when business morality was doubtless a very elastic article, he is never, *in* that elastic set-up, accused of over-sharpness (except of course by Grisling and the French and Portuguese—but these hardly count): no great sinner, but no saint either, save perhaps in that unlooked-for enlightenment described above: rather, a fine example of a good, and growing, type: the merchant who took his own ship to sea and to whom in her formative years England owed so large a debt—more, a very integral part in the process of forming. For Old William and his like were the masters who taught the Elizabethan seamen their trade: and not only his own sons and grandsons, but also Francis Drake and Martin Frobisher, Fenton, Crosse, Cavendish and all the Fenners—all those incomparable sea-dogs who made England great under the first Queen Elizabeth. For evidently, 'Olde Mr Hawkins of Plimmouth' was the pioneer and sea-daddy of them all.

CHAPTER III

William Hawkins II

ༀༀༀ

'Olde Mr William Hawkins of Plymouth' was, as we have seen, a sturdy local magnate who by his own exertions became a considerable national figure too. So did both his sons: the younger, Sir John, and his much older brother William II. Both, before they were through with life, were wealthy and honoured burgesses of Plymouth, and both rose into the higher realms of national life. Speaking generally, however, we find that, whereas John passed at a comparatively early age into the main stream of English history, while still remaining to the last a foremost burgess in his own town, his brother William, while becoming well before his end a big man in the wider field, yet remained to the last mainly the Plymouth Merchant and Burgess. He was in fact the member of the family who, in the truest sense, was the heir to Old William, as befitted the elder son. Unlike Sir John, he spent by far the greater part of his life in the Devon town and, though in the end he neither died nor was buried in Plymouth, he made that place the focus of his work and his affections. There was in fact much more of the Old William in the young one than there was in John.

Not a great deal about his boyhood and youth has survived. That he was educated in the town, and well-educated too, is certain, and though neither his school nor his schoolmaster is known, the best guess is that a chantry priest from the near-by House of the Grey Friars taught him his letters, and, from the evidence of surviving writings, taught him thoroughly and well. But a lad's education in a town like Plymouth in an age like Henry VIII's was not a lengthy business, because a man of twenty had little if any longer expectation of life than a man of forty or even fifty has now. So it was inevitably regarded as wasteful to keep him at his books beyond, say, the age of ten or eleven. The true university of the sixteenth century to boys like William and John was the university of life: and in the maritime atmosphere which must have existed in that old Hawkins home in Kinterbury Street, a lad was apt, at an age no greater than that at which a Victorian youth would be leaving his preparatory school, to find himself plunged into the vortex of 'affairs'; already learning to use his hands as well as his brains in his parent's shipyard, or even in that parent's sea-going ship, serving (probably under the eye of his father) his apprentice-ship afloat.

Since William was at least twelve, and perhaps thirteen years older than his brother, he must have finished his strict book-learning before John was born. So, for all the natural affection which so clearly united them, they were certainly not brought up together. Indeed, though the fact is nowhere noted, there can really be but little doubt that, even before his brother's birth, William II was accompanying his father on his Brazil voyages—even on the first, when he was eleven years old, but almost certainly on the second and third (in 1532, the year of John's birth). But this does not mean, as it would now, that William, and John after him, were uneducated, still less illiterate. Only consider the alleged—yet almost certainly true—list of accom-plishments of a person like the little King Edward VI, or the apparently astonishing erudition of a girl like the unfortunate Lady Jane Grey, and one will appreciate the fact that a Tudor lad who 'left school' at, say, twelve years old was not necessarily uneducated, even in the 'three R's', let alone in the practical application of his talents.

On the other side of the picture it is usually taken for granted that John was from his earliest youth a dedicated seaman, knowing all there was to know about shipbuilding, ship repair, ship management and navigation—and loving them all. This is without doubt true: but that William, with just the same back-ground and upbringing somehow missed this same corpus of knowledge and expertise is hardly likely, though he probably had less practice in them than his younger brother. It may be surprising to learn that, as far as we know, William II never actually commanded at sea until he was fifty years old, or very nearly; but that, when he did, he acquitted himself as to the manner born. It should not be forgotten that, when the sea is in a man's blood during all his really formative years, the sea-trade will come natural to him however late in life he takes it up.

All through the 1530s, there were William I's oceanic undertakings to give William II employment, not to mention the gradual growth of his influence in Plymouth as his father's heir. And—after 1545, when he was still a young man, though his father was 'getting on'—the paternal heritage of privateering came more and more his way. It is true that we do not hear of his commanding at sea as yet: but that is not to say that he did not do so now and again. From the moment, however, when John grew to manhood—say from 1550—we must regard the two brothers as working hand in hand, with William's dozen years of seniority tending to make him specialist in the administrative and the municipal, leaving the executive and the purely maritime side of things more to John: and all under the now ageing eye of Old William I. And when the latter at length died, this arrangement crystallized still further, with old William's civic duties mainly descending upon the elder son and heir. William II, for instance, found himself in 1558, four years after his father's death, a privy councillor of the borough, though John had only just reached the grade of common councillor. Certainly, during most of the 1550s the town records show William to be resident in Plymouth while John seems to be frequently absent.

The brothers remained partners until, perhaps, 1558, when John went off to London, or perhaps later—possibly as late as 1565. Then the 'firm' officially broke up. But they did not quarrel. So far as we know neither then nor thereafter did hard words pass between them. But there were then two businesses—William Hawkins and John Hawkins—both quite Unlimited! And again and again John invested his money in William's concerns, while again and again William backed John actively: financially, and even at times fanatically. John went further and further afield, both geographically in the Crown's good opinion, and in the eyes of Englishmen. But all the time, through thick and through thin, there, at the heart of the homeland, was William, more and more soundly entrenched in wealth, local prestige—he was Mayor for the first time in 1567—and com-

mercial enterprise. It remained a great, if rather looser partnership than before.

The business mantle, then, of Old William fell more and
more on to the younger William's shoulders. More, the elder
son seems to have inherited certain of the father's characteristics
as well. Old William, we saw, was of rather a litigious disposition; and so at times was the son—in this respect very different
from the younger brother who was, by comparison, quite
pacific in ordinary life though not where his public duty called.
Thus, in 1555–6 William brought a suit for debt against a
certain Thomas Hampton; and the story of this affair takes up
much space in the town records for some months on end. Again
in 1557 he had one Raynold Wendon up for slander, claiming
1,000 marks in damages, merely, it appears, because Raynold
called him 'a traitor, a thief and a very villain'; nor, like his
father before him, did he always win his cases—it is not clear
whether he won this one.

Why Old William—and doubtless William II after him—
had braved the wrath of Portugal on the Guinea coast of Africa
and in Brazil, leaving severely alone the even wider colonial
empire of Spain was of course a matter of international politics.
There was no treaty of friendship with the Portuguese, but
there was—and there had been for many years—an important
one with the Emperor Charles V, and, when he abdicated, with
his son Philip II of Spain. So, where the Portuguese regarded
the English merely as odious trespassers, there were no such
feelings in the Spanish camp: and this included the Low
Countries, another possession first of Charles and then of Philip.
So the English carried on a most profitable trade with the
Netherlands, and for a long time with the wider empire of
Spain too. France, not Spain, was the hereditary enemy of
England. In Mary's reign Philip was still making a great effort
to get control of England by strictly peaceful means: by diplomacy but not by war. And that was still the situation when he
married the English Queen and, though shorn of almost all the
power that normally went with the title, actually became King
of England, hoping in his rather cold-blooded way—what Mary
hoped with pathetic eagerness—that the heirs of his body and
hers would in due time inherit everything.

As we now know, no such child appeared; but when, in 1558, Queen Mary died, a disappointed woman, her throne was instantly filled by her half-sister Elizabeth. Even then Philip did not instantly give up hope; the ancient hope of the Hapsburgs to rule not by war, but by marriage.[1] So for a while he angled for the hand of that very tough young lady Elizabeth, the Virgin Queen, and during the first decade of her reign, from 1558 until about 1569, the Spanish Alliance remained the keystone of England's policy. But, during the 1560s, Philip made no progress with his matrimonial diplomacy, and cracks, wider and more ominous as the years went by, began to appear in the structure of Anglo-Spanish friendship. Yet officially, friendship it remained, though often a hollow and uneasy one.

By no means all the fault lay with Philip: for the twin disruptive forces of religion and trade were now pulling the countries apart. Spain of course represented orthodox Catholicism of the most rigid kind. But England, while her Queen was never more than a very moderate Protestant, was moving further and further away from Catholicism until she gradually found herself poised as leader of the reformed churches. Then it was only a question of time before Philip, a bigoted member of the old Church and committed to active persecution, would fall hopelessly foul of the 'heretics' who composed the Protestant communities of Europe. For compromise of any kind was a thing quite unknown to the absolute ruler of Spain and her empire.

Contemporary with, and closely bound to, this religious disruption, there came the startling rise of the English middle classes, and especially of those burgesses and business men who dwelt in the towns. It was this class which was now, as it were, bursting at the seams: in every way too—in wealth, in enterprise, in ambition and in sheer push. And when to this is added the fact that an overwhelming majority of such people inclined to Protestantism, it was inevitable that the new anti-catholic urge would shatter for ever the now rather shadowy concept of 'friendship' with Spain.

For the new English middle-class had for long noted that vast areas of the world were underdeveloped; and they, being traders to the marrow, felt a real itch to develop trade therein:

[1] *'Bella gerant Alii; tu, Felix Austria, Nube!'* men said.

their own robust brand of trade too, which, when dealing with the Portuguese, had always been a rough and ready business. And now that Anglo-Spanish friendship was palpably wearing thin, the Spaniards were tending more and more to interfere in English trade with themselves even to the beating up of individual Englishmen engaged in sea-trade. But those forthright merchants with their equally forthright crews were dangerous people to cross, being always liable to retaliate in kind, and not in the least afraid of using all the weapons which they possessed: in fact, pugnacious to a degree, hot-blooded and positively relishing a good scrap.

During the 1560s 'regrettable incidents' all over the world succeeded each other almost monotonously: and it was not to be expected that the Hawkins brothers would keep clear of them. Far from it. From 1562 onwards the younger Hawkins was very much in the lead, trying first to make friendly trade with the Spaniards, but later, after certain rebuffs, coming back to *take* trade of a much less friendly sort, while his elder brother stood four-square behind him, encouraging him in every step of the way.

The three voyages made to Africa and the West Indies by John between the years 1562 and 1569 will be dealt with in their place. Here we must see what William II, keeping as it were the home-goal, was doing while his brother's roving commission took him far to south and west.

For the first of these expeditions in 1562 the brothers were probably still in partnership. At any rate all the three vessels engaged in it were Hawkins ships, as was a fourth ship which probably sailed with the others. William himself was not to accompany it because already much work remained to be done at home. Though the Hawkinses furnished the ships and looked after the manning of them, many other people in the country helped to finance the affair, because, like almost all the ventures of that day, it was a strictly 'joint-stock company', with shares taken by the promoters of it and dividends paid according to the size of the share. Certainly a 'General Manager', sited in England, was a necessity. So William's role remained strictly that of the merchant with maritime interests who administered this particular venture along with many other activities then being undertaken by the firm. In this undertaking, we know, the other principals were widely drawn from the various people in England who were interested: some from Plymouth itself but others from much further afield; some—and those with the larger business shares—from London: people, indeed, closely connected with the Crown, such as Benjamin Gonson, John's father-in-law and Treasurer of the Queen's own Navy, and William (afterwards Sir William) Winter, the Surveyor of her Navy. This was a very normal pattern for such joint-stock companies. Whether an even more exalted personage—the Queen of England herself—had her share on this occasion is not known for certain. But the chances are that, this time, she had not. The participation of Elizabeth was usually a very closely-guarded secret, because in those earlier days anyway, when the fiction of friendship with Spain had at all costs to be maintained, it was of the greatest consequence to the Crown that the Spanish Ambassador should be kept in the dark as to whether she was in it at all.

The same general arrangements, and the same close secrecy covered both the second and the third voyages too: with one big difference, however. The backers of the second voyage included, in addition to Gonson and Winter, a number of even more highly-placed subjects, including the Earl of Pembroke, Lord Robert Dudley (the Queen's particular darling, now created Earl of Leicester), Lord Clinton (the Lord Admiral), and—but with his share most carefully concealed—Sir William Cecil, the Queen's Chief Minister and Adviser. And to this galaxy of English talent we now know must be added the name of the Queen herself who—but still with the greatest secrecy— actually contributed by lending the Syndicate a ship of her own, in lieu of a financial subscription. This ship was the *Jesus of Lubeck*, a large, though already elderly vessel of 700 tons.

The third voyage, begun in 1567, was in essence similar. Most of the same distinguished Englishmen contributed, and the Queen herself provided, this time, two of her royal ships, though still pretending that she was doing no such thing. This expedition, as we are later to see, was a costly failure, with momentous results if only because it put paid to that already fading period of friendship with Spain, and made the great

Anglo-Spanish conflict inevitable. Even then, however, neither side saw fit to declare open war. Instead, both embarked upon a long period of veiled hostilities, which, nowadays, we should designate as 'cold war'. It lasted to within three years of Philip's full-blooded assault on England in 1588.

From our immediate point of view, however, the importance of the last two voyages lies in the change they brought about in the status of the Hawkins brothers. They remained what they always had been—great merchants carrying on what seemed to them their lawful occasions in the field of trade: but now, in addition, they began to become the direct servants of the Crown engaged in ever more and more formal 'naval operations'. With John this happened first: for when in 1564 he sailed upon his second voyage, he went carrying what we should now call 'the Queen's Commission'. He went, in fact, as the nearest thing then existing to a 'naval officer', commanding a warship of the Royal Navy, though of course quite unpaid for it: and in the third voyage he was in the same position. But during both voyages, in which he did not participate in person, William II remained officially nothing but the private merchant, though gradually drawn more and more into the vortex of purely state affairs. Nor did he ever become, in the sense that John did, a 'naval officer', though once the cold war began he cheerfully took his orders more and more often from London—from Cecil, from the Lord Admiral and from the Queen herself. He became, in fact, the official (and of course unpaid) Government Agent in the West. While still remaining in name, and in essence, a merchant, he began to take an ever-increasing part in a major English war—because, of course, that war itself was, to the last, waged largely by 'joint-stock company'.

Meanwhile his civic duties continued unabated, and in 1567–8 he became Mayor of Plymouth for the first time. It was just at the moment when his year of office was up that several things began to happen almost simultaneously. In November 1568 the Spanish Government was guilty of a great folly. In order to pay the troops of the Duke of Alba, now operating against the Protestants in the Low Countries, it sent out, in an unarmed merchantman and a number of pinnaces, also unarmed, a very large treasure in coined money. They had no escort at all, though they must have known that literally scores of privateers from the Low Countries and the English Channel-ports were prowling in the narrow seas on the look-out for just this. November in those climes was a notorious month for storms, and a gale struck the precious flotilla. The ship stood it out until she was opposite the Isle of Wight, when she could make no more headway and turned into the Solent and so up to Southampton. The little pinnaces did not get so far, but ran into the western ports of Falmouth, Fowey and Plymouth, pursued by the ravenous pack. The ship was instantly detained, on the grounds that the Government could not protect her from the privateers, even when she was lying under the guns of Southampton. Fifty-nine chests of treasure were therefore landed, to be held in the 'safe keeping' of the English authorities. The pinnaces, with ninety-eight chests of money between them, were also brought ashore and placed in the equally 'safe' custody of William the Mayor.

Meanwhile, many thousands of miles away in the New World, although no one in England was certain of it, John had just been set upon, most treacherously, at San Juan de Ulua in Mexico. But already foul play was suspected in Plymouth, and the officers in charge of the Spanish pinnaces were straightly questioned by William. One of them, a certain Captain Diaz, finding himself in Plymouth harbour surrounded by a score or more privateers, all armed to the teeth, and all carrying the commission of the Protestant Prince of Condé, feared the worst. Knowing that John had escaped in person and was even now drawing near home, he span for William's benefit an ingenious yarn, true in some minor details yet basically a lie of the first water.

John Hawkins, so the story ran, 'has been in the enchanted garden of Aladdin, and has loaded himself with gold and jewels. He had taken a ship with 800,000 ducats, sacked a town, and taken heaps of pearls and jewels. A Spanish fleet of forty-four sail had passed a harbour where he was dressing his ships. On board the Spanish fleet'—corroborative detail intended to give verisimilitude to an otherwise bald and unconvincing narrative, as Pooh-Bah once said—'a council of war had been held to consider the prudence of attacking him: but the Admiral had said, "For the ships that be in harbour I will not deal with them, for they, being monstrous ships will sink some of us and put us to the worst. Wherefore, let us depart on our voyage"—adding, for good measure, the worst boy in those ships might be a captain for riches. And he (Diaz) wished he had been one of his men!'[1]

But alas for the clever Diaz! A day or two later John, in the *Minion*, limped into sight, and the real facts, basically different from those of Diaz, quickly emerged. And William was still holding grimly on to the frigates and their chests!

While anxiously awaiting news, William, whose love for his brother was very real, suffered agonies of apprehension which are clearly expressed in a letter written to Sir William Cecil five days before John reappeared, but on the very day when Francis Drake, who had escaped from San Juan in another ship, had reached Plymouth. Even then William was still in doubt about John's fate: for Drake, though he knew all about the treacherous Spanish attack in Mexico, did not then know what had happened to his commanding officer.

> Right Honorable.
> My bounden dewtye alwayes had in Remembrance it may please your honor to be advertisyd that this present hour there is come to Plymouth one of the small barkes of my brothers fleat and, for that I have neither wrytynge nor anything else from him, I thought it good and moste my dewty to send you the capetayne of the same barke, being our kinsman called Fransyes Dracke for that he shall thoroughly informe your honor of the whole proceedyngs of these affayres to the end the Queenes Ma— may be advertisyd of the same, and for that it doth plainly appear of their manyfest injuries from time to time offered, and our losses only in this voyage two thousand pounds at least, besydes my brothers absense, which unto me is more grefe than any other thing in this world, whom I trust, as god hathe preserved, will likewise preserve, and send well home in safety.
> In the meane tyme my humble suit unto your honor is that the Quenes Majeste will when time shall serve, see me, her humble and obedyent subjecte, partly recompenssed, of those Spanyards goods here stayd.
> And further if it shall please her grace to give me leave to work my own selfe against them, to the end I may be better recompenssed, I shall be the more bownde unto her highnes which I pray god long to live, to the glory of god, and the comfort of her subjectes. If I may have any warrant from her Matie or from your honor I shall be glad

---

[1] State Papers, Dom., Eliz., vol. 49, No. 3.

to set forth four ships of mine own presently I have already commission in these things from the Cardanal Shatyllyon[1] for one ship to serve the princes of Navarre and Coundye but I may not presume any futher without commission in these things I shall desire your honors to be advertisyd by my servant Francis Dracke and I shall daily pray for your honors estate long to endure.

From Plymouth the xxth of january at night 1468

By your honors always to command

Wm Hawkins.

As for the pay of Alba's troops, it naturally never reached them. The truth came out just too soon for that! As it was, the treasure remained for a long time a diplomatic talking-point between England and Spain. But then Elizabeth and her lawyers made a considerable, and convenient, discovery—that, legally, it had never really belonged to Spain at all, but was still the property of certain Genoese bankers. Thereupon the Queen cut the Gordian knot by borrowing it herself from the bankers!

William's letter just quoted raises the knotty point of the relationship of Francis Drake with the Hawkins clan. That some relationship did exist seems certain, but what exactly it was has remained unknown. At first it sounds odd to hear William referring to the greatest Elizabethan seaman as 'my servant'. But it must be remembered that Drake was still a very young man, still with his name to make, perhaps ten years younger than John, and more than twenty the junior of William.

Both the first John Hawkins and Edmund Drake, the father of Francis, were 'of Tavistock', which, in the sixteenth century was quite a small place. Sir Julian Corbett, who went into the question in some detail,[2] concluded that Edmund was 'possibly his (William's) first cousin, or perhaps brother-in-law', but then admits that 'the exact relationship is not ascertained'. On the Hawkins side at least, he does not seem to be very well informed. He says, for instance, that 'John and William, the old Captain's sons, were now (i.e. when Francis was born) some twelve or thirteen years old.' This is approximately true of John; but Corbett seems unconscious of the fact that William was much older than John, again by some twelve or thirteen

---

[1] Chatillon, brother of Coligny, the Admiral of France.
[2] In *Drake and the Tudor Navy*, vol. I, p. 62.

years. All, however, is merely guess-work, with Corbett's first alternative likelier than his second.

As soon as John, weak from starvation and exhaustion, reached Mount's Bay, he got into touch with William, who instantly sent thither, to bring the storm-wracked *Minion* into Plymouth, 'a barque with xxxiiij mariners, store of flesh vytles, two ankers, iij cables and store of small warps, with other necessaries as I thought good'. Then, having apparently received leave from London to dispatch his ships against the people whom he now regarded as his worst enemies, William proceeded to fit out no less than eight of his own private fleet for the purpose of retaliation, indeed, in his eyes, of revenge; and John, dauntless as ever, allowed himself only a few days with his brother in which to recuperate and then set out instantly for London. Here he found the Court and Council in some confusion, with Elizabeth (as usual) hovering between a strong policy against Spain, and the weaker one of letting sleeping dogs lie for a while. In the end, however, she compromised, deciding to send an expedition to the aid of the Huguenots at La Rochelle, and not even yet against Spain herself; and it is fairly certain that John was put in command of it. This was a very powerful fleet, containing a number of Royal Ships, with a strong squadron of merchantmen from Plymouth, including William's contingent of eight. It sailed in April and returned, its business satisfactorily accomplished, in July.

But such half-measures did not satisfy the angry William, who also had out, all through that summer, a large force of his own privateers carrying on the usual reprisals in the Channel. In that year, in fact, William was engaged up to the neck in organizing all the activities of the Channel privateers. And this meant much more than being a mere merchant, or even privateer owner. He was virtually commander-in-chief of what was already becoming a Protestant navy in its own right, based upon Plymouth, and completely cosmopolitan in personnel, winked at and probably supported by the Queen of England, though she was very careful never to let her name to appear 'on the bills'. In this year, then, William was essentially conducting the Queen's business, albeit incognito, by proxy, and quite unpaid.

For good measure, too, at the end of this hectic year of 1569, William decided to go to sea himself, and did so. No record of this voyage survives on the English side, but Spanish sources vouch for it.[1] He was already fifty years old, for those days an ageing man, and he had never, so far as is known, commanded at sea before. Yet sea life was no novelty to him, and certain Spanish prisoners whom he took bear witness to the fact that he treated them well: which only serves to show that, like his father and brother, he must have been at heart a kindly man. They also say that his own underlings treated him with real respect. He cruised, it seems, between Spain and the Canaries; but, though the Spaniards suspected him of designs on Brazil, there is no evidence that he ever got so far.

Once home again, he reverted quite naturally to his normal life, as John's agent in Plymouth, and as the local merchant prince taking every opportunity to improve his native town, and confer benefits upon his fellow-townsmen. Already during his Mayoral year he had made a set of rules for the cleansing and keeping clean of the port. Then, in 1570, he built at his own expense a new conduit, to improve the water-supply; and three years later he and John farmed the town mills, which in that day were still built across the mouth of the Mill Bay and worked by tide-power. They provided a special house to weigh the grain before it was milled, and a horse, cart and man, to bring the sacks of corn from the private houses of the people—a great boon to the ordinary Plymothian. No wonder the townsmen honoured him by making him their Mayor twice more, and to the last loved and admired him.

In associating the Hawkinses with Plymouth, J. A. Williamson, the talented biographer of John, goes even further. Why, he asks, was it Plymouth, and not one of the other Channel ports, which became in Tudor times 'an ocean port, a naval base, a privateers' mart, the western bastion of England's defences?' Why not Dartmouth, why not Southampton, both of which had maritime facilities at least as great? His answer is, simply, that it was the Hawkinses who made sixteenth-century Plymouth.

If they had chanced to be Dartmouth men they might have made Dartmouth all that; for it had natural advantages as good as Ply-

[1] *Vide* Miss I. A. Wright, *Spanish Main Documents*, p. 26.

mouth's. Geography has for some purposes given Southampton a
better position than either, but its merchants and captains had fallen
so sleepy in the later Tudor period that we hear little of them. . . .
Natural science alone does not explain human affairs. Personality
counts for much.[1]

Without doubt Williamson is right: and of all the Hawkins
family the man who performed this feat, almost single-handed,
was William II. He, more than any other, gave his life-work to
his much-loved town. And more than any other he was Plymouth's 'big man'.

In 1574 a fresh character appears on the Plymouth scene in the
person of Sir Richard Grenville. He was a great landowner who
lived just across the Cornish border at Stowe, and he had important interests in the north Devon port of Bideford, as well as
properties (including Buckland Abbey) in South Devon too.
Then again, though not a merchant quite like William, coming
as he did from an older and much more gentle family, he was also
a very considerable shipowner. His famous sea action at the very
end of his life has deceived many who are unfamiliar with the
period into thinking of him as a seaman, and a commander of
ships and fleets afloat. He was not such, however, but in his own
day was regarded rather as a soldier, a big landowner, a J.P.
and large shipowner. His actual sea-time was probably a good
deal shorter than that of William II. Yet it was in connection
with one particular ship that he became associated with the
Hawkinses. In 1574 William and he each bought a half-share in
the *Castle of Comfort*, a fine ship of that day which, though
euphemistically called a merchantman, is not once in her long
and troubled story found to be engaged upon ordinary trading
ventures. Yet the contemporary records contain her name more
often than that of any other ship. Indeed, wherever there was
trouble, there was the *Castle of Comfort* in the thick of it.

It was so now. Almost as soon as she became their joint
property, they sent her off to that hot-spot of confused all-in
fighting, the port of Flushing from which the Sea-Beggars
operated. From the very beginning she became deeply involved
in the feats of those all-but mythical people who were already—

[1] *Hawkins of Plymouth*, p. 196.

and were to remain—the very core of the Low Countries' resistance to Spain. It was deliberate fishing in troubled waters. In 1576, for instance, the bellicose *Castle* took a Breton ship from St Malo. Her outraged owners brought the matter to the notice of the Admiralty Court in London. In law, the partners had not a leg to stand upon. Though neither of them had been present in the *Castle* at the time of the capture, Sir Richard was put up by the 'syndicate' to plead in defence of their action, and, though right was very clearly *not* on their side, Grenville's somewhat dominating personality made a great impression upon the judges, if it did not actually get the delinquents off—the exact verdict is nowhere recorded. It must be admitted that this class of activity does not greatly redound to the credit of either of them. But it was all too symptomatic of the evils implicit in the whole privateering set-up. We should remember too that—as usual—at that very time William II had out whole fleets of *true* merchantmen busily engaged upon their really lawful occasions. Thereafter for a while their ways parted. Grenville busied himself with a fascinating project (which, however, came to nothing at that time) to discover and possess the vast land of 'Terra Australis Incognita'—a land which, in the main, did not actually exist at all—while William returned to his home chores, and was, in 1578–9, once more appointed Mayor of Plymouth.

But now the period of cold war was coming to its troubled and predestined end; and the Government, not without startling bouts of shilly-shallying, began to turn its attention to the vexed problem of the defence of England against a probable invasion from Spain. Once more the indefatigable William emerges into the limelight. The safeguarding of the port seemed to everyone —the Crown, all good Plymothians and the Hawkinses themselves—to be a part of the Hawkins responsibility. So, in 1580, William II undertook to see to the defences of St Nicholas's (afterwards Drake's) Island which lay athwart the very entrances to the port. Five years later, just as the hot war started, he was granted the somewhat derisory sum of £39 10s 0d annually for the provision of four permanent gunners for the island battery. It seems most inadequate, but two things must be remembered. First, any surplus expenditure—and there must have been quite a lot—was, tacitly, to be shouldered by William:

and second, the true safeguards of a place like Plymouth cannot be measured by its four permanent gunners. The real defences were every able-bodied man in the town, all legally bound to serve, and fanatically prepared to do so.

King Philip was now becoming really formidable. In 1580, taking advantage of a disputed succession in Portugal, he had put in a claim to the whole of that country, and had, almost without resistance, sent in troops to occupy it. This was an immense acquisition of strength, especially of naval strength, because the Portuguese Royal Navy was a first-class one. Swallowing also the whole Empire of the East, Philip added enormously to the resources of Spain.

At much the same time Drake returned from his highly successful voyage of circumnavigation, his holds bulging with the spoils of Spanish America. These losses, it hardly needs saying, were bitterly resented by Philip. And when Elizabeth almost fell upon the arch-pirate's neck, and knighted him on the deck of the *Golden Hind*, war looked absolutely certain. And so it was, though it was still delayed for another five years because neither Elizabeth nor Philip wanted it just yet. So, with utterly hollow expressions of regret, the protagonists returned to their old game of stabbing at each other where they thought it would most hurt, pretending the while to be the greatest friends. Philip made a dead set at such English merchantmen as were in his ports: Elizabeth (after her usual vacillations) sent out her seamen to repeat, if that were possible, the feats of El Draque.

Amongst others to fit out expeditions was, of course, William II. And this time he himself went out again in command. It was a sporting thing to do, because he was, by the standard of those days, a really old man, sixty-three in 1582 when he started, and sixty-four when he returned the following year. He seems, however, to have shown no signs of mental decline, but to have conducted himself with all propriety and his expedition with all skill. Fourteen years later his brother was to make the sad trip which proved to be his last. He too was sixty-four, but he was by this time noticeably past his best. The difference probably lay in the fact that John, the spear-head of the family, had a much harder and more exhausting life than his 'administrative' elder brother, having braved the perils of sea-life much more often, not to mention experiencing the frustrations of his public life—much more trying than anything which had come William's way. For where William was grappling, mostly, with only one town's problems, or at most one district's, John, uncomplaining, had for the last decade borne the much more wearing, more responsible duty of building up the whole English fleet to face up to a vast national war, and thereafter the task of sustaining it at war strength.

Again this voyage of William II in 1582–3 is very badly documented in English sources. In them, in fact, virtually the only mention of it occurs as a mere reminiscence in the great work of Richard Hawkins[1] published some forty years later when Richard himself was just dead, and William had been gone for well over thirty. Save for this reference to his uncle, whom Richard accompanied in 1582, we must reserve all account of this remarkable book until we come to discuss the career of the author himself. Otherwise our only knowledge of what occurred is derived from Spanish writings, especially those of Pedro Sarmiento, recorded by the Hakluyt Society,[2] and some surviving reports of the municipal authorities of Puerto Rico.

William's original intention, it seems, was to work in conjunction with Don Antonio, an (illegitimate) ecclesiastic who claimed to be the rightful heir of Portugal, and whom, for purposes of policy, Elizabeth was backing. He was not the most satisfactory of claimants, but he was the best then available. At this time certain strategic Portuguese islands (e.g. the Azores and Cape Verdes) had declared for Don Antonio, under whose commission William was sailing. His squadron consisted of seven ships, two of which belonged to Drake and others to the Hawkinses. It is not clear where exactly they went, but they did turn up, first of all, at Cape Verde. Here, it seems, there was severe fighting, in which the English did not come off best—there are accusations of ill-faith on the enemy side, including the murder of a number of Englishmen, mostly Drake's. Then the expedition certainly proceeded to Brazil, which was still, as in Old William's time, but sparsely settled by the Portuguese. Moreover quite a

---

[1] *The Observations of Sir Richard Hawkins, Knight, in his Voyage into the Southern Seas, Anno Domino, 1593.*
[2] *The Voyages of Sarmiento*, pp. 179, 182–3.

number of the European inhabitants were actually English. One party had settled near Rio de Janeiro, but, having suddenly been attacked by the Portuguese five years before, they had vanished into the interior—of the upland natives, it was firmly believed in England! But another party still survived at Santos,[1] where they traded with the natives in, among other things, 'barrels of the leaf called *petune*', that is, tobacco. He probably made contact with these men; but he did not stay for long on the mainland, making his way into the Caribbean. He is next reported as being on the Island of Margarita, the pearl centre. Here, Richard Hawkins tells us, he dredged for pearl oysters 'after the manner we dredge oysters in England', that is, with nets, and not by employing native divers.

Next they appeared in the island of Puerto Rico where the inhabitants were very disappointed at not finding Don Antonio on board, but only William, of whom they were very nervous. But he seems to have left the island without doing any damage. This happy ending, according to the report of one of the Spanish captains named Castellanos, was solely due to the prowess and enterprise of—Captain Castellanos! The English, he alleged, sent a watering-party 150 strong, on shore. But with only seven men the intrepid fellow stole so quietly upon them and took them so completely by surprise, that the whole 150 bolted as one man. Two days later, however, the Governor himself sent in his report telling a somewhat different story. The gallant captain, in this version, came upon *two* Englishmen and, taking them by surprise, killed one and took the other prisoner. Somehow it seems the likelier version of the two!

It was still four months before the expedition reached home; and it would be interesting to know what it did or where it went during that time because, apparently, much must have happened. So far our authorities have mentioned no solid gains accruing to the voyage. 'We had profitted the adventurers nothing,' says Sir Richard. Yet only four months later the Spanish Ambassador is writing to his master to say that William's ship was back at Plymouth laden with vast spoils of pearls and treasure, not to mention many mercantile commodities like hides

[1] Not the modern place of that name in lat. 24° S., but another rather further north at 20½° S.

and sugar. A Dutch merchant, writing from London, assesses his booty at 800,000 crowns. The Ambassador further reported that William was busy fitting out another expedition. It sounds not unlikely. After all William was primarily a business man, and dividends like this would certainly prove *very* tempting! But if he did go again, History is quite silent on the point.

It is in fact pretty clear that William himself never went to sea again. Mary Hawkins, indeed, anxious to crown as many Hawkinses as possible with Armada laurels, declares that he did—that he commanded the *Griffin*, a vessel of 200 tons in all the Anti-Armada actions. But this is extremely unlikely. William was now sixty-nine, and within a year of his end. It is true that, in the English lists, there was a *Griffen*, and she was commanded by a William Hawkins. But it was not William II who, from November, 1587 to November, 1588 was serving as Mayor of Plymouth for the third and last time. And all through those busy months he was doing what we should expect him to be doing, and in the doing of which he can have had no equal. He was doing the less spectacular but equally vital work of fitting out ships for the emergency. On the other hand, to command a ship of war in a naval fleet action was certainly not his forte. It is in fact almost certain that he never did any such thing.

Who then was the William Hawkins who commanded the *Griffin*? The obvious man is William's eldest son, William III. The date of his birth is not known, but he was probably much the same age as his cousin Richard, John's only son. We shall have a great deal to say of him later, because he is the fifth and last of the famous Hawkinses of Plymouth.

Our knowledge of William II's married life is curiously sketchy. We do not even know the maiden name of his first wife, but his second, who outlived him was Mary, daughter of John Halse of Kenedon and Efford. Between them the two wives bore William 11 children, of whom the first-born, by several years, was William III.

The grand old man of Plymouth just reached his three score years and ten. He died on October 7, 1589. But he did not die in his beloved Plymouth: nor were his bones laid there. This may have grieved him, but it is not very surprising. Though he was much less of a national figure than his brother, he still had a good deal of business to transact in Town, both his own merchant's business and—as a J.P. and Government agent—the State's business too. Inevitably he was often in London, and naturally, when there, went to stay with John, who had at least two houses in Town, the main one near the Tower and another one at Deptford, a few miles down-Thames from it: and it was here that death caught up with William II.

He was buried in the graveyard of St. Nicholas at Deptford, that church so intimately associated with English seamen of all ages. Within it John caused a monument to be erected, which, unfortunately, has since been removed. The original was in latin, a translation of which reads as follows:

> To the ever living memory of William Hawkins
> of Plymouth esquire,
> Who was a worshipper of the true religion;
> benefactor to poor mariners;
> skilled in navigation;
> oftentimes undertaking long voyages;
> a just arbiter in difficult causes
> and a man of singular faith, probity and prudence.
> He had two wives,
> Four children by one and seven by the other.
> John Hawkins, Knight, Treasurer of the Queen's Navy,
> his brother, most sorrowfully erected this.
> He died in the sure and certain hope of resurrection
> on the 7th day of October, in the year of Our Lord, 1589.

So William II passed on seven years before his better-known brother. There was unquestionably a distinct fraternal likeness between them: but John was the greater man of the two, if only because his main activities covered a wider—a nation-wide—field. It is perhaps no accident that, in his memorial to his brother, he laid some stress upon the navigational skill of William and his undertaking of long voyages. But his order of stresses is interesting, and since they knew each other so well, they bear the stamp of truth.

They are, *first*, that William was 'a worshipper of the true religion'. He certainly was that, and he shared it with John. Next he was 'a benefactor to poor mariners', and here again John had the same trait, strongly marked—both, one presumes, having inherited it from their own father. Then, after bearing witness to his maritime enterprise, comes a significant reference to William's work as Mayor and local Justice of the Peace. And here the elder brother's contribution to local affairs was definitely greater than John's own, because he spent more of his time and energies upon them. Then, finally, comes his witness to William's abiding characteristics: he was a man of singular faith, probity and prudence. These are well-chosen words, covering William's duty towards God, his duty towards his neighbour, and his mercantile wisdom.

It is of course notorious that epitaphs tend to flatter the deceased, and here real respect and affection for his only brother may well have coloured John's picture of William. But John was too honest and true-hearted merely to 'write up' the dead. And surely anyone in the world would be proud of such a testimonial from such a man as John Hawkins!

The portrait reproduced between pp. 16 and 17 hangs in the Lord Mayor's Parlour in Plymouth. It is inscribed '[aetatis su] ae 74, Año Dñi 1596'. It shows an old man's face, beautiful and exceptionally well-painted. The dates on it correspond with none of the Hawkins family, but the Corporation has always called it— and still does—John Hawkins, though he was dead in 1596: nor was he then seventy-four years old; nor, of course, was he born in 1522, but in 1532.

But Mary Hawkins has a more interesting theory, that it represents the elder brother William, of whom no other likeness exists. She finds a striking resemblance in it to other portraits of John. Of that the reader may judge for himself if he will compare it with the two almost-certain likenesses of John: the 'Chatham' one which is the Frontispiece of this book, and the Buckland Abbey one reproduced at p. 17. The dates, of course, are still wrong: William II's were 1519–89. But at least he did arrive at three score years and ten, which none of the others did. And old men in those days often seemed to lose track of their real ages: which might account for his saying that he was seventy-four. The date too, 1596, may have been inserted later.

There can be no certainty here: nor perhaps shall we ever know the truth. But this face remains the nearest we are ever likely to get to a portrait of John's merchant-brother, thrice Mayor of Plymouth.

CHAPTER IV

John Hawkins

✍︎

a. EARLY DAYS

THERE can be little doubt that John was born, and passed his childhood in the old Hawkins home in Kinterbury Street, where his father, William I lived, and was destined to go on living for over twenty more years. He must also have received the rudiments of his education in Plymouth, though probably not, like his brother William, at the hands of a chantry priest from the House of the Greyfriars: for, between the times of William and John, the chantry, and even the House itself, had disappeared. This state of things must have prevailed for a number of years throughout the country, because one immediate effect of the Dissolution of the Monasteries was to cause a hiatus in ordinary education, such as it then was. John must have been ready for schooling round about 1538–9, having been born in 1532. But the Edwardian Grammar Schools, the earliest attempt to provide lay (as opposed to Church) education, did not as a rule get under way before the 1550s. Yet, on the whole, the most likely educator of John would be an *ex*-chantry priest. When deprived of their livelihoods, most of them stayed on in their own localities as lay teachers, at which task they were already comparatively qualified. So one of them may well have had the task of teaching young John his 'three R's'. Moreover, if so, he must have done his job well, because John did somehow get well grounded in them, quite as well as, if not better than, his elder brother. In fact, of the two, John was the superior in the art of self-expression. But this may have been because, by and large, John had rather the better mind than William, and so was more capable of assimilating what he was taught.

71

Yet otherwise the early careers of the boys were essentially the same. If, as we have supposed, William had ceased his primary education in, say, 1530, in time to accompany his father on his first voyage of that year, then John would have finished his in or about 1543, and then would have embarked upon his wider education in one of his father's ships. In the 1540s those ships were very active, whether the elder William accompanied them or not. Then, in 1545, the French Wars began and the Hawkins clan found itself committed to the privateering programme in the Channel and elsewhere. Here were obvious opportunities for the lad to serve his apprenticeship in trade, in seamanship, in navigation and in fighting.

Even as early as 1542, when John was barely ten years old, there survives a tantalizing scrap of information. In that year a certain John Hawkins was made a 'farmer of the wynewits', and paid at the rate of ten shillings for his work. There were in Plymouth a number of people called Hawkins, some of whom were probably called John. So it cannot be certain that our John was the boy who secured this unimportant and ill-paid post. But it may well be the future Sir John, appointed to the job by the influence of the leading merchant and burgess of the town, his own father. It is quite in character, too, for William I to have done this, because he would certainly realize the importance to his child of having this kind of experience in real 'business', earning money (however little) at a very tender age.

Our next notice of a Hawkins, who this time is almost certainly our John comes in 1552 when the lad had just turned twenty. In that year one of this name was granted a royal pardon for the manslaughter of one John White. It comes as rather a shock, perhaps, to learn that a man whose nature throughout life was essentially gentle had already at so tender an age taken a human life. But this should not put us off. For one thing the Coroner's verdict makes it pretty clear that White was the aggressor; and that John was only defending himself. But even if this was not so, the essential crudity of the times must not be overlooked. In those days, and in a town like Plymouth, even manslaughter was an incident far from abnormal. For, at the time, the sanctity of human life was not very well appreciated: not, at any rate, as it is now. In fact, if the fatal fracas took place, as it almost certainly did, in fair fight—and still more if it were in self-defence—we should be very wrong if we regarded young John as anything in the least like a modern murderer.

The next news we have of John is in 1556, when he spent a considerable time in France, trying in the law courts of Brest to get the *Peter*, a ship belonging to the family, restored to its owners. It is not known whether he succeeded, but it is known that on this occasion he made the acquaintance of several people —the English Ambassador in France, for instance, and the French Ambassador in England, who recommended him to his own Government. Here is a good line on his character, and on what people were already thinking about him. Here he was acting in a novel capacity, and a responsible one too, for a young fellow of only twenty-four. Already, it seems, he was leaving behind his primary avocations of seaman and merchant, and becoming involved in a higher sphere, that of diplomacy, to which he already seemed to show a natural aptitude.

It was some time in the late 1550s that he ceased to call himself 'of Plymouth', and became 'of London'. This, however does not mean that he severed all links with the town of his birth and transferred his allegiance to the greater city. It was not, in fact very much more than a change of address, or even of acquiring an alternative address, because he still remained a burgess and a merchant of Plymouth, and he still passed a good deal of his time there. Moreover he retained till the day of his death his properties in the town, including his share of wharfage in Sutton Pool. He also still maintained many of his ships in the western port. The exact date of this apparent move is not known: nor does it greatly matter except as an indication that his interests were already feeling outwards. It is not even very important that the firm of Hawkins Brothers now split into the two firms of William Hawkins and John Hawkins, because, as we saw, the split itself was more apparent than real, John never doing anything to thwart William, nor William John. Yet this *is* a sort of landmark in John's life because he now bought a house in Deptford— somewhere, it must be presumed, near the Royal Dock and Victualling Yard established a few years earlier by King Henry VIII. A little later he took a house in the City, in the parish of St Dunstan's-in-the-East, which he retained for the rest of his life. This is why his monument was placed in St Dunstan's Church, where it perished during the Great Fire of 1666.

The move was probably made in 1558; and it is not altogether accidental if it happened in that year—the year in which Queen Mary died, to be succeeded by her half-sister Elizabeth. For that event led inevitably, but at first rather slowly, to a great change in the relationships of the Western European Powers. For a while, it is true, France remained our Enemy Number One—there was a new outbreak of war in 1559—and Spain remained our ally, though an uneasy one, with Anglo-Spanish relations becoming yearly more and more soured. Yet the turning-point had really already come in 1558, when the English Government ceased to frown upon the efforts of English merchants and seamen to trade with foreigners, especially Catholic ones. Indeed it may well have been this fact which induced John to set up an establishment in the heart of things.

Another inevitable result of the move was an enlargement in John's circle of acquaintances. He moved first, it would seem, into what might be called the 'Navy Board Circle'—those important people who filled the four official posts, created by Henry VIII, of Treasurer of the Navy, Comptroller of the Navy, Surveyor of the Navy, and Clerk of the Ships (later of the Acts). They were not the titular heads of the Navy—there was the Lord Admiral who occupied that position—but they were the effective administrators of the Queen's ships, and, whenever the Monarch possessed a strong fleet of royal vessels, they were people who carried a very real responsibility. At this time the Treasurer of the Navy was the most important of these officers, followed by the Comptroller, the Surveyor and the Board's secretary, the Clerk of the Ships. At the time when John appeared in London, the Treasurer was a man called Benjamin Gonson. Moreover, Benjamin had a daughter, Katherine, and in 1559 John married her. There can be no suggestion that the marriage, as they say, was one of convenience, or that John expected to gain anything from it. It has all the appearance of being a love-match which lasted, with true affection on both sides, until 1591, when she died, having been his helpmeet for thirty-two years. She seems to have been a good and amiable woman who provided for him a model home, to which he could retire when overpressed by harsh business. He himself declared his affection for her:

> Touching mine own worldly contentation, in my wife I am as well pleased and contented as I desire.

The testimony of the only child of the union survives too. Richard calls her 'a religious and most vertuous lady'. In his declining years John was married again, as we shall see, but this time not so happily. He had no children by the second wife, and the only thing that we really know of her does not greatly redound to her credit. But that belongs to the story of her step-son Richard.

So Katherine presided over John's city home. Yet she too was often to be found at his other and older home. It was in fact there that she gave birth to Richard, who, born in 1560, always regarded himself as a native of Plymouth.

Meanwhile, John fell in with a syndicate of rich City merchants of whom Gonson was one. In the group also was Sir William Winter who was not only Surveyor of the Navy but also Master of the Ordnance, and two wealthy Londoners, Sir Lionel Ducket and Sir Thomas Lodge. These men specialized in the Gold Coast Trade which operated in Lower Guinea, at some distance from Upper Guinea, whence the slavers of Portugal and Spain took their supplies of negroes; a trade already flourishing for those who used it long before John thought of entering it. It has been said that this slave trade cut across that of the gold-trade; but this is hardly so, because the relative sources of supply were a good thousand miles apart: and anyway, it was the Gold Syndicate which now put up the capital for a slaving venture.

A new phase in John's career now opened. It must be emphasized at once that, in the early 1560s, both trades were already long-standing. From time to time, ever since the days of William Hawkins I, various English expeditions braved the wrath of the Portuguese monopolists by going after the gold in Lower Guinea. But now John and his friends were about to make history by combining the two trades: the oft-tried English search for gold and the very profitable trade in 'black ivory' from Upper Guinea. This latter trade had always been the perquisite of the

Portuguese, though for some time other Europeans, including the French, the Dutch, and later the Spaniards had been intervening. So, though John must bear the responsibility of being the first *English* slaver, he was very far from being the first slaver. The other end of the route was, of course, Latin America— Central and South, though not yet North—where both the colonial powers of Portugal and Spain were crying aloud for black labour in their plantations.

In this business, which opened the three famous slaving voyages of the Hawkins clan, John's share was nothing if not original. He knew that he would have to face the opposition of Portugal, of which he had no fear. But he also intended to weigh in to what was in effect the monopoly of a much more powerful potentate, the King of Spain, the inscrutable Philip II, who, we must recall, had only just ceased to be the King of England too. And what made John's venture the more daring was the fact the Spanish trade in black ivory was already something of a personal vested interest in the hands of Philip! But John was no privateer here; and still less was he, in his own view, a pirate. For he was relying from the start upon certain old treaties of friendship between his own Government and that of Charles V's Empire—treaties dating back to the days of *real* friendship with Spain. Now that power had long since made a definite distinction between trading with the English (and others) in the Old World—which it was quite prepared to allow—and trading, in any form, with them in its new colonial empire of the New World. In a word, what John was hoping to do was to insinuate himself into the New World slave trade by blandly quoting the old treaties (made mainly with the Low Countires, still an integral part of Philip's Empire), trusting that Philip would not call his bluff—even though he now meant to enter the New World to secure a share in the Spanish slave trade: even though the trade had become Philip's personal monopoly.

It was quite an ambitious programme: and we know now that it failed, though not perhaps by much—by much less than we should expect. His pretensions ultimately foundered on the one solid fact that his success depended upon violating the King's own monopoly, so wounding Philip in a more than ordinarily tender spot. He failed then, thus going a long way towards making war with Spain inevitable. But he had a good run for his money first.

One big psychological interest in this attempt lies in the fact that John positively believed that right was on his side, and that Philip would play his game. He based this belief, it would seem, on two very different grounds. The first was more or less personal. He never tired of referring to Philip as 'the King my old Master' and like phrases, showing that he *expected* preferential treatment. There is even reason for supposing that, at some period in his career, he had earned the King's gratitude by performing for him some particular service. This is quite possible—there are distinct gaps in our knowledge of John's early life, and in any one of these he could have performed his service. Perhaps the most likely moment would have been when Philip first came to England, an unpopular stranger, to wed Queen Mary. He landed at Southampton after a miserably wet and rough passage. There is an odd bit of evidence that the two men's path crossed just then. A certain Spanish pilot named Juanes de Urquiza stated[1] that John as a young man was an officer in the royal ship which brought Philip to England; and that, on this occasion, he performed some signal service to the wretched seasick prince for which he was rewarded with a knighthood when Philip at length reached England. To believe the whole of this story is surely going a little far, if only because it is much too well-known that John's knighthood came to him only during the Armada campaign. But it remains quite possible, and even rather likely, that on this or some other occasion the two had been acquainted, and that some honour, perhaps only a minor one, had then been conferred upon him. Moreover, in 1554, when friendship with Spain was not only possible but even highly respectable, John may well have cherished a feeling of true loyalty to his Sovereign's husband; so that, when he came to make his voyage in the 1560s, he may well have been quite genuine in referring to Philip as 'my old Master'.

His other reason for half-expecting a successful issue to his plunge into the Spanish monopoly is much better documented. For many years past a thoroughly nasty internecine struggle had

[1] *Spanish Documents concerning English Voyages in the Caribbean*, ed. I. A. Wright, Hakluyt Society, 1929.

been going on all over the Spanish New World, between the
Catholic defenders of their monopoly and the mainly Calvinist
freebooters out of France, largely from La Rochelle. All such
exchanges had gone very much against the Spaniards. The
French corsairs had captured, sacked and burned Cartagena,
Santa Marta (twice), Santiago de Cuba, Havana and a score of
other places. No holds were barred. Prisoners were never taken.
All were put to the sword, or mercilessly tortured before being
slaughtered. There was every reason, then, in 1560, for thinking
that the Spanish Government had no chance of protecting its own
subjects, and, as a result, it might well be prepared to listen to
some offer of outside help. Unquestionably this was John's plan
—to enter the arena, boldly and openly, showing himself as a
respectable and bona fide merchant who always traded fair, and
to say in effect to Philip, 'See how much better we are than those
butchers, the French. Accept our help against them, and let us
enter into a formal partnership. In exchange for you buying our
merchandise (including slaves) and we being welcomed by you
in your markets, we will take over the task of protecting you
from the attacks of all other nationals.'

It was quite a reasonable gamble for John to take. But in the
end it did not come off, for a reason which John could not possibly
anticipate. In the 1560s there appeared a Spanish champion who
could—and did—deal successfully with the French interlopers,
and that without any help from the English. This was the great
captain Pero Menéndez de Avilés: and it was his prowess which
finally decided Philip not to agree to John's terms, so humiliating
to the pride of Spain.

There can be no doubt that John spared no effort to make his
plan work. For he courted not only Philip and the Spanish
Government but also a large number of private Spanish citizens,
mostly of the mercantile fraternity. With this end in view he
even made voyages—probably more than one—to the Canary
Islands, where he sedulously cultivated the acquaintance of some
of the leading Spaniards in residence there. One of these is not
without interest. His name was Pedro de Ponte, and he lived in
Tenerife. Quite a large number of these so-called Spaniards
were of English extraction, and very likely Pedro was one of
them, 'Ponte' being a mere Spanish rendering of 'Bridges' or

'Briggs'. It is worth noting that one prominent alderman of the City of London at that time was Sir John Bridges, who is known to have had a brother domiciled in Spain. Anyway, Pedro de Ponte was completely won over to John's point of view; and when the first expedition sailed he welcomed its arrival at Tenerife, and furnished John with an expert pilot from Cadiz, having earlier written to friends in Hispaniola to invite them to treat the expedition with sympathy and to do business with it. By such means John secured at least the promise of fair barter on the other side of the Atlantic.

The expedition was on such a small scale that the Hawkins interest alone could easily have managed it, and, in the matter of both ships and men, it actually did. All the vessels which comprised it—the *Saloman* (120 tons), the *Swallow* (100 tons), and the bark *Jonas* (40 tons), with perhaps a fourth and smaller one, unnamed—belonged to one or other of the brothers; while the crews, a mere one hundred seamen in all, were to a man local to Plymouth. But John let the London syndicate put up some of the money because he regarded the whole thing as a trial run, to gain experience for a bigger one to follow, in which he *would* need more financial and political backing.

John's 'prentice days were now over. He was entering the world—and at a distinctly higher level than his brother William ever reached. He needed for success the courage of the fighter, the flair of the leader of men, the sea-craft of the sailor, the astuteness of the merchant, and something of the suavity of the diplomat. He was not found wanting. He had them all.

b. THE FIRST SLAVING VOYAGE 1562

John himself gave Richard Hakluyt an account of his journey. Unfortunately, however, he wrote it only just in time for its inclusion in the first edition (1588–9) of the *Principal Voyages*. It reflects, therefore, the political background, not of 1562, but of 1588. And the two were radically different. In 1562 Spain was still England's oldest ally, so that, whatever befell, Spaniards were not to be molested or ill-treated by Englishmen. The Portuguese, on the other hand, were of little account, and were floutable almost at will. But twenty-six years later all had changed. Now Spain was the mortal enemy, to be flouted at all costs if we would survive: and Portugal, in the person of her luckless Pretender Don Antonio, was to be fostered and pandered to in every way, because we hoped that she and her people would take sides with us against Spain. So John's dealings with the Portuguese—which from the nature of the case were extremely rough and rude—are deliberately played down; indeed hardly mentioned.

This is a pity because, not only in this voyage but also in both its successors, the Portuguese were very vocal indeed in their lamentations and in their claims on the English Government for reparations. These are without any doubt grossly exaggerated; and there is every reason to suppose that many of the Portuguese on the spot—broken-down half-breeds for the most part—actually acquiesced in John's alleged brutalities, loudly pretending that he used force against them only after he had gone. Thus where John, in the account he gave to Hakluyt, says that he secured only 300 negroes, the Portuguese accusations put the figure at 910, not counting an unspecified number from one of his alleged prizes, which would bring the total up to well over 1,000: and not to mention large quantities of other commodities like gold and ivory. They also alleged that he violently seized one of their ships and carried it off with him to America. That would amount to arrant piracy: and indeed he probably did acquire a ship there, for there would not have been room in his three (or four) tiny ships for even so many as 300 negroes.

But John's story—which, knowing him as we do, sounds far more likely—is that he did not seize the ship in question, but chartered it from its owners, paying a fair price for it. He also, very possibly, sent his fourth ship (if he had one) directly back to England with the gold and ivory, 'stolen from them' (said the Portuguese) but much more likely 'Traded with them' (as John says). There is clearly ample room in this kind of situation for vast divergencies of evidence. For with the Portuguese claiming as they did a total monopoly on all the coasts of Africa, the very fact of Hawkins being there at all constituted a flagrant trespass and an arrant breach of the law of nations. In fact, to them John was just a pirate. But to John, who did not admit the existence of any monopoly at all, he was only exercising his inalienable rights under that same law. And it is abundantly clear that the only force he used was in making the Portuguese trade with him. For John was, in essence, an honest tradesman, as all his other actions go to prove; so that we are bound to believe that *every-thing* which he took he scrupulously paid for.

Yet this accusation of piracy, so constantly hurled not only at John but at every Englishman who, throughout Elizabeth's reign made sail either to Africa or to America, is worthy of a moment's examination. There were at the time, and there still are now, two broadly different meanings of that word 'pirate'. There is, first, the ordinary definition: 'one who commits robbery on the high seas'. And this man, according to all the jurists, is *hostis sui generis*—the enemy of all other sea-users. And he must be ruthlessly dealt with by all mankind. This is the most widely used meaning of the word today, and in this sense the Portuguese used it in the sixteenth century. And they believed it too! For, once allowing the legality of their premise, the action of a man like John *was* an act of piracy. It was piracy to the Portuguese: but not to the Englishman, who never for one instant subscribed to the monopolist idea, holding rather that the seas of the world were open for all to use and to sail upon.

This goes far towards explaining the Portuguese use of the term. But, almost from the first, and always thereafter, the Spaniards used the term too, and used it not only in the above sense, but also in order to describe all the actions of all the interlopers from all nations. But this was a radically different use of the word pirate: and, at the time when John was beginning his slaving voyages, it was really a little far-fetched to call him *hostis sui generis*, for they were then only just beginning to subscribe to the monopolist idea. Moreover, in those early days, when they used the word to describe a man like John Hawkins, they were not accusing him of indiscriminate robbery at sea, though later they came to do so. No: what they were doing at first was to use the word in a much milder sense—a sense in which it is still used to this day, though nowadays rather more rarely.

Let us consider for the moment this secondary meaning. We speak even now of a man who infringes the copyright of another man as 'pirating' that man's copyright. He prints, say, the

musical compositions of another man without paying any fee
for them. This, it is true, is thieving, but it is, as far as the Law
is concerned, a comparatively minor bit of thieving. There is at
least a wide difference between such a man and the out-and-out
skull and cross-bones man. The latter we want to shoot at sight:
the former we are quite content to 'take the law on', and to
prosecute him in a court of Justice. Or again, we hear from time
to time—or have very recently heard—of 'pirate buses'. But do
we mean by this armed and armoured vehicles gone berserk and
roaming the roads, holding up with pistols and machine-guns
legitimate Green-Line coaches or London Transport buses on
lonely stretches of roads across Blackheath or the M.1? Of
course we do not. We mean vehicles whose owners are trying to
crash in on the accepted routes of legitimate bus or coach lines.
And again the outraged owner of the supposed monopoly takes
suitable action against them in the Law Courts.

Now this, *mutatis mutandis* (and there is singularly little that
needs changing), is what was happening when John began to
crash in on what Philip regarded as his legitimate monopoly—
the trans-Atlantic carriage of slaves between Africa and Spanish
America. Of course the King knew that there was precious little
skull and cross-bones about the eminently respectable merchant
who took fifty suits of clothes to sea with him. Yet, from Philip's
point of view, John *was* trying to crash in on his monopoly, and
so, in his eyes, was the equivalent of the pirate bus or the
modern musical pirater. Later, the thing is considerably com-
plicated by the appearance of Englishmen who were not nearly
so considerate or so respectable as John invariably was. And
there were all sorts of them, from rank pirates in every sense of
that word, to that remarkable Englishman—in Philip's eyes the
arch-pirate—Sir Francis Drake. Not that, in English eyes, Sir
Francis was a skull and cross-bones man, because he never
attacked *all* the ships he met with at sea, but only those belonging to Spaniards. So—to be perfectly accurate in an age when
accuracy was very important—he was not a pirate, but he was,
sometimes, a privateer. The difference was a very real one, which
made an immense difference to the man himself. The pirate—in
International Law when it came in, and before that in the Law of
the Sea (and in practice)—could expect to be, and when caught

was, hanged by the neck at his own yard-arm. But the privateer, waging private war by warrant from his sovereign, was, by contrast, a most respectable person and a true belligerent fighting his country's enemies, though he used, for fighting, his own private resources rather than those of his often penurious sovereign.

But we must return to John, and his first slaving venture.

It was, we saw, something of a dress-rehearsal, and, after leaving Africa, he conducted it quite impeccably. He found, throughout the West Indies, that the Spanish colonists had a strong desire to do trade with him. This is in fact only natural, because he could afford, in selling his main wares—his negroes— to undercut the self-styled monopoly-holder, Philip. All monopolies are like that. The sole monopolist can, and almost always does, raise the price of his commodity to such a height that it is quite easy for an interloper to undersell him. The governing class, as represented by the Spanish governors, were not quite so forthcoming. True, they too liked the thought of getting their black labour cheap, and many of them succeeded in doing so. But it behoved them to watch their step, because they had orders from home not to play!

At Hispaniola, whither John went first, a rather transparent farce was enacted. First, he met a group of officials and colonists from San Domingo, the capital, who seem to have agreed, tacitly, that the town itself was rather too public a place for the trade. John therefore repaired to certain isolated settlements on the north shore of the island, where negroes and other merchandise changed hands freely, even the officials participating. Then another farce was perpetrated. A certain captain named Lorenzo Bernaldez, a converted Jew, went out—or said he went out—against the English intruders, and captured two of them. Thereupon—still the captain's tale—he secured their ransom in exchange for one hundred slaves; and then, in order to get rid of the Englishmen, gave Hawkins written leave to trade, if he would then clear out. This was, of course, blatant collusion, and John knew it. But he wanted that written permission, insisting upon several more of such documents at subsequent ports of call. For these, he thought, would be useful documents in proving both his own fair dealing and the colonists' disposition to trade. He also insisted upon certificates of fair dealing from the local magnates and officials; and he punctiliously paid all customs duties asked of him.

In such ways he soon got rid both of the merchandise which he had brought and of most of the negroes. In return, there was very little hard cash available: but he loaded up with such local commodities as pearls, ginger and hides: and a little gold—there was not much of that about—and a little sugar. These more than filled up the English holds: but he also filled two more ships, one locally hired and the other that Portuguese vessel which he was supposed to have stolen in Africa. He then did what looks at first sight a strange, indeed a foolish thing. He brought his own ships safely home; but he sent the other two, the one into Lisbon, the other to San Lucar in Spain. Both were immediately confiscated!

Why did he do it? John was certainly no fool: so his action is explicable only on one hypothesis—a perfectly clear conscience. He must have honestly believed in what he was doing. As regards the Portuguese part of the trip, he must have been very confident that he had *not* acted in an arbitrary way, but had followed only the accepted rules of barter. As for the Spanish ship sent to Spain, he must still have had real hopes that the King would be prepared to come to terms with him.

Even after the loss of the two cargoes, the expedition had evidently made a handsome profit, though exactly what it was is unknown. It was good enough anyway to make the promoters feel that the dress rehearsal should be followed by a full-scale performance. But first John, armed with a formal protest from the English Government, himself went to Spain, to see whether he could get the confiscation reversed. It was rather a bold thing to do: a little later anyway the Spanish authorities, having turned down his plea, would almost certainly have held on to his person! As it was, however, though he lost his case he retained his liberty, and returned to England to superintend the preparation of a second voyage.

c. THE SECOND SLAVING VOYAGE 1564

This was to be a bigger affair altogether, consisting of more ships and more men, and with a stronger syndicate to back it.

There can be little doubt that John still clung to his hope of collaboration with the King of Spain, though we can now see that it was becoming less and less likely. For the French Civil Wars had now begun, which split that unfortunate land into two bitterly warring factions. The maritime element adhered mostly to the Protestant side; but now, instead of furnishing corsairs for raiding the Spanish New World, it spent its best efforts in fighting the Catholics at home. Thus was Philip ever the less likely to seek maritime protection against enemy incursions from Hawkins or from any other foreigner.

The syndicate was altogether stronger, wealthier, and much more influential than the last. The Navy Board party was still in it, but now, also, there were names like the Earl of Pembroke, and Lord Robert Dudley, the Queen's darling, recently created Earl of Leicester. Then there was the Lord Clinton, Lord Admiral of England, and the Chief Secretary of State himself, Sir William Cecil. But one more important than all these rolled together was also interested. Elizabeth herself did not contribute a money-share—she seldom had any ready money to play with—but she did what in these matters was her usual custom: she contributed a unit of her Navy Royal, insisting upon specially favourable terms from the rest of the syndicate. She was probably justified in doing so too, for her contribution, from the very circumstance that it was the Queen of England's, was worth a great deal more than anyone else's. The ship which she supplied was the *Jesus of Lubeck.* a big vessel compared with any of the others in the expedition—probably of 600–700 tons. She was a survivor of Henry VIII's great navy, having been bought into it, even then not quite new, in 1544. So she was an elderly ship, and still more an old-fashioned type, with very high poop and forecastle; built 'high-carged' (as most of Henry's larger ships were) 'for majesty against the enemy'. This was a build rapidly going out of fashion in this country. Indeed it may well be that it was the *Jesus*, which John was fated twice to sail in, which decided him, when he came to be responsible for the build of the Queen's ships, to have no truck with whatever! Her timbers also, although at the time no one thought fit to mention it, were already old and riddled with dry rot. The other ships were much smaller, and they were Hawkins ships: the *Saloman*, flagship of

the first voyage; a 50-ton ex-privateer, one of the several *Tigers*
then afloat, and another (and smaller) *Swallow*—not the one of
the first voyage. This time the crews (still all Hawkins men)
numbered 150 all told, with some twenty extra gentlemen
volunteers. These, by the standards of the time, were very small
numbers—the 600-ton *Jesus*, for instance, carried only eighty
men. But on this vexed question of the size of crews John
already had decided views. Most people (particularly the
Portuguese) carried enormous ship's companies, trying to insure
that the ravages of disease, endemic in all ships, should not
reduce crews to impotence. They tried, in fact, to carry in each
ship a spare complement for replacement purposes. But John's
experience, already, was that a big crew on the foetid decks of a
sixteenth-century ship always led to big casualties, and that a
small crew had a much better chance of keeping itself fit for a
longer period. Indeed, one of the claims to fame, not only of
John but of all the Hawkinses, was their prudent man-manage-
ment and care for the well-being of their people. But as it was
young Richard to whom the lot fell of noting on paper the fruits
of the Hawkinses' sea-skills, the matter will be referred to again
in greater detail when the time comes to look at his famous book.

John left Plymouth on October 18, 1564. He was accompanied
south by another fleet bound on gold-trade business. On reaching
Ferrol, he turned into that port and exchanged courtesies with
the Spanish authorities. Here at once the Queen's participation
in the voyage helped him. He could represent himself as being
exactly what he was—the leader of an English venture, the
Commanding Officer of a Royal Ship, and therefore an officer in
the employ of the Queen of England. He even wore the Queen's
standard. The local authorities did not challenge these facts:
indeed could not, even if they would have liked to, for Spain and
England were still at peace. It was here that he issued his
famous fleet-orders, which incorporate those maxims so economical in words yet so pregnant in meaning:

> Serve God daily, love one another, preserve your victuals, beware of
> fire, and keep good fellowship.

They are characteristic of a good leader who knew his people,
who believed in God and who had at his fingertips that kind of

discipline which brought success. 'Worship God', he says, 'love your neighbour and do not quarrel among yourselves. Be economical with food and drink, for you cannot easily replace them. Guard night and day against the peril of fire, bane of wooden ships; and, at sea always keep together for mutual support, These, to John, were basic disciplines, laws which might not be broken.

At this time John was no bigoted Protestant, and he had little or no desire to persecute the followers of other religions. In Spain, in fact, he still had the reputation of being at heart a Catholic, though he was not that. On the other hand—and the cumulative evidence for it is overwhelmingly strong—he was a good Christian who not only believed in God but was quite determined to see that his men did the same. A testimonial to this fact survives in rather an odd context—the somewhat pathetic evidence of an English prisoner on trial before a Spanish court in Mexico. The extract below is translated from the Spanish.

> Every morning and evening [the prisoner deponed] the Boatswain took a book in English, like those which the Clergy had in England, and went to the main mast where all the soldiers and sailors, with the Captain, knelt on the deck; and all attended under pain of 24 hours in irons. All being on their knees, the said Boatswain recited the Lord's Prayer and the Creed . . . and then made the same prayers as are made in England. . . . And that was done in all the ships of the said fleet of John Hawkins.

Next they called at Tenerife, where, as last time, John wished to get in touch with de Ponte, his go-between with the Spanish colonists in the West. Thence they headed for Africa, in order to pick up their black ivory. Here proceedings followed very much the course of those in the first voyage. On the whole, the local Portuguese aided John; apparently, but as soon as his back was turned pretended that they had done no such thing, but set up a howl of protest and accusation *via* their Government and London. John Sparke, who wrote for Hakluyt an account of this voyage, tells how, and how not, to secure a good bag of negroes. Do not, (he says in effect) go in bald-headed and kidnap them. That only causes trouble and much local resistance. Rather, ally yourselves to one side or the other in their perennial local wars. Even send in your own men to assist one of the combatants. The side so aided will certainly win, and will capture numerous prisoners. These they will offer to sell to you, and by buying them you will be pleasing everybody (except of course the captives). Thus you will be able to load up with all the black ivory you have room for.

Before it reached this conclusion the expedition ran into serious trouble. At the instance of certain renegade Portuguese, John decided to attack a negro town called Bynota. He entered the place with forty of his own men and a few Portuguese. But instead of keeping together they dispersed among the native houses where their guides had told them they would find gold. Fortunately, however, John kept his eye on a party of a dozen or so, and would not let them scatter. Suddenly the natives rallied and, attacking the stragglers separately, drove the whole party back to their boats, killing several of them and drowning others who in panic took to the water. But John, coming up with his twelve, by his steadiness turned the tables. The party returned to the ships with their tails firmly tucked between their legs: for in exchange for nine negroes taken, they had lost seven of their best men killed and twenty-seven wounded. The Captain of the *Salomon* was among the dead. On this occasion Sparke was full praise for the leadership of John, who, he wrote

> showed a singular wise manner, with countenance very cheerful outwardly, as though he did little weigh the death of his men, although his heart inwardly was broken in peeces for it, done to this ende, that the Portugals with him should not presume to resist against him.

John realized that he could afford to lose face neither with the negroes nor with the Portuguese, and so aped a cheerfulness which he certainly did not feel. For there is plenty of evidence that he always took to heart any losses among his men. Indeed, his invariable custom, if he could find the time, was to go down into the dark and stinking hold to visit his wounded and his sick: if they looked like recovering encouraging them by his manifest sympathy; if they were at death's door, praying for and with them, comforting them as best he could and receiving from them messages for their wives and families. There was a simple piety about John which invariably made his people love him, and put up with all sort of hardships just in order to please him. In every way, in fact, he took great care of, and gave great thought to, his subordinates, striving by no means unsuccessfully to mitigate wherever possible the ghastly conditions they lived in.

The whole family possessed this sort of humanity which, in addition to being a very lovable trait, was also—as most of our really great captains have known full well—one of their strengths *as* great captains. Instinctively these Hawkinses seemed to know, as Nelson knew, that what they did for their people—and were seen by them to do—made all the difference, when the pinch came, between success and failure. Here is no mawkishness. It is basic. It marks the difference between the merely capable and the really outstanding sea-captain.

Early in the New Year (1565), John left Africa behind him, carrying a cargo of some 400 to 500 negroes. After eighteen days 'in the doldrums' he picked up the Trade Wind and quickly reached Dominica in the Lesser Antilles. This island was still the headquarters of the Caribs, an indigenous people so well-known for their ferocity that even the Spaniards fought shy of them. Quite recently, Sparke tells us, a Spanish caravel had gone there to water. But the Caribs stole upon them by night, cut their cable and drove the ship ashore. Then they attacked, capturing *and eating* the crew. John, however, was lucky enough to water there without attracting the attention of any of them.

Next he visited the island of Margarita, once a great pearl-fishing centre, but now in danger of being fished out. Here the Governor proved hostile—almost the only one he met who was. This man sent to the Spanish island-capital San Domingo, to warn the authorities there that Hawkins was coming. Doubtless he meant to be vindictive, but in fact was rather kind, because the Council at San Domingo was so corrupt that, in warning the other Spanish settlements, it merely notified them to be ready to trade with John when he appeared!

He now proceeded to the Spanish Main, landing at Cumana. Here the natives came to them bringing cakes made of maize, a cereal quite unknown to them. Also

> now they brought down to us—which we bought for beades, pewter whistles, glasses, knives and other trifles—Hennes, Potatoes and

pines. These potatoes be the most delicate rootes that may be eaten, and doe far exceede their passeneps or carets.

Sparke does not say whether John brought any of these 'delicate rootes' away with him, so that we cannot tell whether we are here assisting at the first importation of this important vegetable. We also learn,

These natives are expert bowmen, tipping their arrows with apples which are very fair and red in colour, but are a strong poison with the which, together with venemous Bats, Vipers, Adders, and other serpents they make a medley and therewith anoint the same.

The Spaniards, greatly fearing the skill of these archers, and the potency of their arrows,

arme themselves and their horses with quilted canvas of two inches thicke, and leave no place of their bodie open to their enemies, saving only the eyes, which they may not hide, and yet oftentimes are they hit in so small a scantling.

Evidently unpleasant, not to say dangerous neighbours! It is quite wrong to suppose that the Conquistadors had it all their own way in the New World.

Thereafter John continued his journey—to Barburata, to the island of Curaçao, to Rio de la Hacha. At all three places he did business, but not without trouble—more than he had experienced on his first voyage. The general procedure at each port of call was substantially the same. As before, the ordinary planters were as keen as ever to enjoy John's black market. So, in the smaller places, were the governors, who were often local men themselves. But, since last time, they had all received warning from home that any trade with the Englishmen was to be regarded as illegal—orders couched more forcibly than they had been before. The governors of the larger settlements, who were mostly more than local big-wigs, were briefed by the central government at San Domingo, and were therefore the more scared at the idea of disobeying orders. Yet none of these parties, whether planters, local governors or true-blooded Spaniards, were immune from the itch to do business with the English on such relatively favourable terms. The result was that, every time, collusion appeared, John beginning by stating what a good friend he was to their Sovereign, then inviting trade, then, if it was refused, going through the motions of using force, and even landing armed men, declaring that he intended to do business whatever the governors thought about it. And, every time, after this show of force, the governors gave way—under protest, they said—and markets were opened on shore.

What happened at Rio de la Hacha is typical of them all. Here the Spanish documents, recently come to light, throw much illumination on what was happening, not from English sources but from those of Spain itself.[1] The leading man here was called Miguel de Castellanos. Having recently received the order from San Domingo, he sought an audience with John, and stated that trading with him was strictly forbidden. John, as usual retaliated with the threat to use force. The leading colonists, also as usual, were quite satisfied with John's good faith, and instantly set up the trade mart. Now comes the direct evidence—from Spain too—of collusion. The colonists agreed that the Governor should speak privately to John, and that he (John)

> should threaten and feign to intend to burn the houses of the town or settlement, in order that they might take deposition of witnesses and prove that they were forced to trade with him.

Needless to say, John went through with the pantomime; and so did the Governor. The earlier British writers, like J. A. Froude and Sir John Laughton (who wrote the article on Hawkins in the *Dictionary of National Biography*), not having available the *Spanish Documents*, and with a Victorian prejudice against John because black ivory was his principal commodity, blame him severely for his proceedings, accusing him of false dealing and high-handed bullying tactics. But now their case no longer holds water. John was only playing his hand according to the rules laid down by de Castellanos!

This worthy now went still further in subterfuge. He sought, on his own, to secure his slaves even cheaper. He told John that he would consent to the trade, but only if he paid half the price per negro that John had received at Barburata. But this attempt to secure his own price cut no ice at all with John, who could be very firm when he wanted to be. He landed 100 men and some

[1] e.g. *Spanish Documents*, pp. 87–91.

artillery. De Castellanos called out 150 foot-men and 30 cavalry. But (as John knew only too well) it was all pure bluff. He fired one gun, being careful to hit no one, and the whole of the Spanish infantry fell flat on their faces, while the horse ran incontinently away! Thereupon a solemn flag of truce was called and de Castellanos gave way, agreeing to John's terms and prices with no further words.

Thereafter things went on as usual. John sold 300 negroes and much merchandise, even booking orders for more slaves and more merchandise against the day when he came again! In exchange he received a certain amount of gold and silver and even of precious stones: also a great number of hides, to the value of £2,000. He insisted, as before, upon a testimonial from de Castellanos, bearing witness to his civility, fair dealing and courtesy. All this, it must be stressed again, comes from purely Spanish sources.

After this, John proposed to visit San Domingo itself— where, doubtless the same kind of farce would have been enacted: for *all* Spaniards on the spot were prepared (with face-saving safeguards) to allow the trade. But during the whole cruise John had felt the effect of having no competent pilot; and now, making for Hispaniola, he contrived to fetch up only at Jamaica: whence, having lost so much offing—for the constant easterly trades made it very difficult to regain either Hispaniola or even Cuba—he gave up his efforts and, having business to do on the shores of Florida, coasted up it. He was now in the latitude of the westerlies, which wafted him at length to the French post at Fort Caroline.

For this part of his voyage he was under direct orders from home. The year before, the French, wearying of sheer buccaneering, and hearing good (if inaccurate) accounts of the gold of Florida, had sent out an expedition which built a fort there, proposing to take a leaf out of the Spaniards' book, and stay there permanently.

They were not particularly good colonists, because they did not like cultivating the soil, but preferred to rely upon periodic victualling from home. But their freebooting habits were still deep-rooted in them, and most of them had already hived off to attack Spanish settlements in the Caribbean. Already they had been repulsed, and only a few of them had got back to Fort Caroline. Now, a bare year after they had arrived, they were half-starved and wholly discouraged. Suspecting some such dénouement, the English Government had ordered John to go there to reconnoitre before returning home. If he found the Frenchmen in a bad way, and if, upon inquiry on the spot, he thought the tales of gold were well-founded he was to offer them a free passage home, leaving Florida untenanted for the moment, to be occupied by Englishmen at some future date.

John duly made his offer, and an overwhelming majority of the French joyfully accepted it. But one man, their leader, a certain Laudonnière, steadfastly refused to leave. These were all the orders that John had. At that moment we were on friendly terms with the French at home; so he was not to force them to accept. But, when they refused, John, though disappointed, was far too humane a man just to sail away and leave them to their fate; though it would have suited both his own book, England's and Spain's to do so. For, we must recall, John was still most anxious to stand well in the eyes of Philip of Spain, and to that monarch the French in Florida were a very considerable menace. But John was not the man to allow future hypothetical advantages to outweigh the certainty of present misery. So he was full of sympathy and kindness to the wretched garrison; and—though in fact they were thwarting him he did all in his power to help them, actually giving them the 50-ton *Tiger*, in which to come away if the worst came to the worst. He also left with them all the provisions which he could spare: indeed rather more than he could safely spare, for he left himself only the barest minimum for his homeward journey. Laudonniere was deeply moved by the treatment which John afforded him, reporting home that Hawkins was a good and charitable man, 'deserving to be esteemed as such of us all as if he had saved all our lives'.

Could Laudonniere but have known it, though, he had much better have accepted John's offer. For the days of the French in Florida were already numbered. The redoubtable Menendez was already at sea, and making for Fort Carolina. Within a year he had taken it, massacring all its garrison save one or two, of which number, fortunately, the gallant Laudonniere was one.

John, however, knew none of these things. As a result of his chivalry he was now so short of food that he was constrained to hug the coast of North America until he came to the Newfoundland Banks, already known and extensively fished by English trawlers. Here he caught enough cod to carry him safely across the North Atlantic. So, on September 20, 1565, he came safely to anchor at Padstow. In doing so, his navigation had rather let him down, since he missed the entrance to the Channel and came in on the wrong side of Cornwall. This, however, was quite a common occurrence in the days before men discovered how to find their longitude at sea.

John's second voyage had been a considerable success; how considerable no English source reveals. But the Spanish Ambassador in England reported to his master that a dividend of 60 per cent was paid to all investors. Still more striking was the dividend which accrued to John personally for the care of his men. It is estimated that, in all those eleven months spent in tropical climes, a bare dozen of his company had died of disease—a fantastically small total for those days. Indeed John Hawkins may fairly be considered the pioneer of ship-hygiene: and his kindly heart must have been delighted at this near-record.

d. NEGOTIATION AND INTRIGUE

There followed two years of rather perplexing diplomatic intrigue. Philip was now served in London by that very able ambassador, Guzman de Silva. Hitherto the King had not quite made up his mind about John Hawkins—whether to toy further with his application to serve him, or whether to lay it down in black and white that all English trade in the West was to be taboo. Meanwhile the Queen of England and her principal adviser, Sir William Cecil, had not made up their minds either; and were not to do so for many a long year. But Elizabeth, and to some rather lesser extent Cecil, greatly appreciated profits in the neighbourhood of 60 per cent: and she hesitated before turning them down flat. Meanwhile John was also very loth to give up his efforts to get himself taken on as Philip's confidential ally, with the great prize of being allowed to exchange those services for recognition of his right to trade with Spanish

America. So, for the next two years, a fierce diplomatic struggle was being waged between the three parties; with victory poised now on one side, now on another: and especially the contest raged between de Silva and John, talented men both. On two occasions the Ambassador invited John to dine with him—proof positive, of course, that de Silva at least did not regard the English merchant as a pirate.

At one of these meals John asked the Ambassador to use his good offices with Philip in forwarding his pet scheme—to serve the Spanish Crown with his own ships of war in the Mediterranean against the Turks and the many corsairs in that sea. John was particularly keen on this project because he thought that, if Philip could be prevailed upon to accept the offer, it would be a big step gained in his main plan to trade in Spanish America with Philip's approval. And, oddly enough, de Silva consented to play John's game, even putting John's case to the King. Moreover John even went down to Plymouth, to organize and equip a squadron for the purpose.

That Philip was seriously considering John's proposition there seems to be no doubt. In the end, however, he decided against it—but deliberately kept him waiting for his answer all through the summer of 1566. John, however, was not the man to be fobbed off thus easily. If, he thought, my expedition cannot go to the Mediterranean, it would be a pity to waste the whole campaigning season doing nothing. So his mind reverted to the West Indies as a good alternative destination. De Silva, however, heard of this, or perhaps only guessed it, and made such a strong protest to the Queen that he succeeded in getting John sent for from Plymouth to London, where he was examined by the Privy Council, and straightly forbidden to sail. Considering that the better part of that Council were members of the Hawkins syndicate, there can be little doubt that this too was collusive. However, John was nothing if not law-abiding: so he promised not to go, entering into a bond to pay £500 if he defaulted.

So he stayed at home. But his ships did not. They were Hawkins ships all right, but, it seems, ships owned by William! So off they went, but not under John's command. The man who took them was John Lovell. The Spaniards said, afterwards, that

Lovell was John's kinsman, but there is no evidence for this. The only menber of this expedition whose name is worth recording was young Francis Drake, now about twenty-three years old and paying his first visit to the New World.

This voyage was on about the same scale as John's first, and its history is not unlike it. But John Lovell was no John Hawkins, and the difference comes out in several ways. For one thing, while still on the African coast, the captain had a fracas with the Portuguese in which some of the latter were killed—a thing which even the Portuguese had never laid to John's charge. Again, when the expedition was at Rio de la Hacha, Lovell seems to have allowed himself to be outsmarted by John's old friend, de Castellanos. Even now it is not easy to discover what really happened: but one day Lovell landed ninety-two negroes on the other side of the river from the town, patently designing to open a collusive market. But he did not quite understand the finer points of this quaint game, and in the end de Castellanos kept the slaves but omitted to pay for them, while Lovell had to sail away a cheated man. He was furious, but it would seem that his rage was as nothing compared with that of young Drake, who never forgot or forgave it. There is in fact good reason for thinking that his abiding hatred for all Spaniards—such a cardinal feature in forming his character—was born on the backside of Rio de la Hacha.

Lovell went on to San Domingo, but what happened there is not known, and probably not important. He returned safely to Plymouth in September, 1567.

In the meantime the syndicate was getting busy again. This time it was organizing a regular treasure-hunt, not on the western side of the Atlantic but on the coast of Africa. It had been approached by two rather seedy Portuguese renegades, named Antonio Luis, a former Guinea merchant, and another man called André Homem, alias Gaspar Caldeiro, perhaps an ex-pilot. These men brought with them the mysterious secret of a sort of African El Dorado, situated some way beyond that part of the coast occupied by Portugal. There, they said, was a very rich gold mine, conveniently sited quite close to a very fine harbour. Was the whole tale mere moonshine, or was there really such a place? And if so, where? The very word 'treasure' invariably breeds speculation and rumour and, both then and since, all sorts of theorists have let themselves go on the subject. One, in quite modern times, has given it as his opinion that what was discovered was the gold of the Transvaal, still many thousands of miles away from the authentic Gold Coast. But none of this matters much because in the end no one found the site or any treasure worth mentioning. Yet since the episode led almost directly to John's third voyage, it must have its mention here.

The renegades had taken their story first to King Philip, who got so far as to invite them to Spain, to discuss the question. This apparently frightened them and they failed to turn up, approaching instead the French Government, which went a little further, sending out a small expedition under a nobleman named de Monluc. He did not get far, however; for, putting in to Madeira for water, he was fired on by the Portuguese at Funchal. He retaliated by landing and taking the town, but he was slain in the assault and the expedition gave up. Then Luis and Homem came to England, where they met some of the syndicate who took more interest. After all, gold was gold, and not only did it allure the syndicate, but the Queen herself fell for the idea. Anyway, Elizabeth sent for prominent members of the syndicate, who decided upon an expedition and began to collect ships.

So John became involved, though there is good reason for thinking that he himself never really fell for that gold mine. A squadron was therefore formed with a rendezvous at Plymouth. It was a strong one too, consisting among others of two Queen's Ships (one of them our old friend the *Jesus of Lubeck* and a smaller vessel called the *Minion*). The latter was even older than the *Jesus*, having been launched in 1536. There were also a number of Hawkins ships—the *William and John* (150 tons), the *Swallow* (100 tons), the *Judith* (50 tons), and the *Angel* (33 tons). The burthen of the whole squadron amounted to 1,333 tons and the total number of men to 408.

Now though the destination of this fleet was given out as being the coast of Africa and nowhere else, there is every reason for supposing that, from the start, it was designed as a slaving voyage of the old sort. A surviving list of the stores put on board makes this all but certain, because there was taken on board a large consignment of beans, the staple food for negro slaves: also a big supply of good-quality cloth and linen, useless in Africa but much sought after in the Spanish Indies. Indeed it is pretty clear that, from the very first, the Queen, Sir William Cecil and the other syndics really intended the expedition to sail for America via Africa. Of course, when tackled by de Silva, they all denied it, swearing black and blue that only the African treasure interested them, and duly trotting out, as evidence, the scoundrelly Luis and Homem. So, though sceptical, de Silva was constrained to believe them.

In late August there took place in Plymouth Sound a most significant incident. Into the harbour sailed a certain Flemish admiral, the Baron de Wachan, with seven armed ships. The *Jesus*, with John on board, and the *Minion*, both showing the royal colours, lay in the narrow Cattewater. There was plenty of other water available for de Wachan to anchor in if (as he afterwards alleged) he had put into the Sound under stress of weather. But to John it certainly did not look like that, and he was not deceived for a moment. As the Spaniards came in, making straight for the Cattewater, he watched their coming intently; and saw, with growing indignation, that they made no attempt to give the customary salute of dipping flags and lowering top-sails. In those days, of course, the newest-joined boy knew what was the correct thing for a visiting fleet to do as it entered a foreign harbour. To fail to do it could not possibly be attributed to ignorance or carelessness. And in that light John read their intentions.

With no hesitation he opened fire. And he fired not at de Wachan's masthead, not at his sails; but he put half a dozen round-shot right into his hull. Thereupon de Wachan sheered off, 'loofing towards East Water'.

John's action was quite instinctive, and absolutely justified. Lucky it was for England just then that the man in charge knew his own mind so well, and could make it up so quickly. For there really can be no doubt at all that de Wachan's fixed intention was to destroy the expedition first and then to apologize for it. It was indeed fortunate for our country that there were already

Elizabethans prepared, like Blake in the next century, 'to keep the foreigner from fooling us'!

But though de Wachan was foiled, nothing could prevent him from complaining bitterly to all who would listen, nor prevent de Silva from taking his case to the Court of England and making as much trouble as possible for John. Here, said both Ambassador and Admiral, was a squadron from Spain, sailing the Channel upon its lawful occasions, but driven by stress of weather into a port in England—her own ally!—only to be gratuitously fired on by an English Admiral! Justice for Spain, and condign punishment for the perfidious, guest-insulting Englishman! Moreover, though Elizabeth in her heart sympathized entirely with John, and indeed, in private, commended his action, such was the precarious state of Anglo-Spanish friendship at that moment—and such, one must admit, the Great Queen's perennial vacillation—that she felt impelled to administer a public reprimand to Hawkins. This meant nothing to those in the know: there was never a thought, for instance, of dismissing the culprit from his command and sending out someone else with the expedition. Such conduct on the Queen's part was, alas, all too typical. She always expected implicit obedience from her unpaid servants. But she seldom gave them the outward support to which they were obviously entitled. And they in their turn did not expect *always* to be supported. Yet they were prepared to perform their service none the less. That was the way in which things were done under the great Queen. On this occasion of course, though her conduct meant nothing, the episode was destined to have a most unfortunate result in the very near future, as in due course we shall see.

When this contretemps occurred the destination of the squadron was still Africa only, ostensibly engaged upon its treasure-hunt, and so it remained up till September 16. On that day, though, the precious pair of rogues, Luis and Homem, simply disappeared. As soon as their absence was known, the Queen, Cecil, Hawkins and the whole syndicate compared notes, and discovered to their chagrin that none of them had the slightest clue as to where this famous mine was situated. Neither of the scamps had imparted any information on this vital point! But the great ones of England were not going to let themselves be fooled by a brace of mountebanks. To sail south with no known destination was manifestly absurd, and John, who had never swallowed the renegades' story, was delighted. At once he wrote a personal letter to the Queen, setting out without any attempt at circumlocution precisely what he meant to do, if the Queen would agree.

> The voyage I pretend is to lade negroes in Guinea and sell them in the West Indies in truck of gold, pearls and emeralds, wherewith I doubt not but to bring home great abundance for the contentation of your Highness. . . . Thus I have advised your Highness the state of the matter, and do humbly pray your Highness to signify your pleasure by the bearer, which I shall most willingly accomplish,
>
> Your Highness' most humble servant,
> John Hawkins.

What her pleasure was is nowhere stated in so many written words; perhaps she knew better than to write them. But it is perfectly clear that what she actually meant was: 'Go, with my blessing'. For that is what he instantly did. What is more, in spite of one school of modern historians who like to regard Cecil as unwilling to make any move against Anglo-Spanish friendship, and to have been by-passed by the Queen whenever any threat to it was mooted, there can be no doubt that the Minister was informed of the change of plan, and agreed to it: for there survives at Hatfield a letter from the Lord Admiral to the Secretary of State in which he remarks that, now that the Portuguese have fled, he is pleased to learn that 'the other voyage' (i.e. to Africa *and* to America) *that Cecil writes of* is to be undertaken— though, he adds, having apparently swallowed the Portuguese story, hook and all, 'it may not be so profitable as that first intended'.[1]

e. THE THIRD SLAVING VOYAGE 1567-8

At last John and his squadron sailed from Plymouth on October 2, 1567. But at the end of the first week the *Jesus* came near to drowning her company. A gale came on, which lasted for four days: whereupon her seams began to open alarmingly and all over the ship. One in the stern gaped so wide that fifteen thicknesses of stout baize from the cargo barely sufficed to fill it. It

[1] Calendar of Hatfield MSS., Part I, no. 1139, 30 9 67.

was touch and go which happened first—whether the storm blew itself out or whether the *Jesus* went to the bottom. Then, according to custom, John called the whole ship's company together and solemnly warned them of their imminent danger, advising them in telling phrases to make their peace with God. The crew did not panic, but they did repent, whole-heartedly and rather noisily. Elizabethan Englishmen were a courageous lot, as brave as, if not braver than, their descendants of today. But they had not yet mastered the technique of the stiff upper lip. Now they wept openly, and John wept with them! When, on the fourth day, the gale subsided with the *Jesus* still afloat, John called them together again and together they thanked God for saving them. Once more, one feels, John must have made an inward vow that, if *he* were ever to have any say in the matter, no ship so high-carged or so crank should ever be built!

At Santa Cruz in the Canaries where the Fleet put in for water there arose a fracas between two of the 'voluntary gentlemen' sailing with John in the *Jesus*. These volunteers were always to be found in every sea-adventure, and they had to be accommodated, not only because they were offering their services and their experience gratis, but also because, as often as not, they had contributed to the general cost of the expedition. They were often, though, more trouble to the man responsible than they were worth. They were almost always young men, often hotheaded, and they had all worn swords from their youth. Now a quarrel flared up between a Master Edward Dudley and a certain George Fitzwilliam, an officer in the Hawkins service.

When John first heard of the dispute, Fitzwilliam had already gone ashore to fight his duel. But Dudley had not, and John sent for him. Then he forbade him to land, as he (John) did not permit duelling (*vide* Article Two of the Hawkins Code: 'love one another'). But Dudley was a hot-tempered youth, and, this time, resenting John's intervention, he actually drew his sword upon him. John, in self-defence, drew his, and each had several passes at one another before the by-standers, horrified, could separate them. Dudley was wounded in the arm, and John over the right eye. What follows shows well the popularity of John among his own people. Dudley was instantly seized, thrown into irons, and would probably have been summarily dealt with by the outraged company had not John sternly ordered them off. But now the captain had the difficult role to play of being at once judge and victim. It was not beyond him. Dudley, as soon as his momentary heat had cooled, pleaded guilty in humble terms, for of course he knew the heinous nature of his crime in drawing upon the leader. John, who never changed his demeanour throughout the proceedings, said firmly that, as a person, he harboured no grudge against the young man: but, as leader of the expedition and representative of the Queen of England, he was bound to take notice of the assault. He therefore pronounced sentence of death, and ordered an arquebus to be loaded and brought to him, which he took into his own hands. Then, according to custom, he cited parallels from other voyages: deliberately, in fact, wasting time, asking the accused whether he had made his peace with God and was ready. Dudley replied that he was, and freely acknowledged that he was only getting his deserts. At length John raised the arquebus and—quietly laid it down again, ordering Dudley's irons to be knocked off. The pardon was absolute, and the young man, duly contrite, protested his future fidelity: whereupon they embraced, and all was forgotten. Unhappily Dudley's future on earth was very limited, becasue he fell ill and died a few weeks later.

The whole story is wonderfully illustrative of John's character. Not once did he become excited nor change his usual manner. His humanity made him realize the extent of Dudley's exasperation, and he was certainly telling the truth when he said that, for himself, he had nothing against him. Yet naturally he knew that drawing a sword on *any* commanding officer was a most serious offence against discipline and good order. And it must be punished as such—but, if he could manage it, not too severely. So he cheerfully took on the roles of judge and executioner, as well as victim, and deliberately spun out the proceedings until he decided that the young man *was* punished. Then he gave way to his natural feelings of humanity and pity, which ended in reconciliation.

Among the witnesses of this very human scene was young Francis Drake, at the time a volunteer in the *Jesus*, though later promoted to the captaincy of the *Judith*. Some ten years later he was to find himself in a comparable position, when no doubt he recalled this case of his cousin and Dudley. Up to the final move he imitated John exactly, even to the length of proposing to execute his criminal—Thomas Doughty—with his own hand. But, this time, the grim drama was allowed to go right through, and Francis Drake executed his man. Perhaps comparisons are not quite fair, because the circumstances of the two cases were not quite the same: and doubtless Thomas Doughty was a much greater menace to Francis and his voyage than Edward Dudley ever was to John and his. Yet one feels that the real difference lay in the relative characters of Francis and of John. Undeniably Francis had the harder, even the more vindictive nature, John the more human, the more naturally forgiving. But then Francis was perhaps the greater man: if greatness consists in remorselessly getting one's own way.

Even before the expedition left Santa Cruz, John had shown commendable foresight, which doubtless saved him much trouble and perhaps material loss. The Governor welcomed him on arrival with very fair words. But John, from past experience, never set much store by fair words, especially from foreigners. So, in coming to anchor in the bay, he had contrived, as though by chance, to put a number of Spanish merchantmen between himself and the castle of Santa Cruz. Then, sure enough, on the last evening of his visit, he was aware of those covering Spaniards being quietly towed aside, thus giving a direct line of fire from the Castle to his squadron. He was always a quick thinker; so now, without any hesitation, he upped anchor as soon as it was dark and, slipping out of the anchorage, brought up a mile or two outside it, doing the last of his watering by boat from there. His suspicions were sound enough. The Governor's intention had been to open fire on him during the night—and, of course (like de Wachan) to apologize the following morning. And John did not make a fuss—not even representations. He treated the Governor to the last with studied politeness: as indeed, thwarted, the Governor treated him.

Thence they made sail and came to Africa. Here John found the going very hard and dangerous, mainly because by this time the Portuguese had ordered their defences, and were at last prepared to defend their monopoly by force. And, hard as he tried, he had succeeded by the end of the year in collecting a beggarly

150 negroes, sustaining in doing so quite heavy casualties among his people. Near Cape Verde, for instance, he attacked a native town with 200 men, hoping to take it by surprise. But that attempt failed sadly. The negroes came back boldly at them, so that, by nightfall, he had taken only nine prisoners for the loss of twenty-two men wounded. One of these was John himself, and another was Edward Dudley, both hit by what seemed to be innocuous arrows. All made light of them at first, but a few days later they discovered that the arrows were poisoned, and they all succumbed to what they took to be lock-jaw. The officers recovered, but eight of the men died. The reason for the relative immunity of John and Dudley was probably because they washed their wounds thoroughly at the first opportunity; which precaution the men did not take. But one eye-witness,[1] a great admirer of John, says that 'our General was taught by a Negro to draw the poison out of his wound with a clove of garlic, whereby he was cured', almost as though the poor benighted heathen himself had become a Hawkins-fan too.

After this reverse John took counsel with his officers, and they concluded that, if they were to proceed to America at all, they *must* take many more slaves. So they decided to push much further down the coast, and to try the former policy of taking sides in a local native quarrel. The opportunity came their way when they were off Sierra Leone. There, its king sent to ask their help against a large town called Conga. John agreed, and a regular plan of campaign was arranged with the king. John was to attack up the river, his native allies simultaneously to assault the land-side. After some desperate fighting, in which the English lost a round dozen more killed, John himself at length broke through the log fortifications of the town. Then his black allies forced their way in from the other side. To modern eyes it was a very sickening business. The thatched roofs of the town were deliberately set ablaze, and the triumphant negroes began a cannibalistic feast which John had to watch— from the wings, as it were—before they would take any notice

---

[1] Job Hortop, an ordinary seaman-gunner, left by John in Mexico after the disastrous fight at San Juan de Ulua. This man's narrative, which reveals a rude natural talent of such a high order as at times almost to amount to literary genius, is printed in the second edition of *Hakluyt* (Everyman's Edition, vol. 6, pp. 336–54). We shall hear more of him later.

of him. They then drove a vast wedge of the wretched defeated into the river where they were drowned wholesale. At last, however, the victorious king would listen to John, and gave him enough survivors to make his total catch up to 470, which was all he wanted. It certainly does make shocking reading, and we can only remember that, to *all* the white races of Europe, the negro was such a great deal less than human. Moreover, the unredeemed beastliness of black victors to black vanquished does give at least some point to the defence invariably put up by Elizabethan, and later, slave-traders: that the conditions then prevailing in the black homelands could not possibly be worse; that, in fact, to carry the residue away to the New World was not tantamount to destroying them, but actually giving them a better deal than they would ever get at home.

Yet, when all is said, one cannot help wishing that John had been like his father, and contented himself with dealing in natural, and not in black ivory!

His slave-holds at last filled, John now turned his back on Africa, and, on February 7, 1568, stood for the West. He now had ten ships with him—four more than the six with which he had started. One was called the *Grace of God*, and it belonged to a French captain named Bland, who seems to have joined the expedition voluntarily. The crossing took more than seven weeks, which even in those days was painfully slow—particularly painful for the poor slaves, though no one thought fit to mention them. All round, in fact, things were going badly for this third voyage—the negroes harder than ever to come by, the Portuguese more intransigent than ever, the Spaniards likely to be more overtly hostile. And now the weather set blankly against them. It was not until the end of March that they reached Dominica, the first port of call in the West Indies.

At first the third voyage followed much the same route as the second, finding the governors more adamant than ever against trading, but the colonists as anxious for it as ever. Yet, slowly, he still got rid of his slaves and his goods, because the governors were still as venal as ever, though now a good deal more careful to cover their tracks, and the planters so eager that in the end they forced the authorities to do their bidding. But such obstructions to free barter all took time, and progress became slower and slower. Next came Barburata again, then Rio de la Hacha. Once more, perhaps, we may take transactions there as typical of them all.

Here the boastful yet subtle Miguel de Castellanos still held the reins, now with the style of Treasurer. John had dealt fairly successfully with him in 1565, but poor Lovell had proved no match for him in 1567. Now, in 1568, it chanced that John did not have the first go at him. Young Francis Drake, promoted to the command of the *Judith*, was, it seems, leading the squadron by some days, and so, with the *Angel*, was the first to sail into the bay: and he still harboured a grudge against both Rio de la Hacha and its Governor. He stood close in with the Treasurer's house and curtly demanded to be allowed to fill his water-butts. Castellanos replied by opening fire—not the way to treat this particular young gentleman! Drake answered him with two roundshots straight through the man's residence. He was not to know, of course, that he was in the presence of a very different man from John Hawkins. Now a caravel arrived from San Domingo. Francis chased it to the shore and then cut it out.

When John came up five days later, he found that all chances of peaceful trade were at an end—a state of affairs which, it seems, he never expected. Castellanos now put up a show which would have done him credit did we not know his two-sidedness. He erected quite substantial field-works and armed all his colonists, negroes and Indians: and he still had his little troop of horse composed of the better sort of planters, who were accustomed to kill wild cattle by running them down with their lances.

John began with a friendly letter asking for leave to trade. Castellanos answered it with defiance. So John landed 200 men two miles from the town, and outflanked one strong work by sending his armed boats past it by sea. Castellanos' main force of arquebusiers, now faced with advancing English, fired a volley from much too long a range and then ran for it. So John's men took the town.

The affair was more serious, however, than that of the previous expedition, for the Spaniards killed two Englishmen with their volley, though again John contrived that there should be no

fatal casualties on the Spanish side. For in spite of all provoca-
tion he was still determined to be the honest merchant and not
the brutal soldier. But one certainly does not get that impression
when one reads the reports of the other side, all inspired, if not
actually written, by Castellanos.

> He [Castellanos] rendered such signal service [says one] that all
> were amazed at his great valour—both his adversaries and his
> countrymen—for certainly it was an action which today, on looking
> back on it, fills with alarm those who were there and those who hear
> the tale told. In good order he withdrew with his small force without
> losing a man. Truly it seemed unavoidable that any should have
> escaped.

Pretty good, considering that the English were not trying—or
rather trying not—to hit the enemy!

For the moment it looked like deadlock. But then one of
Castellanos' negroes deserted to John and offered to show him
where the inhabitants had hidden the town's treasure. John himself went to look for it, and found it. 'Now,' said John, in a letter
sent, unsealed, to the Treasurer by a townsman, 'unless you
trade, the treasure goes on board my ship!' This, he reckoned—
and rightly so—would be too much for the real owners of the
treasure: who now forced the reluctant Castellanos to negotiate.
And this he did, giving at the same time a quite remarkable,
though unsolicited, testimonial to Hawkins himself.

> There is not one of you [he is reported as saying] that knoweth this
> Juan Haquines. He is such a man that no one talking to him hath any
> power to deny him anything that he doth request. This hath made me
> hitherto to be very careful to keep myself from him: not through any
> villainy that I know in him, but because of his great nobility. So do
> not desire me to do any such thing, because therein shall ye be in
> danger of preferring his desire above the commandment of my master
> the King.

This indeed bears wonderful witness to the magnetism of John's
personality, as well as to the impression of honesty which emana-
ted from him: and that in spite of the natural handicap of language, for John invariably conducted his negotiations with the
Spaniards without the aid of an interpreter, but in their own
tongue.

Now once more all was plain sailing, both Castellanos and the colonists doing business henceforth to the satisfaction of all parties, even of the Treasurer himself. He and John now exchanged presents in the most friendly manner, John producing a velvet mantle with gold buttons, de Castellanos 'a woman's girdle of large pearls, a very rich thing'.[1]

John now continued to coast along the Mainland of South America, coming first to Santa Marta. Here was a reasonably compliant Governor who at once asked John to go through the motions of capturing the town. This John, landing in full armour, proceeded to do. To add verisimilitude, an old unoccupied house was mutually selected, which was solemnly destroyed by gunfire, no casualties being inflicted on either side. Then John occupied the market place and came to terms with the Governor, who indeed had no alternative but to allow John to trade, having no force with which to oppose him. And here, in most friendly fashion, most of what was left of the slaves and the general cargo was disposed of, John taking in provisions for the fleet with everything done strictly according to form, and all scrupulously paid for. Thence the squadron moved on to Cartagena, the last possible point of call in South America, and the capital of the Spanish Main.

It was a relatively heavily fortified place with quite a big garrison. The Governor, with such forces at his disposal, was adamant. He would admit no trade: he would not even allow the fleet to water. John reconnoitred the place carefully: but, though he still had a few negroes left on board and a small quantity of merchandise, he realized at once that no attempt to capture the place was worth while, even if he had the strength to do it. So he sailed out of the harbour. Now, being becalmed for a couple of days, he took the opportunity to reduce his fleet by two, keeping only his original six ships, Captain Bland's French caravel, and another caravel found deserted off Cape Blanco in Africa and commandeered by the English. The month of July was running out and the hurricane season was approaching. It was no place

---

[1] The Deposition of Robert Barrett (Caribbean Documents, p. 157) Barrett, Master of the *Jesus*, was subsequently taken prisoner in Mexico and, on the evidence of Job Hortop (*Hakluyt*, Vol. 6, p. 352) was burnt at the stake by the Inquisition at Seville, in or around 1570. This Barrett was evidently an outstanding man who had throughout the expedition often been the spear-head of John's land operations.

for the battered, leaking *Jesus*. He must make sail for home without further dallying.

f. SAN JUAN DE ULUA

John reckoned that he had enough victuals to take him home if he went by the most direct and best-known route, which was to pass round the western end of Cuba and to make for the Florida passage. But luck was against him again. He was still in the Caribbean three weeks after leaving Cartagena, when, not unexpectedly, a gale hit him in mid-August; not too heavy for a well-found fleet, but much too severe for the poor old *Jesus of Lubeck*, which had to turn down-wind and make for the west, right into the depths of the Gulf of Mexico. Six of the other seven sail followed her, but the eighth the *William and John*, lost touch, and never regained it: but, still battling against the wind, continued up the Florida Passage, and at length reached home in safety.

Meanwhile the plight of the *Jesus* was unenviable. According to a survivor, she could no longer endure the sea. Her stern on either side of the sternpost simply opened up, leaving leaks as big as a man's arm, while living fish swam freely in her hold.

And truly [observes this authority,] without his [John's] great experience . . . we had been sunk in the sea in her within six days after we came out of England, and, escaping that, yet she had never been able to have been brought hither but by his industry, the which his trouble and care he had of her may be thought to be because she was the Queen's Majesty's ship, and that she should not perish under his hand.

And that was true enough. Had she been his ship, or the property of anyone else *but* the Queen, he would long since have cleared her of her gear and men, and let her sink. It did not even pay him and his business friends to keep her afloat because, had she been lost, that loss would have fallen on the Crown: but if she were brought home, however battered and leaky, then the cost of her repair would fall upon the syndicate. But John was nothing if not a loyal servant of the Crown. So he thought shame to return without the Queen's ship which, he conceived, she had entrusted to him. There is perhaps no more shining example in his life of his transparent loyalty, his over-riding honesty of purpose.

But now things began to look very grim, and daily they grew grimmer. The storm blew the fleet deeper and deeper into that blind alley, the Mexican Gulf. Its coastline was but sparsely inhabited, and for hundreds of miles there was practically no anchorage for ships. Throughout its length it was a lee shore, with violent winds which blew anti-clockwise round the coast from east and north, and, at that time of year especially, savage blasts from the north. Everywhere the beaches shoaled steeply. John had never been there before and did not know his way: nor had he a pilot to guide him. For days on end he had to claw off with his big ships, sending in the smaller ones to reconnoitre while he made desperate efforts to keep the *Jesus* afloat.

At length he met with a Spanish ship which, with two others, was carrying wine from San Domingo to New Spain. He stopped them and learnt from their captain that the nearest port was Campeache, with a haven which was of no use to him because it had no facilities for docking the Queen's ship. Somewhat to the north of it, he learnt, was the town of Santa Cruz, but that had no port at all. After that, all that was left was the small haven of San Juan de Ulua. The Spaniards used it as the port for Mexico City, which lay on its high plateau some distance to the west. But now the Spanish captain added the ill tidings that the Flota, the annual treasure fleet, was expected to arrive at San Juan de Ulua almost any day. Thither, then, John resolved to sail, having no other course open to him, and for that very restricted anchorage he now made, forcing the Spaniards to accompany him. It was nearly two months since he had left Cartagena, and his supplies were running dangerously low.

At length, on September 15, he sighted the place. As he approached, the Spanish authorities put out in boats to meet him. They were expecting the Plate Fleet, and though John was flying his Sovereign's royal standard, it was so faded and weather-beaten that they failed to recognize it, but came straight on, not doubting for a moment that John's squadron (with the three Spanish merchantmen eleven sail strong) was the fleet they expected. This at least was in John's favour. They came aboard, John detained the lot, and with them, greatly shaken, he entered the harbour.

It was after all but a poor place—a rather shallow bay with, across most of the entrance and stretching roughly parallel with the main coastline, a low bank of shingle raised only some three feet above high water. This Island (as the inhabitants were pleased to call it) was about 240 yards long, and about three-quarters of a mile out from the shore. The inhabitants, who had yearly to welcome the considerable Plate Fleet, had done a little towards improving the facilities of this island. On it they had built a few rather mean houses used for the accommodation of their slaves: and they had deepened the water on its land side so that ships could lie there, strictly in line abreast for lack of room, with their bows projecting over the island, and their stern-anchors warped out in the deeper water on its sheltered-side. They had also mounted a few guns on the island, which could command the only entrance to the harbour. Between the island and the main shore were moored eight Spanish merchant ships, laden with the annual product of the mines—a princely prize, had John been tempted to seize them. But he was not: all *he* wanted was leave to do such repairs as were possible to his lame duck, and to provide himself with the prime necessities of life. More than that, he was, as has so often appeared in these pages, no pirate (in the English sense) but an honest merchant; so that, in all probability, he would not have touched the ships even if he had been well-found and fresh from home.

A single glance as he entered showed him that the island batteries were the key to the whole position, and that at all costs he must acquire them, adding guns of his own. And this he managed to do because the officer in command of them made the same mistake as the rest, and fired a joyous salute of unshotted pieces as John entered the bay: and then, realizing their mistake too late, the gunners with one accord left their charge and bolted for the mainland. Instantly John took over the all-important position and landed men and guns of his own.

The port, for what it was worth, was now his, because his batteries effectively prevented any other ship from coming in. Thereupon he made his demands, which were quite minimal. He asked to be allowed to revictual his ships, paying for everything he received. He was also to be allowed to do such necessary repairs to his fleet as he could. To these terms the port authorities had perforce to agree, especially as, it seems, they did not expect the Flota until the end of the month. That was still a fortnight on; and John was confident that he could revictual, repair and depart before that time elapsed.

Again he was out of luck. The very next day the dawn revealed the Plate Fleet riding outside, having made a near-record passage from Spain. It consisted of thirteen ships, all but two merchantmen; but all very large ships, well-manned, well-gunned, and reasonably fresh from port.

John's dilemma was now extreme. He still had the means to keep the Spaniards out, but he must now make up his mind at once whether to do so or not: for whichever course he took grave danger pressed upon him. In his own account he says:

> . . . Either I must have kept the fleete from entering the Port— that which with Gods helpe I was very well able to do, or else suffer them to enter in with their accustomed treason, which they never fail to execute where they may have opportunity . . . if I had kept them out, then had there been present shipwarke of al the fleete which amounted in value to sixe millions, which was in value of our money 1,800,000 li, which I considered I was not able to aunswer, fearing the Queens Majestie's indignation in so weighty a matter. Thus, with my selfe revolving the doubts, I thought rather better to abide the Jutt of the uncertainty than the certainty.[1]

So, with eyes wide open to the risks involved, he let them in. Does this surprise us? No. It was altogether in character with what we know of him. John was by nature a law-abiding man. All his instinct led him to prefer honest trade to lawless violence: to prefer, in fact, peace to war. It is true that, in the preceeding year, he had used violence against the Spanish fleet that sailed into Plymouth Harbour, but, in doing so, he was merely maintaining the law as he knew it—that it was the Spaniards who had broken the laws and customs of the sea. But, even on that occasion, he had not been supported by authority, which had reprimanded him. What then would happen now, when the Queen was informed by John's bitterest enemies that her representative had kept the rightful owners out of their own port, thereby bringing destruction worth much more than a King's ransom: worse, money which the Queen might well be required to make good. And that would indeed have aroused her indigna-

---

[1] *The Hawkins Voyages*, by C. R. Markham (Hakluyt Society, 1879), p. 75.

tion! It is true also, that though John *expected* treachery, he could not *know* that it would follow. So, in his own words, he preferred 'rather the Jutt of the uncertainty to the certainty'. The decision was perhaps an unwise one: but it shows up John Hawkins at his honourable best.

He was dealing too with a man who, by all the laws which John knew and invariably obeyed, *ought* to have been honourable. As a passenger in the Spanish flagship sailed the new Viceroy of Mexico itself, and a high-born nobleman of Spain, Don Martin Henriquez, destined to rule New Spain for the next ten years. But—what John probably did *not* know—the man was a fanatic, due during his viceroyalty to introduce into his new dominions the full abomination of the Spanish Inquisition. And here was the man with whom, in good faith, John was to have dealings. The result was really a foregone conclusion.

Before he would admit him, John took every possible precaution. The terms of entry were drawn up with meticulous care, and subscribed to by both parties. And the Viceroy, 'with many fair words' understanding how 'passing the coast of the Indies' we had 'by our honest behaviour towards the inhabitants' universally kept faith, engaged on his honour to keep faith himself. Hostages were to be exchanged 'for the maintenance of peace'. The Island 'for our better safety was to be left in our owne possession'. There was precious little room for all the ships to ride along the island even when lying abreast: yet a space was to be left between the *Minion* anchored at the end of the English line and the nearest of the Spaniards. And John engaged—and Henriquez agreed—to victual his ships as quickly as possible, paying for everything he had, and to depart as soon as this was done. So were all the arrangements made, and for two days apparent amity prevailed, the English and the Spaniards, during that time, actually fraternizing on the Island.

But then John began to notice movements which he could not but suspect. A very large ship—of 900 tons, John says—was being inserted into the space between the *Minion* and the first Spanish vessel, completely filling the gap. Troops from the mainland were surreptitiously introduced into it: guns were seen to be shifted so that they could command the Island batteries. At last, now more than suspicious, John sent Robert Barrett, the master of the *Jesus* who spoke Spanish, to the enemy's flagship, to inquire what these moves portended. Then, finding their design discovered, the Viceroy detained Barrett and threw all disguise to the winds. At that very moment John was sitting down to a hurried meal in the cabin of the *Jesus* when an English-man noticed that one of the Spanish hostages on board that ship had a dagger in his sleeve, and, snatching it from him, revealed the treachery just in time to save John's life. Then, as the English leader hurried on deck, the Spanish trumpets sounded and the action began.

The fight lasted from 10 a.m. to 4 p.m., all fought out at point-blank range between quite immobile ships. John instantly ordered the cables to the island to be cut, and the ships hauled out by their sternfasts: and while this was doing, some 200 Spaniards boarded the *Minion*,

> Whereat our General [says Hortop] with a loud and fierce voice called unto us saying, 'God and St George! Upon those traitorous villains and rescue the *Minion*! I trust in God the day shall be ours.'

On that the crew of the *Jesus* leaped into the *Minion* and cleared the invaders out. But meanwhile three Spanish ships attacked the flagship herself, and before she got clear she suffered heavy casualties.

But the decision still lay on the Island itself. The English gun-crews, even in the act of fraternizing with the enemy, were assailed from several sides at once. The men to whom they were talking drew concealed weapons: others poured over the high prows of several neighbouring ships. Practically all the English on the Island were immediately killed, wounded or taken pri-soner, and the survivors (which, Hortop says, amounted only to three) retreated to the *Jesus*. So the Island with its batteries was lost, and all the English could hope for was to get out of the harbour as quickly as possible.

Before they went, however, they sold their lives dearly. The two Queen's ships were now clear of the Island, and they poured such a point-blank fire into their enemies that, in a very few minutes, the Spanish Admiral was sunk, though, owing to the shallowness of the harbour, she only rested upon the bottom. The Vice-Admiral too was reduced to a wreck, set on fire and gutted, with thirty-five of her people killed outright. One of the large merchantmen was also sunk.

With his foes thus depleted, John now concentrated upon leaving the harbour. But he found that the poor old *Jesus* could not move at all. Nothing but a caricature of a ship from the start, her rigging was now so completely shattered that she could no longer even leave. John defended her to the last, so that in the end he all but got left behind, scrambling on to the *Minion* only at the very last moment. As he entered her she was being assailed by a fire-ship, at which some of her crew, gallant as they were, showed signs of panic, and cut the cables connecting the two ships, thereby all but deserting their General. He had been striving desperately to the last to transfer provisions, and perhaps some of the proceeds of his trading, from the *Jesus* to the *Minion*. But with the work quite incomplete, he had to give it up, and to sail in the only Queen's ship left. Even then, however, he did not leave the coast at once, but stopped a quarter of a mile outside the port, whither all the survivors from all the other ships who could manage it, rowed out in boats, or even swam out, and joined him. So with virtually no food on board, the *Minion* was seriously overcrowded with men.

Otherwise, only the *Judith*, a little bark of 50 tons, escaped. Something of a mystery still hangs over that ship. It seems that the *Minion* lost touch with her at once, and never saw her again until, long afterwards, she reached England. John was evidently a little bitter about her. All he says in his official account is that this bark 'the same night forsook us in our great misery'. That is all: and it is again very typical of John Hawkins. It is the nearest thing to a reproach, let alone an accusation, that he is ever known to have made. He was invariably slow to criticize his juniors: but that only adds weight to this very mild censure. No record of the *Judith*'s doings, or her journey home, is recorded: nor have we any idea as to why she forsook her General in his distress. And the odd thing about it is that her captain was not, as it were, just any old officer. It was Francis Drake himself! And, under all the circumstances, it is difficult to think of any adequate reason why he sailed away thus thoughtlessly, as though shirking the duty of accompanying the *Minion* and of sharing her privations. It is not even as though bad weather drove them apart. We are expressly told that they left San Juan de Ulua in tolerably fair weather. The following night, it is true, a gale did arise: but by then Francis had been missing for many hours. Did the greatest of all the Elizabethan seamen for once think too much of his own safety? At that time he was still a very young man who had not then made his mark. So it does begin to look very much like real desertion. However, as his defence is not known, it would probably be wrong to condemn him unheard.

From the first, after leaving San Juan, the *Minion's* company had been on starvation diet. There was virtually no proper food at all, the people subsisting at first on the rats which abounded on board, together with the cats normally kept to keep down the rats: there were also the pets, mainly parrots, the property of the men who had once hoped to bring them back to England as curiosities. But after a fortnight, and the ship still a very long way short of the Florida Passage, it became clear both to John and to the men themselves that something quite drastic must be done if anyone at all was to reach home. So, with the utmost difficulty, John landed at lat. $23\frac{1}{2}°$N., just beyond the northern range of the Spanish settlements. He found, when he came to inquire, that two parties existed on board: those who wished to stay there and to take their chance of reaching home, and those who preferred to be put on shore, to starve on land, or else to submit to the tender mercies of the Spaniard. At that moment, roughly, the swollen company of the *Minion* numbered about 200 souls: half wishful to go, half wanting to stay. Somewhat more exact figures are given by Job Hortop, who says that 96 elected to land (he being one of them); while another who landed, finally got home, and has left an account[1] puts the landing party at 114. Both reveal the voluntariness of the choice, and their admiration for their General. Neither throws any blame on to him at all, but, recognizing the inevitability of their leaving the ship, both tell how John did all in his power to soften

---

[1] Miles Philip, then a lad of fourteen, who only made his escape to England in 1582. His account of his adventures is also in *Hakluyt* (vol. 6, pp. 296–336). His story is more detailed than Hortop's, being more than twice as long, but not quite so interesting because he lacked Hortop's literary talent. Between them, however, they give a wonderful lower-deck view of the cruel treatment meted out to them by their captors, their pluck and their ultimate escape.

the blow and to relieve their distress, giving to all those left
behind money (if they wanted it) and six yards of cloth each, to
barter with the natives. Then, before he departed, he inter-
viewed the men who were staying behind, praying with each of
them separately, and promising to do everything he could to
secure their release. We shall see all in good time in just what
these efforts consisted, and we shall have to admit that they were
such that no one but a thoroughly good and conscientious man
could have undertaken. Nor must we forget that, while he
was comforting his departing men, he was himself facing the
near certainty of a long and lingering death from starvation.

So the two halves of that forlorn company separated, and, on
October 16 the *Minion* continued on her way. At last a little
good fortune favoured her. By mid-November she was clear of
the Florida Passage. It was of no use, as it had been on his last
voyage, to visit the Newfoundland Banks, because by now all
fishermen had left them for home. So he sailed directly for
Europe, and even so was greeted by adverse weather conditions
to the last because the normal easterlies failed to blow that year.

The survivors were now rapidly dying off, and the best they
could do was, on the last day of 1568, to make the north-west
corner of Spain, where they put into Vigo Bay. This, as none
knew better than John, was a thoroughly dangerous thing to do.
But there was no help for it: and, once there, he put up a remarkable bluff. He had plenty of ready money, and so had no
difficulty in buying food for all. But, not surprisingly, the poor
starving Englishmen 'with excess of fresh meat grew into
miserable diseases, and died a great part of them'.[1] It seems that
no less than forty-five fell to this unlooked-for surfeit. But to
the very last John was his own splendid self, and the provincial
authorities at Vigo could not cope with him at all. He went
ashore dressed in all his finery—'in breeches of crimson velvet'
says another Spanish account, 'a jacket of scarlet leather trimmed
with silver braid, a silken cloak and a long gold chain.'[2] It was
not fine clothes that John lacked, but simply bread and meat!
Though they had been warned by Madrid that they were to

[1] Quoted by J. A. Williamson in *Hawkins of Plymouth*, from an article by C.
Sanz Arizmendi in *Boletin del Instituto de Estudios Americanistas*—a work I have
not myself seen.
[2] *ibid.*

arrest him, his vivid presence, starving as he was, utterly overawed them, and they let him go. Philip, when he heard of it, was furious and ordered searching inquiries to be made as to why 'Haquines' had been allowed to depart. But it was too late. Soon after leaving Vigo he met with an English ship and borrowed twelve men from her. With these he struggled on, to arrive, at Mount's Bay in Cornwall, on January 25, 1569. Hither, as we saw, William hurried off men for his relief, and so at last he came home to Plymouth.

How many of the 408 souls who had sailed from the town ever reached it again is not known. De Silva reported to Philip that there were fifteen! But as Drake in the *Judith* had already arrived—on the day that the *Minion* put into Vigo—there were probably a few more.

John, then, had tasted all the bitterness of defeat. But it was a defeat which, as far as he himself was concerned, was much more like a victory—the victory of the Mind and the Will over mere circumstance.

g. AN EXCURSION INTO DIPLOMACY

San Juan de Ulua was in many ways the turning point in Anglo-Spanish relations, and the principal watershed in John's life. At the moment of his return he was thirty-six years old, and still, even by Tudor standards, in the prime of life. The Spaniards at Vigo had noticed that, despite the hardships which he had undergone, he looked quite young, and so, both in physique and in spirit, he certainly was—though young, a seasoned warrior, a consummate leader with all the sea-skill of a mature man. Now, however, his position was due for a considerable, if a subtle change. Hitherto, though already a true and trusted servant to Elizabeth, he had still been, primarily, the shrewd and honourable merchant who took his own ships to sea, with a mind bent, mainly, on selling his merchandise: selling it too to Philip of Spain, and most anxious to stand well with that monarch; most anxious, in fact, to preserve England's old relations with Spain, thereby carrying his own country, with Philip's goodwill, into the heart of the New World. San Juan de Ulua, however, had now taught him in no uncertain way that such dreams were quite unrealistic: that there was now no longer room for a *peaceful*

passage into that trade: that, if England still wanted to participate in it, she would have to do so, not by virtue of honest mercantile dealings, but only at the point of her sword. In fact, he
now realized at last that there was no future at all for the
honest merchant pure and simple. So, very wisely, he decided to
give up that role: or rather, perhaps, to hand over this particular
role to men not quite so scrupulous as he was. There were many
such in England, and foremost among them, as history was to
show, was his young kinsman, Francis Drake, who was, emphatically, a great deal less scrupulous where Philip was concerned,
and a great deal more willing to use the argument of the great
guns.

After a time, then, Drake became England's spearhead in her
effort to penetrate into the Spanish monopoly, and brilliantly he
was destined to do so. Yet the rise of Francis by no means meant
the fall of John. It merely made the last-named change the
direction of his aim. As Drake emerged more and more clearly as
the spearhead, John became more and more the trusted servant
of the Crown who, unostentatiously, made that spearhead sharp
enough to do its work. In fact John was now about to enter upon
the greatest service which he ever gave to his country: he was
about to forge for her that overwhelming weapon which was to
see her safely through the most serious crisis which had ever
faced her. In a word, he was about to give her a fleet capable of
humbling Spain.

The transition of John, however, from merchant to weapon
forger did not take place overnight; and that for two reasons.
The first was the reluctance of both Philip and Elizabeth to make
that sudden change which would convert Anglo-Spanish friendship into a full-blooded Anglo-Spanish war. Neither had quite
the nerve to do that. Philip held his hand partly from fear of his
old rival France, and partly from an inherited predilection for that
policy which had always, hitherto stood him in such good stead—
the policy, not of war *à l'outrance*, but of diplomacy based upon
marriage: the slower, but in his view the equally sure way of
attaining his ends by replacing the unsatisfactory heretic who
ruled over England with an altogether (he thought) more pliable
candidate—in this case the out and out Catholic ruler of England's northern neighbour—Mary, Queen of Scots. Meanwhile

Elizabeth held her hand, partly from a very real fear of Spain, who *appeared* to be the most formidable power on earth, and partly from her constitutional inability to 'grasp the nettle danger': she feared that her little David would never stand up for long against the Goliath which was Spain, nor her country's poverty against the riches of Mexico and Peru. So, for no less than sixteen years after San Juan de Ulua, there stretched a seemingly endless period, not of real friendship, but of veiled hostility; not of downright war, but of what we should now describe as 'cold war'. And it was during this long twilight period that Francis appeared as England's champion on the seas, and John emerged as England's less spectacular but equally important champion in dockland, forging her war-winning weapon there. It was a division of labour which worked *à merveille*—especially John's part of the partnership.

The second reason why John did not change over at once from merchant prince to creator of fleets was a much more personal one. He had a little business to do first with his erstwhile friend Philip—the business which concerned the unfortunates left behind in Mexico, and the impulse to redeem the solemn promise he had made to them as he left them. This lay heavy on his conscience: this was the first thing he had to do: and this, in an altogether original way, was the first thing he did.

In 1569 there appeared for the first time a western defence squadron, which has, at intervals, been appearing ever since. It was based upon Plymouth, and it was to be the opposite number in the West to the Queen's Ships based on the Thames in the East. But it should be noted that, in 1569, this new western force consisted entirely of merchant ships, mainly of Hawkins ships, kept up for the most part at the Hawkinses' expense and out of the proceeds of the Channel privateers, which was, as we have seen, very largely a Hawkins concern too. Anyway, normally the Queen had nothing to pay!

John's first idea was very typical of the times. He proposed to assemble a fleet—a Hawkins fleet too—to attack the Spanish Plate Fleet: not, ostensibly, as a private venture of John's, but as that of the representative of the Queen's Majesty, who had lost her ship, the *Jesus*, by treachery at San Juan; and who was entitled, under the old concept of law then current, to 'take reprisals' upon the said dastardly traitors. Unfortunately for the project, however, it clashed somewhat with the Royal policy of using John's fleet as a Western defence force. If, in the Government's eyes, it went off chasing flotas, it would not be available for the exclusive defence of the Western approaches. So John found himself strictly forbidden to leave the Channel.

It was now that he began to work seriously on the scheme which ever since his return from the third voyage, had been nearest to his heart—the release of his Mexican captives, thirty-one of whom had been brought back to Spain during 1569. Coolly and patiently he went to work. His first move was to persuade the Spanish Ambassador (now no longer de Silva, but the more gullible Don Guerau de Spes) that he was a deeply disappointed and disillusioned man—a man with a grievance. He was forbidden—most unreasonably, he said—to lead out his own ships to take reprisals in order to cover his losses in the preceding year. It was, for an essentially honest soul like John, a difficult furrow to plough, this pretence of disloyalty to the Crown. Yet this is what he did, and he did it most successfully. He persuaded the rash—indeed somewhat brash—Ambassador that his discontent was such that he was prepared to throw in his lot with the other party at home—that is, with Mary Queen of Scotland and the English Catholics: and that of course, in those days, was tantamount to saying that he threw in his lot with *all* Catholics, including those of Spain. Treachery? Nowadays, if seriously intended, yes—arrant treachery: but in 1570 by no means so arrant, because there were still thousands of Englishmen (perhaps even hundreds of thousands) who had not adopted the New Faith, and who regarded the self-styled Queen of England as a pestilent heretic and a bastard who had no business at all to be sitting where she was. He probably made this approach on his own initiative, but actually, of course, it was no treachery at all towards the Queen of England, because he certainly kept both her and Cecil informed of what he was doing from the very start and throughout. And they, in their turn, encouraged him and played his game at every move.

The Ambassador, who was not nearly so acute as he imagined, swallowed the bait at once. So did the Spanish Government when the Ambassador passed on the good news. It had always half-suspected John of being a Catholic—perhaps after all he was pro-Spanish too—and the King had always thought of him as being potentially pro-Philip: John himself had been busy fostering that illusion for years. And this means that no Englishman *but* John could possibly have played this game with any chance of succeeding.

He had an ideal go-between in the person of a certain George FitzWilliam, a long-standing Hawkins retainer. He had been one of the hostages given by John to the Spaniards at San Juan de Ulua, and had been treacherously held by them and brought over a prisoner to Spain along with the other survivors. He had, however, the advantage of being related to the English wife of a high-born Don, the Duke of Feria. So now he received preferential treatment. He was released from his dungeon in Seville some time in 1570, and allowed to return to England. With such contacts he seems to have been equally welcome in London and in Madrid: for now he returned to Spain bearing a letter from John to the King. It suggested that Philip, in return for John's promised allegiance *and* the Western Squadron of England, might be prepared to release the San Juan captives.

On receiving this missive, Philip was duly impressed. But with his customary prudence he refused to order the men's release until such time as he could be shown an autograph letter from the Scottish Queen vouching for John's 'conversion'. So Fitz-William returned to England, where he must now be introduced into the presence of Queen Mary, already a close prisoner in England with her correspondence closely scrutinized by her gaolers. And then she must be persuaded to write the necessary letter. The writing itself proved to be no difficulty, because the temperament of the Scottish queen was so sanguine that she cheerfully accepted John's account of himself. Nor, with Burghley in the plot, was there any real difficulty about 'smuggling' out the letter when written. The only difficulty lay in persuading the Spanish Ambassador that Burghley knew nothing about the 'betrayal': and this John managed very cleverly by telling de Spes that Burghley knew already of his (John's) efforts to get his men released, but did *not* know of his proposed treachery. And this the infatuated Ambassador, now blindly believing all that John told him, accepted too. So Mary, when she wrote, went through what was the farce (unknown to her) of writing her letter in secret ink which became visible only when heat was applied to it. FitzWilliam now carried this missive with him to Spain, and gave it to Philip.

So all Catholic parties were deceived, and Philip ordered the instant release of the prisoners, assuming that, any day now, John would leave Plymouth with his squadron, and, proceeding up-Channel to Flanders, get in touch with the Duke of Alba who lay there only awaiting the signal to invade Kent, with John's English fleet to escort him. At the same time, too, as John defected there was to be a wholesale rising of English Catholics under the titular leadership of England's premier peer, the Catholic Duke of Norfolk. For good measure, moreover, a murderous Italian diplomat named Ridolfi was to attempt the life of the Queen herself. All was to hinge, in the first place, upon John's treachery, which was to set the rest in motion.

This brilliant deception fooled not only de Spes, but also both Mary of Scotland and Philip of Spain. It has also fooled many subsequent writers, including the partially deceived J. A. Froude himself, who, in his day, only knew half the facts. But of course it never for a single moment fooled either Burghley or the Queen, who were in the know from the first, following every move in the game.

Meanwhile Philip, in his enthusiasm at having landed such an important fish as John Hawkins, proposed to confer princely rewards, or bribes, upon him. He made out a patent for Spanish nobility for him: he granted him a free pardon for all the damage he had inflicted upon Spain in the past: he even designed to bestow a very handsome gift of money upon him—as an encouragement, perhaps, to other Englishmen to do likewise.

John was mildly amused. On receiving a copy of the Spanish Pardon which was going to be given to him, he sent it on to Burghley with a covering letter in which he thus described it, 'Large enough! with very great titles and honours from the King: from which, may God deliver me!'[1]

John had done a great deal more than to secure the release of his captives. He had worked himself so deeply into the Spanish

---

[1] Quoted by R. N. Worth in his article on Sir John Hawkins, in *Transactions of the Devonshire Association*, vol. XV, p. 266.

plot as to render it impossible for the enemy to proceed with it. At the critical moment Burghley had struck by arresting the Duke of Norfolk, and had exposed the dastardly assassination conspiracy: which in its turn so discouraged Philip that he decided then and there to give up the invasion part of his scheme. So in the end it was these moves of Burghley's, and not John's defection (now unnecessary) which *seemed* to defeat the plans of Spain. In fact John's share remained undetected for a very long time, so that Philip himself never knew how he had been fooled! On the other hand that poor dupe, the egregious de Spes, found his complicity exposed by evidence brought to light at the trials of Norfolk and Ridolfi; and he was ignominiously sent packing from England—seen off affectionately from Dover by his *dear* friend John Hawkins whom, even then, he did not begin to suspect!

John never actually received any of the personal fruits of his deception: either the Spanish title, the Spanish pardon or the Spanish gold. What did accrue to him was twofold. He restored to their homes and loved ones most of the survivors from San Juan—and this was, by a very great deal, the principal object of his manoeuvres. But also he established himself as not only—what he had been before—a leader of men and a master of war, but also as an adept in that subtle kind of diplomacy so frequently practised during the 'cold war'. And, as well, he gained the reputation of being one of Her Grace's most valuable and most trustworthy public servants.

Even now, however, John still had some five years to run before, as Treasurer of the Navy, he emerged, in effect if not in name, in charge of the Queen's Ships. And during all the 1570s, from 1572 onwards, he continued ostensibly in his former occupations, spending his time perhaps equally between Plymouth and London. It cannot be said for certain that during these years he never went to sea himself. In fact almost certainly, and for brief periods, he did. But it is broadly true to say that during this time the Hawkins interest in Plymouth was conducted by brother William, while John himself ranged more widely afield. We must very briefly, then, follow him along three separate paths.

The first, in conjunction with William, concerns him still as a

Plymouth merchant, busy with such chores as shipping, the conduct of the Channel privateers, and the very complex voyages,
part trading, part discovery and part warlike, which were pro-
jected, mainly but not exclusively, from the western port;
partly carried in Hawkins ships, partly in the vessels of other
kindred spirits like Sir Richard Grenville, Sir Walter Raleigh,
Martin Frobisher, Sir Arthur and Henry Champernoune,
Edward Fenton, Sir Humphrey Gilbert, John Oxenham, James
Raunse and—a small part at first, growing gradually larger
until it became the largest of all—Sir Francis Drake. There is
not here the space to chronicle in detail the doings of this great
group of men who were gradually putting England more and
more firmly on the sea-map of the world, especially during the
1570s. Here we can only note in passing that the hands of
William and John were readily discernible in financing, fitting
out and even manning the expeditions. Thus, to quote but two of
such voyages, it is likely that Drake, in his first violent and
successful raid into the West Indies in 1572–3 was largely
operating with Hawkins money, and even, possibly, acting as a
Hawkins captain. And again, in his even more famous voyage of
cirumnavigation in the *Golden Hind* in 1577–80, there are
still many traces of Hawkins participation, as well as that of a
wide syndicate including the very greatest in the land—but
always including the names of one or both Hawkinses among
them.

Secondly, through it all, it must not be forgotten that John's
interests were not directed solely towards the Western Seas.
During most of that decade, for example, he was one of the two
parliamentary members for the town of his birth, his first partner
being Sir Humphrey Gilbert, his second Edmund Tremayne. It
was this post, of course, which brought him directly into contact
with the key Englishman of them all, Sir William Cecil, now
Lord Burghley, and which kept him in touch with the Government of England; and with the Crown of England too, because
he was now very well known at Court, and he must have had
constant relations with the Queen.

That she appreciated his sterling qualities one well-known
incident proves. In 1573, while in Town, he came within an ace
of death by assassination. A certain Peter Burchet, a barrister

of the Inner Temple, was to all intents and purposes a homicidal maniac. Suspecting the Queen's favourite, Sir Christopher Hatton, of Catholic tendencies, and of exercising over Elizabeth an undue Catholic influence, he was roaming the Strand one morning, armed with a dagger, when he met (as he thought) this Hatton, and without more ado plunged his knife into him. But the victim was not Hatton. It was John Hawkins. (It was an instructive error, very prejudicial to Charles Kingsley's portrait of our John on Plymouth Hoe in 1588, because the man for whom John was mistaken was a famous dandy, and reputed to be the best-dressed gentleman in Town. So, that day, John must have been well-dressed too—as indeed he always was.) The wound was deep, and for some days his life was in danger. The Queen was horrified when she heard of it, and she instantly sent her own surgeon to cure his body, and her own chaplain to attend to his soul. But John, who was a tough man, and only then forty-one years old, quickly recovered. Peter was hustled off to the Tower, but contrived, before he could be executed, to murder one of the beef-eaters with a blazing log of wood snatched from the grate in his cell.

And now John began to collect a third and new set of duties— that of naval adviser to the Government, making submission to that body on how to wage a maritime war when the inevitable moment for it came. He was now—before the full emergence of Francis Drake—Elizabeth's most experienced naval commander who had already undertaken voyages and actions at sea on her behalf. He was therefore, more than any other subject of hers, in a position to advise her on naval strategy and naval policy— much better qualified to do so than any minister of the Crown, including even Burghley, whose knowledge and experience did not cover the practical side of 'operations' at all, nor the highly technical side of ship construction.

His first appearance in this role of adviser had occurred as early as 1570 when, smarting from his treatment at San Juan de Ulua, he had suggested to Burghley an attack on the Flotas of Spain. At that moment we were very near to war with her: but, then, Elizabeth had not come round to such a drastic policy which would have made that war a certainty. So, after much earnest discussion in the Council, his scheme was turned down or, rather, postponed until another day.

It was only in 1577 that John's full strategic ideas began to become plainly visible: and when they did, they involved radical alterations in the strength and the destribution of the English Navy. By then he had decided that our naval might must be built up, and must be in a high state of readiness, before ever the war was begun. And this, his experience in the *Jesus* and elsewhere had convinced him, meant a new type of warship altogether, consisting of ships which were much less 'Ships of Majesty' and much more real sea-keepers, much more answerable to helm and sail, much better able to manoeuvre on the seas of the world: in fact, a new kind of navy altogether. And, such was the intuition of the man that he saw, if he was ever to get his way, he must himself take over the duties of Fleet-architect and Ship-builder. This, almost certainly, is the reason why John emerges in 1577 as Treasurer of the Navy Board. It was the fourth of his many duties, and it was destined to become by far the most important of them.

By then the immediate crisis of impending war had for the moment subsided. But, before the 1570s were out, there was to be another crisis, which led, among other things, to Drake's voyage of circumnavigation. When he returned in 1580 war was again very near. Yet once more it was postponed, largely for the same reason as before—the unwillingness (for various reasons) of Philip and Elizabeth to take the plunge. But, this time, there was an additional reason. In this year the very considerable plum which was Portugal was growing ripe for plucking from its tree: and at that moment Philip, deciding to garner it, did not want other international complications which would distract his aim and make it harder for him to digest it. Yet postponement could not be for very long now, if only because the might of Philip, having successfully swallowed Portugal, was yearly growing excessive, and yearly more dangerous to his neighbours, especially to England.

h. TREASURER OF THE NAVY

For many years, in fact during the bulk of his adult life, John had been quite intimately associated with that Navy Board which

Henry VIII had created to look after the Royal Ships of England. He had, as it were, married into it, his wife Katherine being the daughter of Benjamin Gonson. This man, indeed, was almost hereditarily attached to it. His father, 'old William Gonson', had served Henry VIII as his chief Naval official for some twenty years, and when he grew too old for the place, he had been succeeded by his son Benjamin who seems, oddly enough, to have been brought up in Holy Orders, having, as early as 1542, been Rector of St Mary Colechurch in London.[1] But he soon gave up his cure of souls to become, first Clerk of the Ships in 1545, then Surveyor (in 1546) and finally (in 1549) Treasurer of the Board. This office he held for twenty-eight years. It was, in his case, a purely administrative post, and though he certainly dabbled in commerce, he never so far as is known left his London office to go to sea. By 1577 he was old and worn out, and in November of that year John was appointed Joint-Treasurer with his father-in-law: who, perhaps providentially, died ten days later.

This appointment, however, did not automatically make John the head of the Board. In Henry VIII's original arrangement, all the Board's officials were supposed to be co-equals, and in fact it was a question of personality which official was at any given moment predominant. At the time of John's entry there was another family almost equally hereditary within the Board. It was the family of Winter and, in 1577, its senior representative was a certain Sir William (knighted in 1573). He filled two important posts, and had long filled them. One was Master of the Ordnance—not a Navy Board post, but closely connected with it, since he was responsible to the Crown for all naval guns. His Navy Board post, which he also held, was Surveyor of the Navy. When John came on the scene, too, he had for some time been the master-spirit of the whole outfit. He was supported by his younger brother George, now Clerk of the Ships, a somewhat less masterful figure, yet always supporting his elder brother.

It would be wrong, probably, to regard the Winter clique as basically dishonest, though there can be no question that, by 1577, they were running the Board in a way which would be

[1] A. W. Johns (Article in *Mariner's Mirror*, vol. XIV, 1, p. 34).

scandalous nowadays but was not so then. In plain fact they were making a very good thing out of it. But, in Tudor times, everyone—always excepting John—did that, and was expected to do it. But during his years in power, Sir William had done, full and by, an efficient job, according to his own limited lights: and the small navy of Elizabeth's early years had not been noticeably neglected—always, that is, according to the standards of the day as then understood. In short, it was not Winter who was the exception: it was John, about to set a new pattern of honesty.

It was his fixed intention from the start to attack and to destroy the Winter monopoly: and it was an action which required considerable moral courage, because the Winters were old friends of his own with whom he had often worked in commercial undertakings, with no thought of fighting them. And he knew from the very beginning what he would be up against. Old Benjamin had warned him in no uncertain way. 'I shall pluck out a thorn from my foot,' he had told John on his deathbed, 'and set it in yours.'

The only other member of the Navy Board was one William Holstocke, the Comptroller of the Navy and, by comparison with the others, a nonentity.

John opened fire with a report to Burghley in which he did not pull his punches at all. The 'ordinary' (normal yearly expenditure on ships) was at the moment costing the Crown some £6,000 a year. This, said John, could easily be done for £4,000, and better done at that. The 'extraordinary' (heavy repairs in dry-dock and new building) was 'in great confusion'. Repairs charged on six ships cost £4,845, which was more than enough: yet Her Majesty was to be charged £1,600 more— 'which proceedeth of the wilful covetousness of one man' (name not mentioned yet no doubt tacitly understood) 'and to set forth his glory'. Of new buildings, ships that should cost only £2,200 are costing £4,000. Her Majesty has paid for 900 loads of timber where 500 loads would have been ample, while 'the Surveyor (Winter) keeps all such business in his private books, and the Office knows nothing of what is supplied to the Ships.'

Thereafter all sorts of abuses pile up one upon another. The Queen, these last seven years, has paid £7,000 for certain materials: but only £4,000 of them have been used in her service. The royal buyers of timber, misusing their position, make enormous profits which go into their own pockets. They keep the best timbers, selling them to private builders, while the Queen, at extortionate prices, has to make do with the inferior stuff. In quality, the Queen gets only one-third of the value of what she pays for.

Then his charges become more personal. The *Mary Fortune*, a Winter ship, was very largely built of the wood paid for by the Queen, while the *Edward*, another ship of Winter's, was built entirely from the Queen's timber. Winter builds wharves of his own with royal timber. In Drake's voyage of circumnavigation, the *Elizabeth*, commanded by Captain John Winter, the Surveyor's nephew, though built mostly of royal timber, was the subject of a charge of £120, payable by Drake to the Surveyor. The same happened to two pinnaces for which Mr Frobisher paid £24 to the Surveyor, though they were built entirely of the Queen's timber. Cables and other 'Baltic stores' are surveyed at the moment when Winter chooses, and condemned without reference to anyone else. They are then sold out of the service, the price never being paid into the Treasury. Then as to personnel, many of the clerks in the Yard are paid double wages, as well as being in a position to pick up unreasonable perquisites. All gunners', boatswains' and pursers' posts are at the Surveyor's disposal, so that they can be punished, or rewarded, by him at will.

In short, corruption of all sorts was rife, not only among the workmen and lesser officials, but—much worse because it all began there—among the principal officers themselves. And of course this was true—save under exceptional leadership or the exceptional vigilance of our own day, the administration in dockyards tended *always* to be corrupt. The only chance of honesty, as John saw very clearly, was to eliminate the jiggery-pokery at the top, so that the principals could, with a clear conscience, pounce upon petty pilfering among their subordinates. And what John was proclaiming—for the benefit of Burghley and the Queen's ministers, though of course it would soon get round to everybody—including the Winters of this world—was 'Purge the Navy Board, the Dockyards, and everyone who works in them. Then you will find that, for half the money which the Queen has to spend, she will get a better fleet for less money—or (and this perhaps was his main point) a much bigger and better fleet for the *same* money'.

Thus did John throw down his challenge. Why did he do it? What were his real motives? Well, there can be no doubt what the Winters thought, and said loudly and often both *coram populo* and by private innuendo. They were not obscure men either, but influential officers of the Crown, dangerous to thwart: men of good substance and of outstanding personality, with the reputation, largely deserved, of possessing the monopoly of know-how in naval administration. Of course they resented it! Who, in any age, likes to be pilloried in public—and whether he deserves it or not makes but little difference? So they used every weapon in their armoury, to justify themselves and to vilify their accuser; both by blank denials and by the more insidious method of depicting him as the snake in the grass, the viper in the bosom, untrue to his own kind and even to his own kin. Moreover they tried to carry the war into the enemy's country by misrepresenting his motives. Jealous of the Powers that be, they alleged, he was working for their overthrow so that the said power and the legitimate profits which were theirs by right might pass to himself. And of course they misrepresented his actions too. They watched lynx-eyed to see if they could catch him out playing any of their old tricks! Nor were they above inventing dishonesties of all kinds. In a word, who can doubt but that John, in doing what he did, was putting his hand into a hornets' nest, which is never a particularly pleasant thing to do. An immense amount of mud was thrown at him—and notoriously mud, once flung, sticks, however undeserved the flinging of it.

So it was with John Hawkins. For all the rest of his own life, there were not wanting those who impugned his honesty (though even then they did not include in their number anyone who really mattered). Yet pure honesty and real altruism were so rare in John's days (and probably still are) that many of those who in aftertimes discussed the problem of his motives, have not had the honesty, or the good sense, to clear him completely. Until nearly our own day in fact, *some* of that mud has clung.

Even in the nineteenth century, we have seen distinguished historians like Froude and Laughton discolouring their pages with it. But now it is washed off: and it is only right that tribute should be paid to the man who performed the cleansing process. This, much more than anyone else, was the late James A. Williamson whose two great works on John Hawkins at length did the trick.[1]

If then it was not love of perquisites and power which made John take the path he did, what was his real motive? The whole tenor of his life seems, to this author anyway, to give the answer: which is love of country, loyalty to his Queen, and an upbringing which, in peace and in war, had forced him to the conclusion that everything which was dear to him and his depended in the last resort, upon a Royal Navy as large and as efficient as possible; to be the nucleus of a much larger navy (furnished by Protestants like himself and Brother William) which, joining with it, alone could save everything he loved from the colossus of Catholic Spain. He was among the first, though perhaps not quite the first, to realize these things. But he may certainly be considered as the first man to implement them, the first man to provide such a fleet.

If nowadays such accusations as John levied against Winter and Co. were sustained by authority, then, of course Winter and Co. would instantly have been dismissed while John (with a new team if necessary) would have been left to carry out his plans. But in Tudor times there was not as yet such a concept as collective responsibility. So the Winters were not discharged, still less punished. They continued in the Board Room of the Navy Office along with the victorious John, and still—theoretically—his equals. But in fact there can be no doubt that a sensible man like Burghley saw to it that, in future, John should be the real boss of the Navy Board. And though the Winters continued to calumniate him, doing everything in their power to get him ousted, as far as authority was concerned they never questioned his primacy.

His charge as Treasurer of the Navy involved an immense head of work, and materially changed the course of his daily life.

---

[1] *Sir John Hawkins* (Oxford, 1927) and *Hawkins of Plymouth* (Black, 1949). The present author's debt to these two studies is immense.

Hitherto he had spent his days, roughly, between Plymouth and London, with perhaps an equal time passed in each. But now he was committed to live and work in or near Town. Nor must it be forgotten how supremely competent he was to undertake his great task. All his life he had been connected with ships, at all levels—building them, fitting them out, manning them, victualling them and sailing in them. There was in fact singularly little about ships which he did not have at his finger-tips, and there was certainly no other man in the land better qualified to administer them. Yet now he was giving up his own fleets (probably to his brother) in order to concentrate on that one collection of them which was the only real bulwark of his country. His private ships, his brother's and those of all his contemporaries would still be needed when the hour struck. But the collection of the Queen's ships, gathered in the Medway and based on Chatham was the only State Navy that then existed in England, and on these ships England must depend absolutely when the day came. His work and responsibility were such that he could not afford to leave them. So, though he still lived in his house in the City, he almost certainly had quarters in Chatham dockyard too, where he dwelt at the heart of his work, learning to know, even by name, the few hundreds of permanent shipwrights, seamen and clerks who busied themselves with the actual tasks of maintenance. There was little chance now for even occasional trips into Devon, and none for any hope of enjoying a sea-command.

There were, when first he took over, only twenty-five ships, large and small, lying 'in ordinary', and all riding high in the water, unballasted, innocent of stores and provisions, with their spars safely stored on shore, and their guns, though ready for use, unmounted and almost all housed in the Tower of London. His purpose was to be sure that these vital component parts could all be assembled at the shortest notice, and the fleet fully mobilized. It was a very big task for one man, however knowledgeable he might be. Moreover, even then there was plenty of 'paper-work'; for the Board met weekly on Tower Hill and reported monthly to the one and only true 'executive' officer in the Navy, the Lord Admiral. (Lord Clinton had occupied that lonely eminence ever since the last year of Queen Mary's reign.

He died in 1585, however, when John had been for eight years in *his* lonely office, to be succeeded by one who was to prove himself a really great man—Charles, Lord Howard of Effingham.)

For the first eighteen months John shouldered the burden alone, constantly snarled at by almost all his colleagues on the Board and other ill-wishers, yet staunchly supported by both Burghley and Elizabeth. Then—surprisingly to modern eyes—he landed himself in still further responsibility of a very personal kind. He proposed to Burghley a new scheme, to which, the Queen, one feels, agreed gratefully. He proposed—and Minister and Crown accepted—what is usually known as the First Bargain. Two agreements were signed, one between Elizabeth and John, the other between Elizabeth and the two master shipwrights, Peter Pett and Matthew Baker, John's lieutenants at Chatham. By the first agreement John undertook to shoulder half the 'ordinary' expenses, paying for them out of his own pocket; and for this he was to receive £1,200 a year, without the obligation of sending in detailed accounts of the money spent to the Queen. But the other three officers—Comptroller, Surveyor and Clerk of the Ships—were empowered to oversee his expenditure, and report on it to Burghley and Clinton. This overseeing was customary: but now it savoured rather of making his enemies his judges! By the second part of the agreement, the other half of the 'ordinary' expenses were farmed out to the master shipwrights, in exchange for a yearly payment of £1,000. Thus the Queen was to shed all her 'ordinary' expenses, which used to cost her £4,000, in exchange for fixed payments—to John and the shipwrights—amounting to £2,200 only. The 'extraordinary' expenses were left out of both the agreements which formed 'the Bargain', and were to be superintended, as before, by the whole Board. But, in addition, John specifically informed Burghley that he would save the Queen £4,000 every year.

What John was doing in effect was to sign a contract to maintain the old Navy at a given rate—a rate which was much lower than (barely half) that hitherto borne by the Crown. And he did it, we may be very sure, with his eyes wide open. If he could manage it—and he thought, if he cut out all waste, that he could—well and good. If he did not manage it, then he, John Hawkins, would make up the difference out of his own private resources.

It would be impossible nowadays to envisage any government shedding its inalienable responsibility for the whole of one of the armed forces of the Crown, and allowing a private individual to take it on. Yet such farming of governmental expenses was by no means unknown in Tudor times, when the resources of the Crown were often too exiguous to meet the extra strain of war. It was by analogy, in fact, exactly on a par with the Crown's (then customary) habit of fighting a major war by letting—indeed expecting—its maritime subjects shoulder a large share of its costs. It was really, in fact, the only way in which the Crown *could* manage it and yet remain solvent. In this odd lay-out, of course, the private warrior was allowed, and was expected, to take his profit. So it came about that men like Francis Drake made very considerable fortunes out of 'war', as well as making a great contribution towards winning it. But here John's case was rather different. On such a tight schedule of profit possible in the First Bargain, in no circumstance can he have made much out of his contract. Indeed, what he made probably was a minus quantity: he was almost certainly out of pocket over the whole business.

So mere monetary gain cannot have come into it. Also the whole thing was essentially a risky business. What would have happened, one wonders, had Burghley faded out, to be succeeded by one of John's ill-wishers? Or what would have happened if John himself had fallen down badly on his agreement? The Queen was never one to lose money with a smiling countenance, and she was consistently hard on those who seemed to fail her, though she could be very gracious to those who succeeded in her service.

But John did not fail, and that in spite of the fact that, on his own volition, he had chosen as team-mates some of his bitterest enemies, who were also his permitted critics and the overseers of all his actions. At first, indeed, he had a great deal of trouble with these people, especially with the Winters, who were for ever on the watch to prove him wrong and false: for ever carping at all he did, for ever trying to trip him up, and to set

his champions against him. But they never succeeded: and that
goes far towards proving the essential honesty of the man.

Only once, it would seem, did they come within sight of
accomplishing their ends. In 1583 they—but expecially Sir
William—got so far as to induce the Privy Council to appoint a
commission to inquire into the State of the Navy. This John
welcomed, and probably Burghley did too, because he always
believed in him. And John emerged triumphant from that
inquiry: indeed, so strengthened his position that, soon afterwards, the elder Winter, hitherto his principal critic, at last
gave up the uncongenial task of being in more or less permanent
opposition; and, making an all-but complete *volteface*, became
again a firm friend. Old Sir William was like that: venal
enough in everyday affairs when venality was all the fashion,
but at heart a decent and sensible soul, even a generous one. It
is pleasant for us to know, as it must have been pleasant for
John to experience, that the two became fast friends again, and
took their place side by side in perfect amity when the real
crunch came. Indeed we see here another illustration of John's
natural charm. It almost looks as though nobody, not even a
rather difficult character like Winter, could keep up a hate
against him while daily rubbing shoulders with him on the
dockside or in the board room. Just before he relented and
became John's friend, he left behind a reminder of how John
appeared to everyday acquaintances, even hostile ones. He
wrote to Burghley,

> He hath charmed the Queen, your equals and inferiors, for he careth
> not to whom he speaketh, nor what he saith. Blush he will not.

This was Winter's last kick, because he ends the same letter by
declaring that he is 'tired of these quarrels'.

It was now that John entered into his second 'bargain' with the
Crown: for now it was 1585, and everyone in England, save
only the Queen, realized that war with Spain—hot war too—
was only just round the corner. The Prince of Parma had all but
subdued the Southern Netherlands, and next he would crush the
United Provinces. Once they were defeated we should have no
ally in the West at all. Even Portugal was already duly swallowed and digested. Now in the Channel and all over western

Europe there would come that head-on confrontation of the conquering Catholic and the hard-pressed Protestant which everybody in the Reformed Faith dreaded. Already Philip of Spain was the Catholic Champion, and already Elizabeth of England was finding herself in the unwelcome role of Ultimate Protestant Hope. Now he had only the heretic Queen to crush. Then the Counter Revolution would triumph, Protestantism wither away and England become a mere province of Spain.

In face of such a threat all that was best in England was drawing together in self-defence—even (as it were every other month) the Queen herself; though, in the alternate months, she continued her ditherings, desperately clinging to notions of possible appeasement. Burghley and Walsingham had at last given up hope of any remedy other than the drawing of the sword, and were already busy preparing the country for inevitable invasion. Leicester, the Queen's favourite, with part of the rather amateurish English Army, had sailed for the Low Countries, hoping to stave off the collapse of the Dutch. Drake, taking advantage of a temporary veer towards war on Elizabeth's part, had skilfully seized his chance of carrying hostilities into the Spanish camp, and was now on the high seas with a considerable expeditionary force aimed at the West Indian sources of the enemy's power. Sir Walter Raleigh was soon to be put in charge of the Devon defences. Sir Richard Grenville was about to be charged with the similar defence of Cornwall. William Hawkins was, as ever, in Plymouth, mobilizing for war his private fleets and those of his friends. The new Lord Admiral, Howard of Effingham, had just taken over from the dead Lord Clinton, and was already beginning to master his new trade.

And John—what was *he* doing at this critical time? Probably the most important task of them all. Now, by the making of the Second Bargain, he had undertaken, almost single-handed, to put England's only naval bastion—the Queen's Ships—into a posture of defence. And his idea of defence was, like Drake's, not a mere cringing in harbour to await the blow, but attack! For the two most prominent of England's seamen had both realized that, in this particular crisis, the best, the only sort of defence lay in attack.

By the second bargain the contract with the master ship-wrights was cancelled, and they reverted to their former status of maritime servants of the Crown; and John now became responsible for both the ordinary and the extraordinary expenses of the Queen's fleet, at a very considerable saving to the Crown. In fact the whole cost of both the 'ordinary' and the 'extra-ordinary' were now undertaken at a charge equivalent to that which, formerly, had been expended upon the 'ordinary' only.

Moreover John was determined that, with this saving, the Queen's fleet should grow, not only in efficiency but actually in numbers too. And this growth, in the course of the years 1585, 1586 and 1587 he succeeded in bringing about. In 1586 he added a new ship altogether, the 150-ton *Tremontana*, while in 1587—and out of his accumulated savings too—he added no less than three more 'capital' ships. There was first a very fine new galleon of 800 tons, recently privately built for Sir Walter Raleigh. This—all out of his savings—he bought for the Queen. It was a great moment for John, and a great triumph too, when the Queen changed the name of the new acquisition from *Ark Raleigh* to *Ark Royal*: and, with the new Lord Admiral hoisting his flag in her, she became flagship of all England's anti-Armada Fleet. In the same year too Pett and Baker built two more brand-new, up-to-date galleons, both ships of John's dreams. They were named the *Vanguard* and the *Rainbow*, and they did not cost the Queen or the country a penny. They were both built out of the proceeds of John's economies! For good measure he also added several 50-ton pinnaces, his aim being to build at least one new pinnace for each new 'great ship'.

When in 1585 he made his second bargain with the Queen—and what a bargain it was for her!—there had been in the Med-way, all told, twenty-one ships of 100 tons and over, with ten pinnaces of 50 tons and under. By the end of 1587, however, all ready for sea and in first-class shape, there were twenty-five fighting ships of over 100 tons apiece and eighteen sea-going pinnaces. This is the measure of John's achievement, made at no cost to the Queen whatever.

One last achievement. He had his fleet in such a state of readiness that, when the Armada finally appeared, in the late summer of 1588, he was able to fulfil his heart's desire and take his place in one of the ships of his repairing, to acquit himself as manfully in the fight as he had acquitted himself against all home opposition.

We can measure his success to some degree by means of a table. In the last decade of Henry VIII's reign his Royal Ships had increased enormously both in number and in power. But during the reigns of his son and his elder daughter, they had been neglected and maladministered. In Edward VI's time speculation and dishonesty were rife, and many vessels rotted away at their moorings. In the last year of Mary's reign there had been an effort to improve the ships when Calais was being attacked. But before the Navy could be invigorated the town was lost. It is of course notorious that no state can build up its naval strength in a hurry.

Since Elizabeth had been on the throne there had been no such neglect as had disgraced Edward's day. But the fleet had not grown any larger, while, by 1577 (when Hawkins arrived on the scene) it had grown nineteen years older. In the later stages of wooden ship building old age came but slowly upon them. Good English oak, it was found, would last almost for ever: even up to 100 years. But this was not so in the sixteenth century, when the indifferent adjustment of weights caused excessive strains in ships, where proper sheathing was in its infancy, and where rot, both wet and dry, was neither understood nor remedied. There had been a small enlargement of the fleet coinciding with the beginnings of the Spanish threat in the early 1570s, when the *Bull* and the *Tiger* had been rebuilt, thus adding two useful ships of 400 tons. But it was only in 1577, the very year in which John became Treasurer, that a really worthwhile addition had been made—a vessel which was to prove quite revolutionary to the whole art of shipbuilding. This was the *Revenge*, a ship whose career was destined to be at once exciting, unfortunate and short. For after being Drake's flagship in the Armada campaign she was lost only three years later by Richard Grenville in the best-known action of the whole Elizabethan Age.

Yet in the story of shipbuilding the *Revenge* is epoch-making. She contrived in her short life to change not only the structure of fighting-vessels but even their very nature and purpose.

Hitherto the warship had been little more than a platform for the housing of what had even then become the chief weapon of naval warfare, the Great Gun. Her predecessors had been what that thoughtful genius, Sir Walter Raleigh, was to call 'Ships of Majesty'—striking-looking structures rising very high out of the water, with immense raised poops and forecastles, heavily armed with numerous, though relatively small pieces in bow and stern: yet lumbering and leewardly vessels which man-oeuvred with difficulty; top-heavy and unstable with their 'high carges', and far from serviceable when it came to action. Of such a sort had been Henry VII's *Regent* and Henry VIII's monstrous *Great Harry*; and of such a sort was the later *Jesus of Lubeck* which had proved John's undoing at San Juan de Ulua: mighty gun-platforms indeed but of very little use to sea-going fleets, because so constructed as to render them liable to unfortunate stresses and strains, due largely to the fact that their centres of gravity were placed too high. They were also wretched sailers and indifferent steerers, which could not keep the seas for any long periods and were very vulnerable as targets for the enemy's fire.

Already, however, seamen who habitually used the sea for purposes of both war and peace—like John himself and Drake—were gradually coming to realize that England's commitments afloat required ships—even considerably smaller ships—which were not just 'built for majesty', but which must be able to ride out the storms all over the outer oceans, and to manoeuvre there *as ships*, capable of hugging the wind and tacking quickly when required: in fact, to be no longer floating fortresses, but ships which could be manoeuvred in their own right. This was in fact *the* discovery of the Englishmen of the Tudor period. This it is which raised their vessels so far above the ships of other nations: which, when the time came, allowed them to make rings round the clumsy carracks of the Armada. For we had, in 1588, vir-tually a monopoly of the new galleons.

The older ships which John inherited when he took over the Royal Fleet in 1577 were all of them of the 'carrack' kind. The *Mary Rose*, the *Elizabeth Jonas*, the *Victory*, *Triumph* and *Bear* were very 'majestic' and often very large: the *Triumph* and the *Bear*, for instance, both displaced a thousand tons or more. Now a glance at the table opposite will reveal one inescapable fact.

THE QUEEN'S SHIPS IN 1588[1]

Category I. Old and old-fashioned 'high-charged' ships, already out of date and unpopular in Hawkins' time—'Ships of Majesty'

Name	Built or bought	Re-built	Burden in tons
Mary Rose	1556	(1589)	600
Elizabeth Jonas	1559	—	900
Victory	1560	1586	800
Triumph	1561	—	1,100
(White) Bear	1564	—	1,000

Category II. 'Middling Ships'. Either ships of the modern (Hawkins) build or old ships completely re-built under Hawkins

Nonpareil ex. Philip and Mary	1556	1584	500
(Golden) Lion	1558	1582	500
Hope	1559	1584	600
Elizabeth Bonaventure	1567	1581	600
Revenge	1577	—	500
Vanguard	1586	—	500
Rainbow	1586	—	500
Ark Royal	1587	—	800

Category III. Smaller ships from 400 tons downwards, either old and re-built or new in (or just before) Hawkins' time

Antelope	1546	1581	400
Bull	1546	1570	200
Tiger	1546	1570	200
Swallow	1558	1580	360
Aid	1562	1580	250
Foresight	1570	—	300
Swiftsure	1573	—	400
Dreadnought	1573	—	400
Achates	1573	—	100
Scout	1577	—	120
Merlin	1579	—	50
George (hoy)	1585	—	100
Tramontana	1586	—	150

Category IV. Pinnaces of Hawkins' building

Brigantine	1583	—	90
Cygnet	1585	—	30
Moon	1586	—	60
Charles	1586	—	70
Advice	1586	—	50
Spy	1586	—	50
Sun	1586	—	40

Category V. A true—but useless—galley, left in Thames Estuary.

Galley Bonavolio	1584	—	—

Names of ships built or rebuilt while Hawkins was Treasurer are in italics.

[1] Names and dates mostly from Oppenheim's *Administration of the Navy*, p. 120. Tonnage from the Armada List in Laughton's *Defeat of the Spanish Armada*, Navy Records Society, vol. II, pp. 324–5.

John had no use for these big ships, and, with one exception—the *Victory*—he did nothing whatever about bringing them up to date. Nor did it occur to him to build any more of this class.

(It should be mentioned here *en passant* that, in Tudor times, 'rebuilding' might mean almost anything, from a rather extensive refit to the taking to pieces of the whole old structure, taking out of her such timbers as were still deemed to be sound, and starting on her quite afresh, with completely new lines and completely new dimensions. This is what was done to the *Victory* in 1586. She went into the shipwrights' hands a 'carrack', and emerged a 'galleon'.)

But to return to the *Revenge*, that key-ship which marks the change from floating fortress to usable warship. This type was already, even in John's day, coming to be called 'galleon-built', that word implying not the *old* galleon-type first used long ago by the Spaniards, but the smaller, low-built, nearly flush-decked vessel, relatively long in comparison with its breadth (with a rough proportion of one to three-and-a-half) and therefore a very much improved sailer: with its castles removed partly from the stern and entirely from the bows: withal an incomparably better sea-boat.

The *Revenge* was laid down just before John took over the Treasurership. So it is not possible to say for certain how far he was responsible for her design and building. Yet, in this author's view, the chances are that he was responsible for both. For one thing, she was just the type of ship to suit his known views and purposes. For another, we know how disgusted he was with the performance of the *Jesus*—the *Revenge*'s antithesis. Lastly, he was, and for many years had been, very much in the circle of old Benjamin Gonson (in the last of whose days the *Revenge* was laid down), and a known *habitué* of Deptford where her keel was laid.

The very first ship of the new galleon-build was probably the *Foresight*, laid down in 1570, soon after John's return from San Juan. Even this ship may have been influenced by John's views, though this is not so certain. It is perhaps significant, though, that the two ships of the 1573 programme, the *Dreadnought* and the *Swiftsure*, reverted partially to the old type. All the later ships which we know he had the building of were galleon-built.

We may note too that the nine ships which he rebuilt on galleon lines—the *Victory, Mary Rose, Lion, Hope, Elizabeth Bonaventure, Antelope, Nonpareil, Swallow* and *Aid*—all emerged in galleon-form.

So the whole Royal Navy which went to sea in the summer of 1588 was not only in superb battle trim to the last rope, sail, and bolt; it was also the best designed, the most competent collection of ships that had ever left the English dockyards, and the best able to acquit itself well in the face of the enemy. And that is the debt which his country owes to John.

This, the cynic may say, is all very well. But how do we know it *now*? The answer to that legitimate question is that every Englishman, and not least the users of the ships, were unanimous in saying so. Even that erstwhile foe and captious critic, Sir William Winter, can now write to his colleagues at the Navy Office from his cabin in the *Vanguard*—John's latest addition to the fleet—and say,

> Our ships doth show themselves like gallants here. I assure you it will do a man's heart good to behold them: and would to God the Prince of Parma were upon the Seas with all his forces, and we in view of them: then I doubt not but that you should hear that we would make his enterprise very unpleasant to him.[1]

An even more wholehearted, and quite spontaneous eulogy comes from the pen of the arch-user, the Commander-in-Chief, Charles, Lord Howard of Effingham, reporting to Lord Burghley. Note too how he gives all the credit to the man to whom it properly belongs:

> For Mr Hawkyns' bargain, he is presently to repair to the Court where he shall best be able to answer in his own defence: but this much I will say to your Lordship: I have been aboard of every ship that goeth out with me, and in every place where any may krype [creep], and I do thank God that they be in the estate they be in: and there is never a one of them that knows what a leak means. I have known when an Admiral of England hath gone out and two ships in fleet could not say so. There is none that goeth out now but I durst go to the Ryall de Plata [Rio de la Plata] in her: and yet the *Mary Rose* and the *Swallow* be with me, who were ships in the King's Majesty's her father's time. And there I dare presume greatly that those that have

[1] Laughton, *Defeat of the Spanish Armada*, vol. I, pp. 81–2.

been made in Her Majesty's reign be very good and serviceable, and shall prove them arrant liars that have reported the contrary.[1]

Then, to make certain that his words have sunk in, he writes to Burghley again, only eight days later,

> I protest before God and as my soul shall answer for it that I think there were never in any place in the world worthier ships than these are, for so many.

Lord Charles Howard was not a Catholic, as has often been said, but a firm Protestant, and a very religious man of real nobility of character, who would never have written these words if he had not profoundly believed them. He was not a seaman by upbringing, but he was an outstanding leader who knew as well as anyone did, how to make the most of his rather mixed, and on the whole, rather difficult team. We may find a striking modern parallel to him in that well-loved figure who commanded the armies of Britain and the USA in 1945—General 'Ike' Eisenhower.

It seems somehow in keeping with John's modest nature that he did not choose to go to fight the Armada in one of the most modern or the largest ships. Howard, of course, had the *Ark*, which on account both of her size and her modernity was probably the best vessel of all. Drake had the *Revenge*, and Lord Henry Seymour one of the two latest galleon-types, the *Rainbow*. The heaviest ship of all, the *Triumph*, went to Frobisher, the next heaviest, the (*White*) *Bear*, to another nobleman, Lord Sheffield. John was content with the *Victory*, once a 'ship of Majesty' but now converted by John into a galleon of 800 tons. This was the first ship in the Navy to bear that famous name. The Commander-in-Chief of the British fleet at Trafalgar, 217 years later, wore his flag in the fifth and last *Victory*. He was of course a more inspired leader in battle than John Hawkins. But he had not *created* his whole fleet in the same way as John had.

This superb fleet was not John's only achievement either. On

---

[1] Laughton, *The Defeat*, vol. I, p. 79. Howard is wrong, but only just, when he says that the *Mary Rose* and the *Swallow* were built *temp.* Henry VIII. They were both ships of Queen Mary's reign. The former, a 'ship of Majesty', had not been modernized by 1588, but was so treated in the following year. She must, however, have been very thoroughly repaired. In the Armada fights she was commanded by Edward Fenton. The *Swallow*, modernized by John in 1580, was of particular interest to us in that her captain was John's only son, Richard.

December 28, 1585, he had put into the Government's hands a paper headed 'A note to show the Commodity that would grow to her Majesty and Country by increasing the Wages of the Servitors by Sea in Her Highness's ships'. It is a completely new scale of pay for everyone from captain to common mariner. He seems to have had his way too, every rank and rating receiving 50 per cent more wages than he had before. Thus the common mariner would now receive 10 shillings per month where before he had 6s 8d, while the captain would go up from 20s a day to 30s. Moreover John proposed that the Queen should pay no more towards the higher rate than she had paid before, because the complements were to be cut down by one-fifth. His argument runs,

> There is no Captain exercised in Service but will undertake with more courage any enterprise with 250 able men than with 300 of tag and rag, and assure himself of better success.[1]

So John, wizard-like, produced out of his hat, as it were, not only a bigger and better fleet than the Queen had hitherto possessed, and at the same cost to her as before, but also, for no extra cost, he paid both officers and men wages half as large again as they had been before! His rate of 10s a month remained in force until the end of James I's reign when it rose to 14s.

i. THE ARMADA CAMPAIGN

The year 1587 was Drake's year, in which his brilliant manoeuvres off the Spanish coast had forced Philip to postpone his Enterprise of England for a whole year. But the assault was only postponed, not prevented, and Philip proceeded steadily with his preparations through the winter and the following spring.

The traditional defence of England against his scheme was to hold the Queen's Ships in readiness in the Thames estuary, to guard against the Prince of Parma's assault from the Netherlands, while John, or some other English commander, operated from Plymouth in the west to guard the sea-road from Spain. And such were still our dispositions when the critical year

[1] 'Papers Relating to the Spanish War, 1585–7' (*Navy Records Society*, vol. XI. 281 et seq).

arrived. No doubt John thought that the Western Command should go to him, as it had done in earlier crises. But, since then, he had become almost purely administrative, while Drake had established himself as the man to do the fighting: and so, while Howard, as Lord Admiral, commanded the larger and stronger Eastern forces, Francis held sway as C.-in-C. at Plymouth with a numerous, but not particularly strong, squadron, mainly of auxiliaries—armed merchantment. Meanwhile John remained at the Lord Admiral's side in the Thames, still looking after the main body of the ships which had been his special care.

But the seamen-leaders of England, including both John and Francis, already realized very clearly that this arrangement was faulty. For the principal Spanish threat must approach England from the west, by sea, while Parma in the east had virtually no sea forces at all. If then, they argued, England's main strength remained in the Thames, the whole of the Armada could enter the Channel from the West, brush aside the weak Western Squadron, and capture Plymouth, Falmouth or any of the more westerly ports before the main fleet, could beat up against the prevailing westerlies and make its weight felt. They therefore, all of them, put what pressure they could upon the Government to reinforce considerably the vital Western Squadron from the cream of the ships of the Eastern Fleet. Very wisely, then, they made a dead set at Howard, seeking to bring him to their way of thinking: and at length, though not until May, they succeeded. Then Howard, with the bulk of the Queen's Ships and strong lighter forces proceeded down-Channel, and at the end of the month dropped anchor in Plymouth Sound. A redistribution of command now became necessary, because everyone (even Drake) knew that the Lord Admiral *must* be in command of the Main Fleet. Francis Drake can hardly have been pleased, but he had quite enough patriotism and loyalty to his Sovereign to submit, and did so with all cheerfulness. The Queen, who had been rather nervous as to how he would take it, tactfully hastened to send down his commission as Vice-Admiral, and at the same time appointed John as Rear-Admiral. Perhaps John was disappointed too, though of course he never said so, taking his place as junior to Drake in the same spirit as Drake put himself unreservedly under Howard. So, at the critical moment all was peace, because all realized equally the nature of the crisis. John did not sail at once with Howard, remaining in the Thames for last-minute adjustments. But he arrived in Plymouth early in June. Winter, however, remained with the residue of the fleet in the Thames, to give the benefit of his advice and experience to another noble C.-in-C., Lord Henry Seymour. Holstocke, the only other Naval Commissioner, and now a very old man, remained in administrative charge in London.

The move was timely, yet made only just in time. And even so, there is no doubt that the Eastern Squadron remained too strong. For though now most of England's strength lay at Plymouth, there were still missing, left behind in the Thames, the two newest and perhaps most powerful galleons, the *Rainbow* and the *Vanguard*. Also left behind were no less than eleven other Queen's Ships, all of smallish size—eight ships and three pinnaces. All these ships engaged the enemy in the final battle of Gravelines, but all missed the actions up-Channel. The small ships, headed as they were by the *Antelope*, the *Tiger* and the *Bull*, could easily have destroyed any of the puny craft at the disposal of Parma: which means, regretfully, that the two new galleons were to some extent wasted.

It must not be supposed that John, when he joined up with Howard, had grown rusty through not having been to sea for many years. It should be mentioned that he had been afloat as late as 1586, and in command of a squadron too. In that year, while Drake was still away in the West Indies, Elizabeth had once more got the wind up, fearing that Philip had designs in the Channel. So John was taken from his administrative work and given five Queen's Ships (four of the middling sort and one small one) and thirteen merchantmen, all fully armed. He sailed in the *Nonpareil* and had with him in the *Golden Lion* William Borough, at that time Clerk of the Ships, with a seat on the Navy Board. John wasted the summer, not through any fault of his, but because he was watching for an attack which was never mounted: and it was September before he was allowed to do what he wanted, which was to act as a follow-up to the raid of Drake, now safely home again. He did, however, cruise off the Spanish coast—too late to make contact with the Plate Fleet—

and visited the Azores before returning home in October, back
to the Navy Office grind. The voyage was humdrum, but it does
throw rather interesting light on John as a leader and as a man.
We know that Borough had for some time been a confirmed
enemy of John's: but his experience as Second-in-Command of
John's squadron made him completely change his mind. Thereafter he became a confirmed adherent, finding his erstwhile
enemy at once extremely understanding and easy to work with.

This same Borough was not perhaps a very great man: perhaps even rather a tetchy, small-minded individual, whom probably John was not particularly anxious to have as his friend. Yet
he won him with no great effort, but by his natural sympathy
and charm. Here there is a contrast between him and Drake,
who had probably as much natural charm as John—when he
wanted to turn it on. But all too often he did not so want. It
chanced that, in the very next year, Borough went to sea again,
this time as Second to Drake on his 'singeing' expedition.
Borough's rather slow thought-processes and his ultra-conser-
vative views soon got under Drake's skin. They quarrelled
violently, and Drake arrested him, confining him to his cabin
in the *Golden Lion*. Then her crew mutinied and sailed for home.
It was not Borough's doing at all, but Francis, without waiting
for any real evidence, called a court martial and condemned his
second to death in his absence. The authorities at home, of
course, saw to it that the sentence was not carried out: but undoubtedly Drake's conduct on this occasion was violent and
high-handed—entirely different from John's at any moment in
his career.

In this same cruise John took a merchant ship, and, as was his
wont, treated the Spanish master of it with great kindness and
consideration, allowing him—a rare concession this—to keep
all his personal effects. The master naturally fell for such kindness, and has left on record a glowing account of what he saw on
board the *Nonpareil*. Everything was beautifully ship-shape; the
food was wonderful, including even such livestock as sheep and
pigs, and such anti-scorbutics as fresh apples and pears. John
always had great ideas on the subject of diet: but he was not the
victualler of the ships, and there can be no doubt as to where
those apples and pears came from—from his own orchards!

But now—having already seen how one eminent Victorian imagined him, as he participated in that immortal game of bowls on Plymouth Hoe—let us see, if we can, what he was *really* like, discounting the badger's fur, the outlandish rig in which Kingsley thought fit to clothe him, the broad Devon accent, and even the gold mayoral chain which was, in that year, the proper perquisite of his brother William. We should probably find, it is true, the grey beard, for John was already fifty-six years old and prematurely grey in the service of his mistress. But there would be little else that was true in the novelist's portrait. For one thing he would be really well and carefully dressed in garments fashionable to that day. He would command the respect of all his contemporaries: he would hector nobody, quarrel with nobody; not speak in a notably Devonshire accent, and not criticize his well-loved son—who, incidentally, would be dressed in clothes brighter in colour perhaps, but otherwise by no means dissimilar from his father's. For here was one grown old in companionship with men like Burghley, Raleigh and Lord Howard; and who, in all save mere birth, was an essentially noble man, the undoubted equal of any man there present, nobleman or commoner. Here, at what was perhaps the crisis, to which all his past had inevitably been leading, a noble man indeed was John Hawkins of Plymouth, first merchant of his day, leading light in his country's policy-making, famed leader of men, skilled handler of ships, architect of the fleet now about to be tried in the hour of battle.

We may not follow him here through all the vicissitudes of the next fortnight, partly it is true through lack of space, but mainly because, odd though it may seem, historians have contrived to mislay almost all the details of those great days. Many accounts of what happened survive, and from these we should be able to reconstruct a more or less minute to minute account of what was passing. But that may not be. We must content ourselves with the general course of the struggle: how the English fleet was caught, almost at the last minute, in the sad position of being embayed in Plymouth, so that the Spaniards had an excellent chance—which they would not or could not take—of destroying our main strength in the confined waters of the Sound,

We know how, by brilliant seamanship, the English commanders extricated themselves from that grave danger: how they engaged the unwieldy carracks of the enemy in three long and hard pitched battles in the Channel. We know too how the Armada, under a chief with even less skill and experience than that of our Lord Howard, yet contrived to sail the whole length of the Channel, keeping near-perfect formation the while, though decidedly battered and bruised, until at last, arriving practically within sight of their objective, which was the army of the Duke of Parma, it dropped anchor in Calais Roads.

It was after the third and last of the great Channel battles—when the Armada had been cunningly shepherded past the entrance to the Solent, its last safe anchorage in the Channel—that there came a welcome lull in the fighting. In this pause the gallant Howard found time to summon to the deck of the *Ark Royal* some of his leading captains, and one of them was John. Here, by virtue of his Commission as Lord Admiral, he conferred the accolade of knighthood upon them. Nowadays—who can doubt it?—much of the glamour and meaning of knighthood have vanished in a welter of honours which have become so common as to make them a great deal less precious. But in Elizabeth's day there were well-understood rules in the conferring of them. Peerages went to men in reward for wealth or political power. But knighthoods were still the unique rewards for *Service*—fighting service too. And surely, if any of her servants deserved the honour—long overdue, we may think—it was our John, now and henceforward Sir John Hawkins, Knight.

The crux of the fight was still to come, however. As the unbroken array of Spanish ships lay uncomfortably at their dangerous anchorage—for at Calais there was no real harbour at all—Howard's fleet anchored a gun-shot to windward of it. Someone—perhaps it was Drake though it may well have been Sir John—had the idea of fitting out some of the smaller craft as fire-ships, and loosing them down-wind at the enemy. Seven were hastily prepared, one of them belonging to Francis and one to John: and though every fireship missed every Spanish ship, drifting past to ground on Calais sands, the result was none the less a spectacular success, because it did what up till then the whole English fleet had failed to do. Many Spaniards panicked and, in their hurry to escape the flames, cut their cables, falling rapidly down-wind along the treacherous Flemish coast. So, for the first time, the rigid Armada formation was broken.

There followed the decisive Battle of Gravelines.

The English fleet went after them. Lord Henry Seymour and the Thames contingent had joined forces with Howard during the night, and the chase, now under five leaders, was on. The first squadron was Howard's—though he lost valuable time by stopping to take one of the Spanish galleasses which in the confusion had run on to Calais Strand. But Drake's division, Hawkins's, Frobisher's—now Sir Martin, because he had received the accolade along with John—and Seymour's (in which Sir William Winter in the *Vanguard* played a worthy part) made no such mistake. All day the fleets banged away at each other, and came, really for the first time, into effective range. Hitherto the English, probably rightly, had been very careful to keep their distance, partly to ensure that the Spaniards did not board them— which would have proved fatal to us since they had a large army of trained soldiers on board where we had none; but also because they had a much bigger supply of heavy-shotted cannon, where we relied upon the lighter but longer-ranged culverins. Soon, however, on this day of Gravelines, the Spaniards began to run out of powder which, so far from home, they could not replace. Then, as their heavy pieces fell silent, at last the English closed the range.

The effect of our culverins and our demi-culverins, however, was not so great as we had hoped. Even at the new and closer range many of our round-shot failed to penetrate the massive timbers of the enemy ships, and towards evening we too had expended nearly all our powder and shot. Meanwhile most of the Spaniards, though sore battered, damaged aloft and drifting dangerously towards the Flemish shoals, were still afloat. That day, probably, they lost five ships, either sunk outright or stranded in the shallows and taken by the Dutch from the land. But as the loss which the Armada had suffered in ships sunk in all the earlier battles had amounted to only three, they had even now lost a mere eight out of the 126 which had reached our shores.[1]

[1] Four galleys and one large sailing carrack had failed to make the English coast. So, after Gravelines, their total losses of all kinds were thirteen ships. The English lost no ships at all.

As far as ships were concerned, then, the English victory was far from conclusive. But in men, and still more in morale, the Armada's state was forlorn. It was beaten, and every man in it knew it was. As the helpless ships drifted eastwards into ever-shoaling water, every man waited for death with what fortitude he could muster. But in the evening, when all hope was gone, what seemed a miracle happened. The Westerly wind, constant for so long, suddenly swung a few points, enabling the whole fleet to claw off-shore and stand away to the north. So, for the moment anyway, the bulk of the Armada was saved.

Yet its failure was still apparent to its leaders. The wind was now carrying them away up the North Sea, and right away from Parma and his men. Moreover, even if the wind fell or veered they knew they could not go about and attempt another passage of the Straits. For that meant facing again those illusive, satanic galleons that had toyed with them as a cat plays with a mouse. So they kept steadily on up the North Sea, followed by the rather disappointed English captains who, having no ammunition, had resolved (in Drake's words) 'to put a brag upon it'. It was enough. The great fight was over, and the enemy vanished into the misty North, from which a bare half of them ever returned home.

Assuredly England had triumphed. But why? No Englishmen seemed very certain. It was not, as we have been so often told, because her notorious weather unduly favoured her. It did not—at the very best it only broke even: not, as many Englishmen modestly thought at the time, because a Protestant God came to the help of his own, and 'blew with his wind and scattered' our (Catholic) foes. It was not even because the Protestant artillery was so superior in performance: as artillerists both sides had rather noticeably failed. There were two reasons, and only two. The first was because the English seamen, officers and ratings alike, were far more sea-minded, more imaginative, more wedded to a sea life than their Spanish opposite numbers, and used their advantages to the uttermost: and that was a feather in the caps of all Englishmen. The second, and the outstanding reason was that the Queen of England's ships were in every way superior to, in every way better equipped fighting machines than were the King of Spain's. And that was a decisive feather in the cap of one Englishman—the Treasurer of the Navy.

It is sad that we know so little about John's personal share of the fight. But there it is—even though he left a long account of it to Walsyngham. John was never one to advertise his own wares, and the few sightings that we get of the *Victory* in action come to us from other sources. On the first day, we learn, he, Drake and Frobisher were in hot action with a Portuguese flagship and other ships which came to her aid, and on the second day we catch a fleeting glimpse of him going with Lord Thomas Howard in a skiff of the *Victory*'s on board an enemy ship which had been wrecked by an explosion of her own powder,

> where they saw a very pitiful sight—the deck of the ship fallen in, the steerage broken, the stern blown out and about 50 poor wretches burnt with powder in most miserable sort. The stink in the ship was so unsavoury and the sight within board so ugly that they shortly departed.[1]

The *Victory* receives honourable mention again on the third day, when there was a 'great fight' in which she nobly seconded the *Ark*, and again when the main fleet went to the rescue of the *Triumph*, when Frobisher nearly got caught inshore by a change in the wind. On the fourth evening the Admiral decided, wisely, to divide his ships into four divisions and appointed John to command the third of them. Next day, it seems, John opened proceedings by attacking a 'great ship', turning the *Victory* up for the purpose into the wind. Then came the day of the knighting, then that of the fire-ships: then Gravelines. The Lord Admiral tells how the *Victory* plunged into the mêlée, followed (among others) by the *Swallow*, under Richard Hawkins. But thereafter we hear no more of the *Victory*; nor of John, nor of Richard, either from Howard or from John himself. But on that last day, without any doubt at all, everyone behaved well. Is it really so strange though, that we did not do better, seeing that there was no one in the whole fleet who had ever had any experience of a full-fledged naval action?

Every account of the Armada fight reveals, time and again, the astonishing superiority of the English ships in both sheer speed and in manoeuvring. Just one specific example must suffice. Take that occasion when Frobisher got surrounded by practically

---

[1] 'A Relation of Proceedings' (Laughton's *Defeat*, vol. I, p. 9). This account is what we should now probably call 'The Official Dispatch'.

the whole Spanish fleet. All the ships leapt to the kill: but then, quite suddenly, a flaw of wind appeared, and the situation changed in a flash. Even as every Spaniard within reach crowded on sail, 'certain' (says the Spanish official account) 'that we could that day succeed in boarding them, which was the only way to victory', she suddenly left them all standing. 'She began to slip away from us', says one Spanish report, 'and to leave the boats which were towing her'—she had been trying thus to escape while there was no wind. Another Spaniard moans:

> She got out so swiftly that the galleon *San Juan* and another quick-sailing ship—the speediest vessel in the Armada—although they gave chase, *seemed in comparison with her to be standing still.*

And the *Triumph*, we must remember, was a Ship of Majesty untouched by John; indeed perhaps the worst sailer in the fleet! No wonder the galleons and pinnaces of the Hawkins build, far from being sunk, were hardly scratched by the 100,000-odd roundshot fired at them by the enemy!

But now the Spaniards are gone, and the English fleet is come home. Are its leaders duly elated? At first sight strangely they are not. They are uncertain of the future. They do not realize the completeness of their victory, or the damage done to the enemy, either material or moral. They only know that superficial results have been disappointing. For long they had tried to break that stubborn formation, but they had succeeded only at the eleventh hour when their powder was failing them. Individuals were disappointed; and disappointment notoriously breeds discontent. Seymour was sulking because Howard had sent him home (as he thought) too early. Frobisher was using most unparliamentary language about Drake whom he accused of cheating. John, of course, made no accusations against anybody, consoling himself with the reflection that the Armada had been much more powerful than we had expected and yet not powerful enough to do much damage to his beloved ships; and now his only thought was to get them docked before deficiencies got out of hand, yet too wise to suggest demobilization until much more of the Armada's movements were known for certain. Drake was oddly cheerful, confident yet not boastful: Howard greatly concerned for the welfare of his men: they are, he says, without provisions or water, and disease is spreading rapidly through the Fleet.

But the real trouble-maker just then was the Queen. So long as the danger had been at its height she had been magnificent, vowing that she would lead her loving and loyal subjects, if necessary, in the last ditch:

> I know [she cried] I have the body of a weak and feeble woman, but I have the heart and stomach of a King, and a King of England too: and think foul scorn that Parma or any Prince of Europe should dare invade the borders of my Realm: to which, rather than any dishonour shall grow by me, I myself will take up arms. I will be your General, Judge and Rewarder!

Yet, as soon as the peril was past—or rather, in her advisers' eyes well before it was past—the set of her mind reverted to its habitual economy. Her expenses must be instantly reduced, her armies disbanded and sent home; the hired ships discharged, most of her own laid up, and their crews demobilized. So Howard was sent for, to leave the fleet and advise how best, and how quickly, these things could be done. Papers of all kinds were sent for too, and closely scrutinized. Where was the account of the ammunition which Lord Sussex had collected and sent to Howard in the Channel? Who had authorized it? Were Hawkins's latest accounts to the Navy Board in, and, if in, checked? Where was Darell's list of men victualled? Were the dates right? Had he taken every precaution to see that he was not cheated by the contractors? For that matter let him straightly show that he has not been cheating himself. What a mistress! Daily she harried Walsyngham and Burghley who, in their turn, had to harry Darell and Howard and Hawkins. No one was spared, from minor dockyard officials to major executive officers: all were subjected to a ruthless, nagging inquisition, until at last poor old John, most faithful and overworked of her servants, worn to a shadow by most exacting duties both executive and administrative, could only bow his weary head and say, 'God, I trust, will deliver me of it ere it be long, for there is no other hell.' Yet he turned upon the Lord Treasurer when that much-tried minister so far forgot himself as to hint that the men who had died or been discharged sick constituted a good and legitimate saving to the Government, as wages due to them could now go towards paying others. John reminded him with dignity and patience, but with unbending firmness, that these poor people had dependents, to whom the deceased's wages already belonged in both justice and equity.

As Treasurer of the Navy, John bore the main brunt both of the demobilization and of paying the men. Custom demanded that the two should go together—and there was no money for payment. The generous Admiral grew more and more desperate as the vicious circle developed. If the men could not be paid, they must remain: but if they remained, the wage-bill continued to go up too. They must also eat, but there was little food and no money to buy more.[1] Here Howard is shown at his very best. He was honestly attached to his seamen, knowing how well they had acquitted themselves, under shocking conditions too. He refused absolutely to discharge them unpaid and starving. Ordered to hand over a little prize-money collected from Drake, he kept it, without warrant of course, but informing the Government of what he had done. With it he paid as many of the men as he could, and then spent as much again out of his own patrimony, which was pretty limited. It was, he wrote, too pitiful to have men starve after such services, and he was sure that Her Majesty would not want it so. He seems, however, to have been doubtful about the efficacy of an appeal to the Queen's sense of justice and fair play, because he followed with an argument of pure expediency. You will be wanting these worthy men again, he said in effect, but if you send them away now, penniless and starving, to die miserably in some ditch, you simply will not get them. Ultimately John got most of the men away, though some of them certainly starved.

This, however, was not the worst evil which struck the luckless men who had just saved England. Far worse, in mortality anyway, was the pestilence which now assailed the fleet. Sickness in ships (with the sole exception, sometimes, of Hawkins ships) was the normal thing, even when they had been only a short time at sea. Already, even before the Armada appeared, we read of mounting sick-lists. But here, it would seem, was

[1] John, we must remember, was not responsible for the victualling, but only for the ships, their upkeep and well-being. Here his record is unique. In the whole nineteen years of the Anglo-Spanish War not a single Queen's ship was lost by leakage or unsoundness of hull or gear.

something even graver than the usual outbreaks. It was a major epidemic. It is never easy to discover the nature of a disease in days when contemporary physicians have failed to identify it. In this case, almost all historians have assumed that it was an exceptionally fierce outbreak of what was then the commonest of sea-diseases: the 'gaol fever' or typhus, a malady which thrives in environments where overcrowded and underwashed humanity congregates, be they gaols or slums or ships: a disease that, for the next three centuries or nearly, was to take more lives at sea than the hottest action or the wildest weather. In both fleets there were unquestionably many cases. But the deadly disorder now under consideration was, according to the latest authority,[1] not typhus at all. It was 'food-poisoning in its most virulent form with rapid death from toxaemia'.

What the actual loss by death was it is quite impossible to say. The official complements of the Queen's Ships at the start add up to 6,705. After all was over John reported to Burghley that the number then in the ships was 4,453. That looks at first sight as though the casualties—all of them but a bare 100 killed in action, due to disease—were 2,252, or about one in three of the original crews. But they were really much heavier than this, because we know that most of the ships had received repeated and substantial reinforcements from first to last. It would probably be truer to estimate that, approximately, two out of every three men in the original crews were lost—some 40 lost by disease for every one slain by the enemy!

j. LAST YEARS

John lived for rather more than seven years after the Armada's overthrow. But they were, on the whole, years of labour and sorrow. Gradually he was overborne by the sheer paper-work of the Treasurer's Office. He was constantly trying to shed his burden but he was much too necessary to the Queen and the Ministers, and they would not let him go. This fact alone, when one comes to consider it, furnishes positive proof of his essential honesty, silencing for good the vile accusations of his ill-wishers.

Most of the actors were, like John, growing old, and now

[1] J. J. Keevil, *Medicine in the Navy*, vol. I, p. 76 (Livingstone, 1957).

gradually quitting the stage. In 1589 Brother William died. So did Sir William Winter, and Holstocke too. The Queen at once filled up the vacancies in the Navy Office occasioned by the deaths of the last two. The Board was reconstituted. It now consisted of John (with the Comptrollership added to the Treasurership), his old enemy—but now firm friend—Borough as Surveyor, and his wife's brother, a younger Benjamin Gonson, as Clerk of the Ships. And that was all: every member of the Board a Hawkins, a relative or a confessed admirer! What a fool the great Queen must have been—and no one yet has ever accused her of financial folly—to let the whole administration of her ships fall into such hands! No: rather did Elizabeth know very well a good and faithful servant when she had one: and well she knew that no one else in England could be better trusted to do the job.

John did ask for, and was granted, however, a year's leave in which, not to take a well-earned holiday, but to grapple with the muddle in the accounts caused by the total mobilization of 1588. And this by dint of infinite labour he now accomplished. By then, as the Exchequer Accounts make it very plain, all were straight again, but for the fact, of course, that he was still trying to make both ends meet on a grossly inadequate Public Revenue. Yet in one direction at least he found repose. Vilifications ceased at once and were never renewed by his contemporaries—only by subsequent historians.

William Hawkins, as we saw, probably died and was certainly buried in Deptford, where, for the time being, John had his principal home. And two years later an even more personal grief was to come to him. Katherine, his faithful spouse for thirty-two years, apparently found Deptford too damp and cold for her. John, fearing it was so, asked once more to be allowed to resign, in order to remove with Katherine to the milder climate of Plymouth; and, his request being turned down once more, Katherine died. Very little is known about her, though what is is good. Her son Richard spoke of her in the highest terms, and we have one small piece of tittle-tattle about her which comes, of all places, from a scurrilous letter written by one of John's detractors in the days of his vilification. She was then, it seems, busily engaged with her maids in cutting out with her own hands the lavish display of flags, banners and pendants for the Fleet. John's vilifier complains that she was taking the bread from some poor devil's mouth: but to us it conjures up a very pleasing domestic scene—*Dame* Hawkins and her girls making themselves useful to her busy husband.

He soon found that he could not live alone. So he took a new wife in the person of Margaret Vaughan, the daughter of an old and wealthy family in Herefordshire. But the match was a much less happy one. Little is known of Margaret either, but the one story which is told of her is, if true, certainly not to her credit.[1]

It was at this time that John, having observed at first-hand the sufferings of the ordinary seamen, decided to do something practical about their future. First, in 1590, with the co-operation of Drake, he founded what came to be called the Chatham Chest, a fund for the relief of ailing and ageing sailors for whom, of course, neither then nor for at least another century, did the authorities make any provision at all. Financially it was sound. It was a contributory scheme, the seamen of the Queen's ships contributing sixpence a month, deducted from their wages: and because banking was then all but unknown, the capital collected was placed in a large chest. The chest itself still survives, and may be seen at the National Maritime Museum in Greenwich. In John's time it played a very useful part in naval life. But later, when corruption again invaded all parts of administrative and governmental life, its contents were used for wrong or unworthy purposes. Then, two years later, Sir John, all by himself, founded, also at Chatham, an almshouse for aged mariners and ship-wrights from the Yard. This foundation never ran into half the trouble of the Chest, and it survives to this day as a monument to the memory of a good man.

Meanwhile they did not let John remain solely in Administration. He was altogether too valuable as an active commander at sea. But he did miss the campaign of 1589, and he was lucky to do so because the main expedition—a descent upon the coasts of Spain and Portugal—was an utter failure. For this reverse Drake, who was in command, was made the scapegoat, though it was by no means entirely his fault. In fact, with the Armada defeated, we can already begin to discern the emergence of the two distinct

[1] See below, p. 217.

schools of strategic thought destined to strive for mastery in this country for several centuries. The one is usually called the Continental School which, in brief, believed that naval power alone was not enough: that we, being a geographic part of the continent of Europe, must take a full share in the concerns and campaigns of that continent, throwing into the struggle, when necessary, not only our navy but also our army. The other school, known later as the Blue Water School, thought that continental entanglements, with military expeditionary forces on the mainland, were never, or hardly ever, necessary: were in fact a weakness rather than a strength.

The expedition of 1589 had been, essentially, a continental effort; for Drake took an army with him which, it was hoped, would provide a permanent bridgehead on the Iberian Peninsula —and Drake's failure lay mainly with the army which was embarked in, and disembarked from, his fleet. Indeed, owning at the time virtually no regular army, we were being rather wildly premature. The failure, however, did seem to prove one thing, that, if Philip could not successfully invade England in 1588, we could not hope to invade his homeland in 1589. Drake was not really a protagonist of the Continental School, yet he had allowed himself, in 1589, to appear as such, and his lack of success on that occasion led to his temporary disgrace. He was not employed again, in fact, until 1595, when he and John made their last, but equally unsuccessful attempt on the overseas Empire of Spain.

John, on the other hand, was from the first a leading spirit— perhaps the leading spirit—of the Blue Water School. In all his surviving advices to the Government he uses the argument that what we now had to do was to follow up our success against the Armada by a series of almost purely naval attacks on the maritime communications of Spain, going wholeheartedly for the cutting of those Atlantic links which brought the wealth of the Indies into Europe. And this, he held, was an object to be persisted in scientifically. The assault *must* be sustained. If we made one spearhead attack upon, say, the more distant sources of the Spaniards' wealth, we must also have a second-line force to prevent the riches from entering the Spanish home ports: or, at least, if we sent out one fleet against the Spanish flotas, we must always have another force standing by, and all ready to operate when the first fleet, for logistic reasons, had to return home. This was John's main plan. It is perhaps not possible to say at this late hour what would have been the success of such continuous maritime pressure upon the enemy, because, in the event, the Queen and her Government thought the effort of maintaining two such forces too expensive to undertake: so John's scheme was never properly tried out. In the end, in fact, we fell noticeably between two stools. The Continental School was allowed no more chances, and the Blue Water School was only allowed to function rather half-heartedly. Indeed, in our efforts to cut his life-lines by capturing his floatas—almost always unsuccessfully —we allowed Philip the breathing-space to organize a new protective system which, as the war grew older, entirely thwarted our efforts. In short, while the war was still on, we allowed him to create a new, and mainly protective, navy which we were never strong enough to defeat.

It is instructive to look into John's detailed proposals. With typical Hawkins good sense, and an eye to a maximum of economy, he laid down in considerable detail what maritime effort was required in order to ensure success, and exactly what it would cost. There must be a continuous patrol of the seas between the Spanish homeland and the Azores, each squadron to consist of six Queen's Ships and six pinnaces, each provisioned for four months, and manned by 1,800 men. The whole, he said— and he was the only man who could say it—would cost, in wages and victuals, £2,730. This sum, he goes on (knowing his Queen) will or should be readily recuperated out of prize-money; of which Her Grace will take one-third, the other two-thirds going into wages and victuals. The whole scheme for eight months in the year—the four winter months were never used for shipping in those days, by either side—would involve twelve ships and twelve pinnaces, which would leave an equal force (of twelve ships and twelve pinnaces) to operate for Channel Defence, as well as a reserve of six ships and six pinnaces which would normally be in port, refitting. Emphatically this scheme was *not* (as Sir Julian Corbett has alleged) mere *guerre de course*—commerce destruction. It was far more scientific. Nor is that same historian correct when he alleges that the scheme was tried out, and that it failed. It did *not* fail, because it was never tried out! What did fail was the Queen's rather parsimonious, and wholly unscientific, modification of the Hawkins scheme—an uncoordinated series of individual raids. It was against this spasmodic short-sightedness that John protested for all the rest of his life; and so unsuccessfully that in the end it almost broke his heart.

In 1590 he thought for a moment that he had got his way. He even went so far as to fit out his six galleons, to sail under his command. But at the last minute the Queen heard reports of Spanish ships making for the Brest peninsula, and her nerve failed her. John was to stay at home—and, next month, the flota with five million ducats on board passed right across the water he should have been occupying, and safely reached home. John's sad comment was that the Queen has placed him 'out of hope that I ever shall perform any royal thing!' Later in this year he *was* allowed to sail: and when Philip heard of it, he cancelled for the year the sailing of further treasure-frigates, almost going bankrupt as a result!

Partly under pressure of his great and growing disappointments, but also partly because he was beginning to feel his age, John seemed during these years to grow more religious-minded: more strictly puritan than he used to be. It was on this occasion that he wrote to Burghley, explaining the failure (which was not his) in making any prizes:

> And thus God's infallible Word is performed, in that the Holy Ghost said, 'Paul doth plant, Apollos doth water, but God giveth the increase.[1]

In his younger days he would not have clothed his thoughts in such biblical language. Nor, probably would his mistress have made her harsh, though immortal, comment,

> God's death! This fool went out a soldier, and is come home a divine!

But this is not, of course, what Elizabeth really thought of John. It was merely a passing tantrum, reflecting her disappointment at getting no dividend. She was no puritan herself, and always apt to give the breed the rough side of her tongue.

For the next four years both Francis and John, as sea-com-

[1] S. P. Dom. Eliz., vol. 233, f. 118.

manders were 'on the beach', so missing all part in the most famous combat of the whole war, Sir Richard's great solo fight in 1591 with Alonzo de Bazon and his 'fifty-three', in which the *Revenge* was taken, and lost, while on the other side four large Spanish ships went down. Also they missed, in 1592, the greatest single capture of treasure by the English, when the vast *Madre de Dios* was taken by a crowd of privateers, with a cargo worth, it is said, half a million pounds. Incidentally the ship that bore the brunt in that action was the *Daintie*, jointly owned by John and Richard Hawkins.

But John, though on the beach during these four years, was by no means on the *shelf*; for he was still the most important half of the Navy Board. But yearly he was growing more weary, and was now longing to give it all up. He tried again in July 1592, and yet again in February 1594. But still it was no good. They would not let him depart. At this time he must have been in very close communion with his son Richard who was engaged, first in building and afterwards in fitting out their jointly-owned ship, the *Daintie*. At the moment, probably, they were living together at Deptford, and there is plenty of evidence that father and son were devoted to each other, as will be shown when Richard's great book comes up for discussion.

k. THE LAST VOYAGE

It remains to tell, though briefly, how the old man sailed away to his death, taking with him his (relatively) young cousin, and hitherto friendly rival, Sir Francis Drake.

It was indeed an error of the first magnitude to allow an expedition to sail under the joint leadership of John and Francis. Both were men with a lifetime of command behind them, both quite unaccustomed to any such division of authority: both men of strong personality, loth to share responsibility with anyone. And, worse perhaps, both were men of genius, but endowed with very different kinds of it. Drake was essentially an opportunist, one to take hold of the occasion whenever it presented itself, and to perform miracles with it—if things went right. Hawkins, on the other hand, had genius in a more Carlylean sense. He had 'an infinite capacity for taking pains', and almost all his success in life had been due to anxious care and forethought—and foresight. They were, if one may venture upon a simile, the brilliant race-horse, on the flat or over the fences, who, on his day, can leave all his rivals standing; and the steady cavalry horse, superbly reliable, superbly unflappable, who takes in his stride the flying cannon-balls of battle or the blaring brass band of the parade ground. What would happen if one tried to drive them in tandem?

Indeed they ought never to have agreed to work in double harness. But for both of them there were temptations which they could not resist. To John, who knew how old he was growing, this must have seemed the last chance to do that 'royal thing' for which he had for so long been pining. To Francis the unaccustomed lack of employment for six long years was growing more and more irksome. He panted to be once again at the heart of the war, repeating, as he hoped, his own old and glorious feats. Nor let it be forgotten that both of them had many beliefs in common, above all the feeling that the war was no longer going right, and that an offensive touch *must* be given to it: just such a touch, surely, as the two greatest living English seamen would be able to give. And so, but for temperament, it might have been. If only they could have pulled together, what might not have happened?

But they could not; and most of the trouble can be traced back to the Queen, who was, as usual, chopping and changing her mind until there was no time left for the original objective, which was the conquest of Panama and the permanent cutting off of all Spanish treasure from Spain. But when, as late as August 28, 1595, she let them sail from Plymouth, the plan had been more or less completely changed. News had arrived that the flagship of the flotas had been badly damaged in the Florida Channel, and had taken refuge at San Juan de Puerto Rico. This then was the new objective, which they thought was well within their compass if they would fulfil yet another of the Queen's conditions: they were to be home again within six months of their departure.

The size of the fleet was much the same as that envisaged by John for his four-monthly operations. There were six Royal Ships and twenty-one privately owned vessels: and they were divided fifty-fifty between John and Francis, who had severally undertaken the manning and victualling of them. John carried his flag in the *Garland*, Francis in the *Defiance*, both of them ships of post-Armada vintage, though of course, as ships of John's building, both of advanced galleon-type. As befitted John's careful mind, a strict schedule of the numbers on board and of the victuals per man was laid down.

The next misfortune must undoubtedly be laid at Drake's door. Only four days out of Plymouth, a council was called in the *Garland* when Francis airily broke the news that he had 300 too many men on board; that he could not hope to feed them all; but would John be so obliging as to take them over and feed them on *his* stocks? To John such conduct was quite unforgivable: it upset all his most rudimentary calculations, his basic ideas of what was right and proper. He absolutely refused to do it, and the council broke up in deadlock.

A few days later Drake, though very unwillingly, had to re-open the question. The council was held in the *Defiance* this time, and he now declared that, as it was impossible for him to cross the Atlantic with so many men and so little food, he intended to turn aside and attack the Canary Islands, there to collect the necessary supplies. John answered tersely that such a course involved a complete change of plan, and that the attack on the Canaries not only wasted precious time, but also would lead to a serious weakening of strength because the islands were powerfully fortified, as well as depriving the expedition of the advantage of surprise. He therefore said that, whatever Drake did, *he* would proceed straight to Puerto Rico. Francis insisted that he must go to the Canaries: so deadlock resulted again.

But it was John who gave way, not because he experienced any change of heart, but because he knew that the division of forces would spell certain ruin. Besides, how could her two most experienced commanders face the Queen and confess to her that they had brought all to nought over what she would probably feel was a petty quarrel?

So the rift was patched up, and all dined amicably together in the *Defiance*. But events proved that John was right. The fleet proceeded to Las Palmas on the Grand Canary, where the soldier in command of the troops, having promised the capture of the town in four hours, now found the place looking so formidable that he recommended not landing at all. And to this the commanders agreed. But the fleet lost precious days in sailing round the island, and in landing, unopposed, on its western side, to take in water. Then they sailed on, watered but with no more food, and with the priceless secret of their destination revealed to the enemy. For some Englishmen taken when they landed to water, revealed it to the Governor, who instantly dispatched a swift caravel to Puerto Rico with the news.

With all hope of surprise gone, and with the commanders barely on speaking terms, the unfortunate expedition crossed the Atlantic and came at last to Guadeloupe. Here it was John who insisted upon a halt, to make good the defects which had developed on the journey. Perhaps it was hardly necessary, but—contrary to what some historians have said about the over-prudence of the older commander cramping the dashing style of the younger—it made no sort of difference, because Puerto Rico had been alerted even before the English reached Guadeloupe.

Two days later, on October 31, John was struck down, apparently quite suddenly. There is no report of any particular epidemic raging, though such things were so common as not always to be mentioned. It is much more likely that he just collapsed, partly from the endless work which he had performed, uncomplaining, for so long, and partly, no doubt from the grim news he had received back in the summer—the news of Richard's fight with the Spaniards in the Pacific and his capture by them. He certainly took these tidings very much to heart. He even had time to add a codicil to his will, leaving new monies for the ransoming of his dear boy. He may also—who knows?—have been dreaming that his present expedition might possibly reach as far as Mexico, where he might—such things *could* happen—gain touch with Richard once more: even rescue him! But his collapse must have been mainly due to the frustration caused by his quarrel with Francis, and by the fear, prominent in his mind, that the expedition—the Queen's expedition—was doomed to failure. In John's halcyon days, of course, no such shadow of defeatism ever clouded his vision. But he was an old man now: knew it—and felt it. He was sixty-three: he had just reached that 'grand climacteric' so feared by all the men in the Tudor Age. He wanted to lay down his burden, and to rest. He may even—

we do not know—have had a stroke, as his son was to have when he was much the same age.

Anyway, he seems to have made no sort of fight for life. On November 2 he took to his bed and never left it again. As the fleet came to anchor off Puerto Rico, John died quietly. Hope was dead: that was all.

As he lay dying, the deepest sentiment of his life was uppermost in his mind. The captain of the *Garland*, when he was gone, wrote to the Queen to tell her that, in a codicil to his will he had bequeathed to her—'if Your Majesty will take it'—£2,000. One does not know for certain that she took it, but can we see Her Majesty refusing?

They threw all that was mortal of John Hawkins into the tropical sea off Puerto Rico: just as, only two months later, they were to sink Francis Drake into the warm waters of Nombre de Dios Bay; as a year earlier, they had disposed of Martin Frobisher, wounded off Brest and alleged to have been slain by the maladroitness of his surgeons, though he just lived to reach Plymouth; as, four years before, the Spaniards had sunk the body of Richard Grenville down into the deep Atlantic; as, eight years before that, there had perished, also in the deep Atlantic, Humphrey Gilbert, departing with those immortal words on his lips: 'We are as near to Heaven by sea as by land.' By 1596, indeed, nearly all the older generation of seamen had gone, paying their last debt to nature with, for the most part, no human memorial to mark their last resting places.

Was William Shakespeare, writing his own swan-song a few years later, perhaps thinking of them when he penned what is surely the finest requiem in the English tongue:

> Full fathom five thy father lies
>   Of his bones are coral made:
> These are pearls that were his eyes,
>   Nothing of him that doth fade
> But doth suffer a sea-change
> Into something rich and strange.
> Sea-nymph timely ring his knell,
> Hark now! Hear them—Ding-dong bell!

CHAPTER V

Richard Hawkins

a. 'THE COMPLEAT SEAMAN'

EVERY schoolboy—and that not the sixth-former only—knows of Sir Richard Grenville: at least knows one thing about him—that with a single ship called the *Revenge* in a fight ('off Flores in the Azores') which lasted half one day and the whole of the following night, he took on a vast Spanish fleet of fifty-three sail. By the end of that immortal fight he was taken prisoner and carried, dying, to the enemy's flagship, where he delivered certain heart-stirring words—last words. Then he died: and the *Revenge* sank in the tempest which followed.

But how many schoolboys have ever heard of another Sir Richard—not Grenville but Hawkins—who three years later put up another stirring resistance to impossibly heavy Spanish odds? Where did this encounter take place, and what was the name of the ship? He has no idea! Why is it that almost every Briton has remembered one Richard and forgotten the other, seeing that the stories of their respective fights are in many ways all but identical? There are two distinct reasons.

First, almost all the 'heroic' trumps are in Grenville's hand. He fights most gloriously against impossible odds—and dies: but not before kindly Fate has given him the inestimable opportunity of rising upon the enemy's deck (whither he has been carried a prisoner) and delivering his immortal 'last words'. But see how scurvy, relatively, is Fate to poor Richard Hawkins. He fights against odds just as gallantly as does the other Richard (and incidentally for four times as long), loses and, like Grenville, is borne half-dead to his enemy's flagship. But since he fails to die—only just—he is denied the enormous psychological asset of having any last words at all. Logically, of course, this should make no difference at all; for both Richards were so sorely hurt that it was not in the power of either to influence events. Yet it *did* make all the difference because, instead, the younger Richard recovered, to endure some eight years of cruel (yet essentially inglorious) captivity, a fatally cold douche to all hero-worship.

The second reason why our Richard never had his due is not far to seek: and it explains, not so much why he has been forgotten as why Grenville has been remembered. It so happened that two writers of real genius have immortalized the *Revenge* story, while Richard Hawkins never found a chronicler in the least comparable with either. It was not that he was neglected, still less disgraced, in his own day. On the contrary, he was praised by his generation and knighted by his sovereign when at length he returned. But meanwhile the war in which both actions occurred had ground to an inglorious halt; and, even then, another score of years was to elapse before anyone but himself and a few of his fellow-survivors knew any details of what had happened. Not so, however, with Grenville. Sir Walter Raleigh's superb account of the Azores action—one of the gems of Elizabethan prose—appeared in the very year of it, and the elder Richard's fame was established for all time, even without the support it received from Sir Robert Markham's poem of 1595, and then Jan Huygen van Lindschoten's narrative of 1598.

But of course this is not all. Our schoolboy did not get his information from Elizabethan literature, however good it might be. No, he had it from *The Revenge: a Ballad of the Fleet*, written nearly three centuries later by Lord Tennyson, dubbed (rightly or wrongly, who shall say?) the greatest sea-ballad in our language, and long since passed (surely rightly) into 'Poetry for use in Schools'. Let nothing in these pages be construed into disparagement of the older Sir Richard. He deserves his immortality. My only point is that the younger Sir Richard deserved some immortality too, and of exactly the same brand. But he did not get it, because he found no Raleigh, let alone a Tennyson.

This is not to say that no detailed account of our Richard's action ever appeared. It did: but only in 1622, and even then from the pen of the hero himself: who; when all is said, is about the worst chronicler of his own exploits that any hero can have the misfortune to choose. For if he is of the kind intent upon doing himself and his exploit full justice, he runs the risk of being accused of bragging. But if (like our Richard) he is modest, he will hardly do *himself* justice. Apart from this, too, no one will pretend that he, though no mean writer, is in the same flight with either Tenyson or Raleigh.

His book is called *The Observations Of Sir Richard Hawkins, Knight*, and it was published posthumously. It is a great book: great enough anyway never to have been quite lost sight of from that day to this. Most, but not all of it, was reprinted by Samuel Purchase in *His Pilgrimes* in 1625. It was the first volume selected for reprint by the newly founded Hakluyt Society in 1848, and it appeared again in 1878, edited by C. E. Markham, as part of *The Hawkins Voyages* and published again by the Hakluyt Society. In this century it has reappeared in the delightful dress of the Argonaut Press, edited by J. A. Williamson.

It is a gold-mine both to students of Elizabethan history (especially naval history) and to anyone who aspires to write about the author. Without it, indeed, no biographer could very well start, because he would know, if possible, even less about Richard than we know about his grandfather; and, even with it, a volume devoted solely to his life would be a thin thing—which perhaps accounts for the fact that nobody has attempted one. True, for the single year covered in the book, we know a very great deal about the man: but of all later years precious little, because Richard himself was not engaged upon an autobiography, and he had far too well-organized a mind to trail off into irrelevancies. Firmly he called his work *The Observations of . . . in his Voyage into the Southern Sea, Anno Domini 1593*: and he stuck to it, though fortunately his 'observations' range widely through time as well as through space.

Later in these pages Richard's biography (in the accepted sense of that word) will be attempted. But first, it chimes in better with our plan to use his work in an attempt to discover the man: and, if we have any success here, we shall also be nearer to answering another vital question: why did his contemporaries, with one voice, acclaim him *'the Compleat Seaman'*?

b. 'THE OBSERVATIONS'

The title, precise and accurate, is entirely characteristic of its author's precise and accurate mind. Its basis is a detailed account of the fatal voyage. But the word is 'observation', not 'narrative': and, throughout, the writer uses that word both in its more restricted sense of 'seeing and recording' and in its wider one of 'considering and commenting upon'. There is therefore far more here than a record of things seen or done. He usually starts with these; but thereafter his observations radiate out in every direction until they seem to embrace pretty nearly everything which concerns the sea, its ways, its customs; the ships which sail upon it with all their appurtenances; and how, from all his wide experience, he concludes that seamen (and especially sea commanders) should conduct themselves thereon. There is no bravado about it, no sign of self-praise or even self-assurance: no particular stress on what 'I' do. It seems to be—was taken then to be, and has ever since been taken to be—a very modest, dispassionate statement of the point reached by his day in the art and craft of the sea: a sort of last word, universally agreed.

To anyone wanting to understand the man himself, too, it is uniquely valuable. Both substance and method seem to reveal a being essentially straight, in deed, in mind, in soul; talented too, but with talents which somehow fall just short of real genius: a careful, fair-minded, humane person, remarkably knowledgeable, both of the contemporary world around him and of his own professional corner of it; withal a really well-educated man who has a trained mind and can use it—though whence the education came is not so clear, since he seems to have taken to the sea at a very tender age.

There is no striking similarity between the three generations of Plymouth Hawkinses. Both the older men, one feels, were cast in a rather more angular mould than Richard. Not that any of them could be called inordinately *hard* men (certainly not John); nor could Richard possibly be regarded as soft. But there is about him a sort of gentleness, sensitivity—almost spirituality—largely lacking in John and, so far as we can judge, entirely lacking in William.

Yet they retain certain traits in common. One is a very marked local patriotism, to be expected in William who always lived in Plymouth, and even in John who came to manhood there; but rather more unlooked-for in Richard who, though almost certainly born there, must have left the West Country for Town when a mere child. Yet his profound and lasting love of home is very evident. Watch his departure from Plymouth bound on his unfortunate voyage, all couched in that near-poetical language which is such a feature of his work, as it is of so much Elizabethan prose:

> . . . all put in order, I looft[1] near the shore, to give my farewell to all the inhabitants of the towne, whereof the most part were gathered together upon the How, to show their gratefull correspondency to the love and zeale which I my father and predecessors have ever borne to that place, as to our naturall and mother towne. And first with my noyse of trumpets, after with my waytes and then with my other musicke, and lastly with the artillery of my shippes I made the best signification I could of a kinde farewell. This they answered with the waytes of the towne and the ordnance on the shore; and with shouting of voyces, which with the fayre evening and the silence of the night, were heard a great distance off.[2]

There is something very pleasing, oddly civilized, in all this, and especially in this possession of no less than three sorts of 'musicke'. Yet it was quite normal for an Elizabethan commander, off on a long voyage into seas and perils unknown, to provide himself with what looks at first sight like mere luxuries: which, however, cost him but little, because his 'musicke' consisted solely of his ordinary crew, who 'made it' when not engaged upon their routine chores.

A very marked trait, almost a keystone, in Richard's character was the intense admiration and love which he had for his famous father. By far the commonest proper name in the *Observations* is 'My father, Sir John Hawkins', or 'Sir John Hawkins, Knight, my Father'. There is pride and affection in every reference to him. If the point at issue is the proper way to conduct a difficult affair, the proper way of managing things is almost always that of 'Sir John, my Father': if it is some new practice which is well worth adopting, it is almost always a case of 'Sir John did this', and often 'Sir John invented it'. Writing to his father when he

---

[1] Plied to windward.   [2] *Observations* (Argonaut Edition), p. 22.

was a captive in the Spaniards' hands, he begins his letter, 'Illustrious and beloved Father'. Later in that letter come the words, 'I console myself that it was such that neither was my Queen dishonoured by such a subject, nor my Father by such a son:' and he ends with the words, '. . . may my prayers prevail that before I die I may see thy face! your unfortunate but loving and obedient son, Richard Hawkins.'

Evidently he was devoted to his father, and it is equally clear that that father was devoted to him. Throughout they invariably played into one another's hands. Whenever anything weighty is toward, Richard always consults John and he almost always follows his advice. Here was true hero-worship. Moreover Richard clearly thought that his father was a really great man—much greater than most of his contemporaries thought him. And of course he was right. John was even a greater man than Richard. For where the son was one of the products—and a fine one—of that great new Elizabethan Age, the father was essentially one of its creators.

Another very marked trait which Richard certainly shared with John was a religious strain of faintly Puritan, yet never aggressive, texture. To the twentieth century this very real streak of piety may appear stranger in John than in his son. We may find it a little hard to associate true Christian belief with our first slave-trader. Yet anyone who imagines that piety and the Trade could not consort together quite comfortably under one Elizabethan doublet, is badly out. They could, and they did. Indeed one already quoted remark of the Great Queen herself seems to show that, of the two, it was she who had less real piety than John. Once, in reporting failure to secure valuable prizes, he fell back upon the Scriptures as was his wont. 'Paul doth plant,' he wrote, 'Apollos doth water, but God giveth the increase.' Her tart comment, we recall, was, 'God's death! This fool went out a soldier and is come home a divine!'

But John was no hypocrite: the whole tenor of his life proves it. Such turns of phrase were the norm just then among the more protestant of her subjects. But they were none the less genuine. A man like Hawkins did believe, profoundly, that the Almighty was wholly on the side, not so much of himself as of his Faith, his Country, his Queen and her cause—and it should be remarked in passing that the corresponding Spaniard held exactly the same view about himself and *his* cause.

Richard had this characteristic too; and its spirit informs the whole of the *Observations*. Only, as being a somewhat more sophisticated person than his father, his claim as recipient of Divine Providence is rather less bald, and therefore may seem rather more genuine, though it is doubtful whether it really was. At any rate, in the sample just cited, Sir John lays himself open to fine fun at the hands of the cynic, who will say that he was excusing his failure by inferring that it was in some sort the Almighty's fault—that, in fact, God must take some share of any blame that is going! But Richard praises God, and freely acknowledges his debt to him when that debt is not nearly so obvious: in fact sometimes so indirect as to be virtually non-existent. Three examples out of many will show the difference.

In the first, his ship, the *Daintie*, had driven suddenly upon an uncharted rock in the Magellan Straits, and

> had wee had but the fourthe part of the wind which we had in all the night past, but a moment before we strucke the rocke, our shippe, doubtlesse, with the blow had broken her selfe all to peeces. But our provident and most gracious God, which commaundeth wind and sea, watched over us, and delivered us with his powerful hand from the unknowne danger and hidden destruction, so that we might prayse him for his fatherly bounty and protection, and with the prophet David say, *Excepte the Lord keepe the cittie, the watch-men watch in vaine* . . . and therefore He for his mercies sake grant that the memoriall of his benefits doe never depart from before our eyes.

And again, very soon afterwards, the Almighty—he was certain of it—intervened once more in the directest possible manner, and, of course, effectively. They were caught by a sudden furious whirlwind in a grim, fiord-like channel, where

> necessitie, not being subject to any law, forced us to put ourselves into the hands of Him who was able to deliver us. We cut our cable and sayle all in one instant; and God, to show his power and gratious bountie towardes us, was pleased that our shippe cast the contrary way towards the shore, seeming that He with his own hand did wend her about; for in lesse than her length she flatted,[1] and in all the voyage but at that instant she flatted with difficultie, for that she was long, the worst propertie she had. On either side we might see the rockes under us, and were not half a shippes length from the shore;
>
> [1] Came round on her heel.

and if she had once touched, it had been impossible to have escaped. Magnified ever be our Lord God which delivered Ionas out of the whales belly; and his Apostle Peter from being overwhelmed in the waves, and us from so certain perishing.

In our last example we may fairly say that God has not directly helped Richard at all; not bodily, anyway. He has not put him in the way of wordly wealth, nor of thrashing the Spaniards nor even of preserving him from drowning. He has merely shown him—a humble believer—what a glorious being he is. Richard, with interest amounting to awe, has been telling of the birds on Penguin Island in the Straits and their marvellous economy; how they behave, nest and breed. Quite simply he ends:

all which are motions of prayse, and magnify the universall Creator who so wondrously manifesteth his wisdom, bountie and provindence in all his creatures; especially for his particular love to ungrateful mankind, for whose contemplation and service He has made them all.

In this there is precious little of self-interest. Here surely is pure and unsolicited praise. Here is every sign of a simple faith.

Such praises spring spontaneously from the heart. More often, however, what he writes comes from the head, and a very level head too. For Richard is thoughtful and practical. Moreover he designs to make his book interesting as well as instructive: one might almost say he has his eye on the sales. So sometimes he tries consciously to attract the then extensive travel-book public. Of this kind is his disquisition on pearls and pearl-fishing, which Richard himself had dregged for off the island of Margarita: on the various wines they swallow (with a note on the deleterious 'new' practice of drinking the fiery fortified products instead of the purer French ones): the strange customs of the natives they meet: the islands, straits and coastlines they explore: the fruits they find and eat: dates, bananas, coconuts, prick pears (artichokes); the animals they see, and sometimes capture: chinchillas, parrots, 'cyvett-catts' and 'munkeyes'; the various fish they watch: the dolphin, bonito, shark, flying fish, sword-fish and thresher; whales, and the breathtaking hunting of them by the Indians, who contrive to hammer wooden pegs into their blow-holes, thus drowning them; seals and 'sea-wolves'; and the albatross, one of which (shades of Coleridge!)

they deliberately catch on hook and line. Then there is the new island they discover, which Richard christens Hawkins Maiden Land—most likely the Falklands, which, unknown to them, however, John Davis had found in the preceding year. Then there is gold, that never-staling topic: how the natives recover it by mining and washing:

> in Coquimbo it rayneth seldome, but every showre is a showre of gold to them . . .

This, however, is no traveller's tale. He instantly explains it away:

> . . . for with the violence of the water falling from the mountains it bringeth from them the gold.

In fact, on 'marvels' as such he is not nearly so strong as are most of his contemporaries. But he does fall occasionally, as in his description of a certain tree in Fierro which, all by itself, supplies the whole island with water. Usually, though, he is above such superstitions; too sensible to believe all he hears and too honest simply to pander to his public.

Yet there is one superstition (for so no doubt it must be called) to which, not surprisingly, he did subscribe—the magic residing in ships' names. And no wonder, seeing that such a view is as old as the oldest ship and, in only very modified form, as new as the newest. To all regular ship-users, they were, they are, and probably always will be, living creatures—always female and individually 'lucky' or 'unlucky'. Richard clearly believes this, but evidently thinks that man may control the situation. He can at least give his ship a good wholesome name.

When he launched the *Daintie*, his own mother, Sir John's first wife,[1] asked to have the naming of her. Richard agreed, and

---

[1] Richard makes an odd mistake here. His phrase is, 'The Lady Hawkyns (my mother-in-law)'. He must have meant his own mother Katherine, and not Sir John's second wife, Margaret, because the *Daintie* was already at sea in 1590, and his mother Katherine died only in July 1591. The explanation of this otherwise curious error in which Richard apparently confuses his true mother with his step-mother, is undoubtedly this: he actually wrote 'Lady Hawkyns'—unqualified—but the words in brackets, 'my mother-in-law', were inserted by the anonymous man who saw the book through the press, Richard having died just before it appeared; and this man, no doubt, did not know the dates of Sir John's respective marriages. Why should he? By 1622 Katherine had already been dead for thirty-one years. Another reason for supposing that this is the explanation for the apparent

she called her the *Repentance*. He acquiesced, but he was not happy. His experience taught him, or so he thought, that ships' names foretell the shape of things to come. As ever, he cites examples. Look, he says, at the *Revenge*: a really ungodly name. Does not Holy Writ itself reserve to the Almighty alone the right to deal in Vengeance? And in plain fact was not the *Revenge*, all through her life, 'ever the unfortunatest shippe'? In five short years, between 1586 and 1591, she had no less than ten near-fatal mishaps (listed); and; of course, *in* 1591, a completely fatal one. Then there was the *Thunderbolt of London*, a sinister name but uncannily apt, seeing that she was struck by one off the Barbary Coast, was the victim of an unexplained explosion in Dartmouth harbour, and finally burnt to cinders in the river of Bordeaux. Or the *Jesus*, whose sacred name is too holy to be conferred on such a man-made thing as a ship. And everybody knows, of course, what befell her ('with my Father on board') at San Juan de Ulua.

But the *Repentance*! What an ill-omen! *What* was Mother thinking of? Surely she knew one only repents having done something wrong? Somehow it fastens upon a ship a pre-acceptance of guilt. Fortunately, however, things turned out rather well, and Richard was able to avoid the unpleasantness of having to break his promise to his mother. Providence intervened. The Queen's Majesty herself, dropping down-river to her palace at Greenwich, was attracted by the ship's beautiful lines as she lay a-fitting off Deptford. She inquired her name, was full of scorn at the ineptitude of it, and herself christened her *Daintie* then and there. Naturally that was that. No one thought to disobey Her Highness in a matter like this,

Nowadays, no doubt, the perversity of calling a lovely ship *Repentance* would pass unnoticed; miraculous trees are long out of fashion; our eyes goggle no more at munkeyes, sea-wolves and prick pears. Yet, so long as they did, the *Observations* was a first-rate travel-book.

---

mistake is that Richard goes on to call the lady 'a religious and most vertuous Lady, and of a very good understanding'. He can have had but little use for his step-mother, she having, as he supposed, tried to do him a very bad turn indeed, (see below, p. 217). On the other hand, there is plenty of evidence to show that he was devoted to his own mother.

But it is much more than this. It is also a compendium, a sort of encyclopaedia-in-little, of all sea knowledge not his, but everybody's. We soon find out that he has developed a technique which, though varied in detail, is invariable. First he allows the subject at issue to emerge from his personal narrative. Then he discusses it as a personal problem: then, becoming historical again, he cites instances of it as they have arisen elsewhere, showing how other eminent sea-folk have tackled them. Finally he summarizes the acknowledged facts, the latest views. And it is entirely characteristic of him that his final verdict by no means always coincides with what he did under like circumstances. The solid candour of the writer, from which nothing will move him, is fascinating, and entirely revealing of the man. Here are three examples out of many, stating several moral problems of officers, mostly senior ones. The first is general, applying equally to his time and ours. The second applies more particularly to his, the third perhaps mainly to ours. Yet he covers all three with equal care and with equal effect.

I Of fleet-discipline, experience and obedience to orders

(*a*) *The case stated.* I sailed down-channel with a party of Hollanders. Their fleet-discipline was superb. This the English taught them; but, to our shame, we often nowadays neglect to observe it ourselves.

(*b*) *Arising therefrom.* The reason is because we often appoint as Commander one who is ignorant of the values of obedience and experience.

(*c*) *Historical.* The right spirit. That fine man, Sir H. Palmer, appointed to a lucrative command off the Spanish coast, refused it simply because he lacked experience, having always served hitherto in the Narrow Seas.

The wrong spirit. The loss of the Burgundy fleet in 1592 was solely due to the indiscipline of the Vice-Admiral who, ordered to bring up the rear, chose to sail with the van. Again, in 'my Father's' fleet off Spain in 1590, the Vice-admiral, contrary to orders, stretched ahead during the night, and cost us at least eight prizes. (I saw it myself.)

(*d*) *Widening the discussion.* There are certain disciplinary obligations which every Commander *must* obey. One is his obligation not to desert those of his company who are ill ashore. This, then, being a first or basic duty, Richard Grenville at Flores was perfectly correct in stopping to pick up his sick and accepting all subsequent risks. And he would still have been correct even if he had not put up a fight so glorious to Englishmen.[1]

Further, the conduct on the same occasion of Captain Vavasour of the *Foresight* is equally worthy of commendation, with, however, a rather subtle reservation. The normal duty of an English captain is, under all possible circumstances, to support his fellows to the best of his ability. This Vavasour did, by casting about upon the whole Spanish fleet in order to give what support he could to Grenville; even though the general order from the Admiral (Lord Thomas Howard) was not to engage.

(*e*) *Conclusion*—(very wise, and surely surprisingly modern):

> Some do say, and I consent with them, that the best valour is to obey, and to follow the head [i.e. the Admiral's order] seeme that good or bad which is commaunded. For God telleth us that obedience is better than sacrifice. Yet, on some occasions . . . it is great discretion and obligation judiciously to take hold of the occasion.

It would be far-fetched to suppose that, off Cape St Vincent in 1797, Commodore Horatio Nelson was influenced by old Sir Richard's *Observations*. Yet there, in leaving the line of battle without his admiral's express orders, he surely gave the classic confirmation of the soundness of Richard's diagnosis: '*It is great discretion and obligation judiciously to take hold of the occasion!*' Indeed it can hardly be denied that this thoughtful Elizabethan has, all by himself, probed pretty well to the heart of one of the hardest problems which confronted commanders—and which confront them still.

II *When to be obstinate, and when to give way*

(Applicable primarily to Richard's day, when, owing to the absence of radio and the general slowness of communications,

---

[1] Here perhaps the author of the *Observations* is in some sort begging the question. He commends Grenville for picking up his invalids—an action for which no one has ever seriously blamed him. But he does not mention—what was almost certainly the fact—that Grenville could, had he liked, have both retrieved his men *and* avoided action.

the commander was, for very long periods, his own master, and arbiter of life and death to all his people.)

(*a*) *The case stated.* It is unwise in a commander, even if it be not quite impossible, for him *always* to persist in what he deems the correct course in face of the views of his subordinates, collectively differing from him. For, if he does so, he may well lose the most important thing of all, their confidence in him.

(*b*) *Illustration.* There were at least three occasions during the voyage of the *Daintie* when this situation arose.

(i) After failing several times to get through the Straits of Magellan, each failure accompanied by ever-increasing discomfort, danger, and fear for the future, by far the greater part of the ship's company wished, vociferously, to turn back. Not to give up the expedition—oh no! Merely *reculer pour mieux sauter.* Now Richard's experience and knowledge of history (instances cited) told him that, in these circumstances, to turn back, even for a moment, was tantamount to sailing home (if possible). He therefore refused, point blank and very firmly, yet urging his case as persuasively as he could. He prevailed. They accepted his leadership, not exactly willingly but, being at heart a very good crew, not too unwillingly.

(ii) After this, they came very near success again and again, at one moment emerging into the Pacific only to be blown back again. Then, heart-breakingly, again and again they were forced back, tossed to and fro by winds and currents which, to the men, seemed plainly diabolical. At length, however, they reached a place where they could anchor in comparative calm, with the gale howling round and over them. Here they remained for a while, shaken, confused. But then, quite suddenly, an inspiration amounting to virtual certainty came to Richard—he attributes it, of course, directly to the Almighty. The gale still howled, but he—Richard—he *knew* that they must up anchor and away at once! Everyone else on board was against it—even, for once, those most trusted of his officers who had hitherto always supported him. In spite of everything, however, so strong was his conviction that he persisted. And again he prevailed—indeed doubly so. Not only did they all obey him but his instinct was abundantly justified. Very soon after they had weighed, the wind moderated, shifted, and set fair in their direction. Then, with no further crises, they sailed clean out into the Pacific. For the moment, of course, his prestige on board was immense.

(iii) But soon there came reaction, natural to the point of inevitability. The company's spirits rose at a bound from Very Stormy to Set Fair. Visible dangers lay all behind them, pleasurable anticipation in front. 'Now,' they argued almost to a man,' we can get down to what we came for, the delectable business of Prize and Pillage. Let's start at once!'

But Richard thought otherwise. Again his experience and knowledge of history stepped in to make him cautious. If they began operations now, he knew, there would be but little to capture at so high a latitude. What they would lose would be the priceless attribute of surprise. All that would happen would be that news of their presence would pass up to Lima and beyond. So, when they did arrive, the enemy would be ready and waiting for them. He therefore said in effect, 'Nothing doing before we pass Lima!' But this did not suit them. They would not take it. They remembered, as uneducated minds will, a part—but only a part—of what had gone before. They forgot, or did not choose to recall, that twice already he had been demonstrably right and they egregiously wrong: they only remembered that he had twice opposed them.

They did not show signs of mutiny, and, he was bound to say, he was doubtful whether under any circumstance they would have gone to quite that length. (This is typical of Richard. He is not going to take the easy way out and say, 'They made me do it.') But it did seem to him that the point had been reached when the dangers of his always being in a minority of one (even though in the right) would, in its effect upon their mutual relations, outweigh the danger of giving way to them. He therefore did give way: fatally as far as the whole expedition was concerned, because once more he was right, and all fell out exactly as he had predicted. 'It was our perdition,' he reflects sadly.

(iv) *The moral*. In the light of hindsight, he considers that he made a mistake—probably: for only the Almighty can say what would have happened had he persisted. But nothing is proven. It may well be that, by insisting, he would have earned an unenviable reputation for over-prudence, if not for pusillanimity, none the less fatal to the venture for being undeserved.

This time there is a comment to make on Richard's handling of the situation, which, however, hardly amounts to a criticism. Had any mere landsman been in his shoes, there would probably have been no difficult problem to face. Much more probably the *Daintie* would already have been at the bottom of the Straits at worst, or, at best, well on her way back to England. Yet in his handling of the affair there does seem to have been a certain weakness, not in deed, nor even in character; but in prescience. In fact we may feel that he did make a mistake; though it was one which he does not even mention. The really heaven-born leader—a Drake, for instance—would surely have foreseen the likely reactions of his men, even before they began to react: and he—a Drake—would have made up his mind long before, in the quiet of his own cabin, what line he would take, when or if the demand was made. Having done so (and when that demand came) he would have been prepared with a firm answer, according as to how he had decided. It might have been, "Pillage, lads ? Aye, that's what we're here for. Off we go!' It might have been, 'We'll take our time'. But, whichever it was, it would have been perfectly clear and unalterable. In either case they would think— a very healthy thought for both commander and commanded— that he was leading them, and not they him. As it was, however, or so it seems to this author, he had the worst of both possible worlds. While letting them see that he wanted to say 'No', he said 'Yes'.

III *When to interfere*

(Applicable much more to the second Elizabethan era than to the first: to our own age of specialization than to Richard's 'salt-horse' days.) Right at the crisis of his affairs, when he found himself all but looking down the muzzles of a far superior enemy's artillery, Richard made the devastating discovery that he had been let down, totally and irredeemably, by the officer in charge of that department upon which all was about to hinge— the gunner. That the man was a bad one he verily believed; that he was actually a traitor he suspected; but that he was a liar he was quite certain because, throughout the entire voyage, he had never ceased to boast of his complete readiness. At a moment's notice every gun, every cartridge, every shot, rammer, sponge, worm and scraper would be there just so. And Richard, who had always believed in a policy of mutual trust, in suspecting not the worst but the best of every man, until that man himself convinced him to the contrary; who had therefore always avoided wherever possible even the shadow of prying into the concerns of his departments—he, Richard, God forgive him, had believed the gunner!

Instantly ghastly shortcomings stood revealed. The powder, which should have been carefully measured out into its canvas cartridge-bags, was lying in bulk below, untouched. The scoundrelly gunner had vaunted his 500 cartridges all ready for use. However, as there were none,

> we were forced to occupie three persons only in making and filling cartridges: and of 500 elles of canvas and other cloth given him for that purpose at sundry times, not one yard was to be found. We therefore could not avoid the danger to charge and discharge with the ladell, especially in so hot a fight.

Then there were the 'brasse balls of artificiall fire to be shott with slurbowes (whereof I had six bowes and two hundreth bals)' peculiarly important for the hand-to-hand work now about to take place and which poor Richard was obviously proud of having furnished:

> he had stowed them in such a manner, though in double barrels, as the salt water had spoyled them all: so that, coming to use them, not one was serviceable.

Moreover,

> few of our pieces were clear when we came to use them, and some had the shott first put in, and after the powder.

To charge any artillery officer with so rudimentary a blunder as this last can only mean one of two things. Either the gunner was indeed a traitor, bent on delivering the ship into the hands of the Spaniards—and Richard does allege that the man had once served in a Spanish ship—or else, in his wrath against him for his other incompetences, he was guilty of exaggeration.

Even so, however, though pardonably bitter about the man, he makes no attempt to evade his own share of the blame. On the contrary, he uses his own discomfiture as a warning to others:

The griefe and remembrance of which oversights once again in-
forceth me to admonish all captains and commanders hereby to take
advice, now and then to survey their officers and store-roomes, the
oftener the better: so that the defects and wants may be supplied in
time: never relying too much upon the vulgar report, nor giving too
much credit to smooth tongues and boasting companions.

Here then is the bald account of the calamity, and the (in this
case) obvious recommendation for avoiding similar troubles
thereafter. But it is not Richard's way to leave it at that. There
are deeper lessons still to be learnt and he must discover them.
How far, he asks, *should* a commander trust his departmental
officers? If he overdoes his superintendence, he sees clearly that
he will

> deprive the other officers of their esteemes, and of that that belongeth
> unto them, which were a great absurdity.

How right he is: how real the dilemma! There is probably no
naval captain, past or present, who will not know what he means,
and freely acknowledge the dilemma's existence. Not to seem to
interfere, yet to know!

But still this thoughtful, painstaking man persists, until he
produces an answer: and in that answer he touches upon what is
one of the great officer-problems of all navies and of all ages;
perhaps most of all the present, and the future. He proceeds

> But my opinion is that he should be more than superficially instructed
> and practised in the imployments (of the various officers' depart-
> ments):

that, in a word, he should know enough about *all* departments to
be able to judge, approximately, what is going on in them.

But, he realizes, he cannot be exactly a specialist in all of
them:

> He cannot be tyed to the actuall toyle, or to intermeddle with all
> offices, for that were to binde him to impossibilities, to diminish and
> abuse his authoritie.

His ideal captain, then, is one who, while too familiar with all
facets of his ship's economy for any of his own subordinates to be
able to pull wool over his eyes, is still prepared, having summed
up his officers' probity and efficiency, to trust them.

Yes, I am verily perswaded that the more absolute authoritie any commander giveth to his under officers, being worthy of it, the sweeter is the command, the more respected and beloved the commander.

But—Heaven knows—it was a sticky enough problem for Richard in his unicellular organism the *Daintie*. What is it for the modern commanding officer in his twenty-odd million pounds-worth of devices and gadgets; wherein any really intimate knowledge of only one in ten of them is clear outside practical politics! Here in fact is one of the most intractable problems facing modern navies. And here is a sixteenth-century Hawkins anticipating and resolutely facing it.

We may now begin to see why his contemporaries dubbed him 'Compleat Seaman', implying a much wider competence than is involved in the mere handling of ships. To them he was the man who had at his finger-tips the whole art of manning, storing, sailing, commanding and fighting them. And so he had: but to show in detail how right they were is hardly possible here. To do so would in fact be to essay some account of all sea-lore as known at the close of Elizabeth's reign. All that we can do here is to summarize brutally.

I *On navigation*

He includes,

(*a*) A disquisition on how to find one's longitude at sea. Naturally he reached no final conclusion here, because another century was to pass before John Harrison solved the problem with his chronometers. But Richard makes a good attempt, retailing as usual the *latest* knowledge.

(*b*) On the supply and training of *Masters*: on steersmen, their training and supervision.

(*c*) On the necessity for satisfactory rendezvous at sea, for all units of all fleets. There is nothing *quite* new here, but it is, as ever, 'the last word'.

II *On the raising, feeding, clothing and management of men*

(*a*) The dangerous futility of offering 'Imprests'—the inducements later called 'bounties'. These should be paid only to *married* men, with families who can thus be provided for during their wage-earners' absence. The alternative for the wretched wives and children is starvation. Here Richard is well over a century ahead of his times.

(*b*) Keeping the ship's company happy. Here he is at his best, his most sensible and perhaps at his most modern; for he shows himself to be a good psychologist.

Exercise, he realizes, they get a-plenty. What they require is recreation, at all costs and in such variety as is practicable. He names such pastimes as fishing—almost always possible—dancing and music: we have already seen him providing the wherewithal for this. Then, though their food can hardly be good, it should be made as good, as palatable and as variegated as possible; and all excesses, especially of drink, must be avoided, not only for health of body, but for health of mind too. There must also be intelligent division of labour—he actually advocates 'watches', and—heavily stressed—a day of rest, as complete as may be, on Sundays. Last—and here speaks the essential puritan in him—they must not take the name of God in vain; and, most ingeniously, he contrives to convert an anti-swearing campaign into a *game* in which the men were willing collaborators.

> So with a general consent of all our companie, it was ordayned that in every shippe there should be a Palmer or Ferula, which should be in the keeping of him who was taken with an oath, and that he who had the Palmer should give to every other that he tooke swearing in the palm of the hand a palmado with it, *and* the Ferula. And whosoever at the time of evening, or morning prayer, was found to have the Palmer, should have three blowss given him by the Captaine or the Master, and that he should still be bound to free himselfe by taking another (in an oath), or else runne in danger of continuing the penaltie: which executed, few days reformed the Vice, so that in three days together was not one oath heard to be sworne. This brought both ferula and swearing out of use.

Say what one will, *if* this device worked—and we have no grounds for doubting it—it can only be described as a remarkable feat of sixteenth-century psychology. The ferula can merely have tickled those horny palms; but, as a game, it tickled their fancy; which was why the scheme succeeded.

Of his other efforts, most of them have doubtless been tried hundreds of times since, but, as far as is known—and this is the point—seldom if ever *before*.

(c) Keeping the company healthy

Here he is as advanced as he is in mind-cure. He fully recognizes the ever-present dangers of bad ventilation, dirt and damp, though he cannot do anything really radical about them beyond routine fumigation and cleansing between-decks. He also insists upon everyone who gets wet changing as soon as possible into dry garments. Indeed, he puts quite a modern faith in the very act of changing clothes, which is even one of his specific remedies for the scurvy.

That grim disease he discusses at length, and singularly scientifically for that unscientific age. He mentions all the known specifics, some of them a little pathetic no doubt, but none of them completely 'quack'. He is probably the first English seaman to describe the symptoms in detail. Clearly he knew a great deal about them, his crew having had a bad epidemic in the Atlantic, before they reached the Straits. So all his deductions are based on experience. And in the end he gets there, or very nearly. He has at least discovered two important truths about scurvy: (1) if you can get your patient ashore, he will almost certainly recover quickly and completely, and (2) he mentions what was destined to be *the* remedy:

> That which I have seene most fruitfull for this sickness is soure Oranges and Limmons.

He was not however, the pioneer in the use of the citrus fruits. In the early 1200's one Albertus de Aquila was more than half-way to the truth: the first Portuguese explorers and the Spanish *Conquistadors* had proved their efficacy from dire necessity after they had started the long oceanic voyages; and even the Englishman Thomas Cavendish had exploited the value of the lemon in his round-the-world trip of 1586.

In one respect, however, so far as we know he was a true pioneer. He had with him on board an elementary apparatus for the distilling of sea-water, thus at a pinch eliminating the agonies of thirst. This is truly extraordinary, because here he is well over 250 years in advance of his day. As late as 1845 an

R.N. ship's company was dying of thirst in the Pacific because it carried no still.

(d) On ships, ship-construction and ship protection

(*a*) He has naturally a good deal to say about ships, and everything to do with them—how to lade them, and how to protect them from the three scourges of fire, rats and worms. Perhaps his most interesting disquisition is on ship protection; and especially on remedies to counteract the ravages in warm seas of that pest *Teredo Navalis* or Sea-Worm. Ships, and especially their bottoms, have to be sheathed with a layer of some material other than their natural oak. He lists the materials used in other lands, but concludes that the English practice is the best. This consists of an outer layer of half-inch board, usually of elm, covered on the inside with a thick coating of tar, and then an equally thick layer of hair 'such as the whitelymers use'; all to be nailed firmly to the outside of the oak planking which forms the ship's bottom. Though he does not expressly say so, this sheathing in England was really a Hawkins patent: and it remained the standard for a long time.

(*b*) He also discusses, and illustrates, the dangers of fire in the wooden ships of his day, giving instances of vessels lost through burning and the chief causes of such outbreaks. He also notes the best methods of mastering the flames at the earliest possible moment. He had, he tells us, a fire in the *Daintie* soon after his cruise began. It was caused by boiling pitch overflowing when it was being used to caulk the seams. He succeeded in extinguishing it by ordering the whole crew to throw overboard their sea-gowns tied to a string (he having provided one for every man on night duty). With these formidable squeegees they all attacked the blaze immediately and together: and though some were 'singed and scalded', they contrived to quench it. On another occasion there was a fire below-deck in the *Jesus* 'when my Father, Sir John Hawkins, Knight, was her General'. He dealt with the crisis by having the 'sloppers' (scuppers) blocked up, pumping several inches of water on to the deck, and then letting it through suddenly on to the flames. But much the greater number of ships, once well alight, were burned to the water's edge.

In fine, his book contains every known specific which made an Elizabethan commander a good one; which made him 'compleat'.

No more can be said here of this great book. When they had it, belatedly, between their hands, all his compatriots agreed upon Richard's 'compleatness '.Yet it is much to be doubted whether, even then, they realized what a superb navigator he was, what a superb man of action he was: what a terrific fighter. For in the *Observations* he fails largely to bring such points out. But they are features in the man's character which must now be stressed.

Let us view him first as a prime navigator.

c. THE STRAITS OF MAGELLAN

Passing from the Atlantic to the Pacific, at any rate before the completion of the Panama Canal, has always been an adventure, even when one navigated a steam-driven vessel round Cape Horn: considerably more so when in a sailing-ship, however large and well-found. But the navigational difficulties were increased a hundredfold before Cape Horn was known and charted; when one had to negotiate the dangers of the passage which Magellan discovered in 1520. The difficulties and dangers then were great and awe-inspiring indeed! And *every* navigator who passed through that Passage Perilous was great. Of all who tried, at least three out of every four failed, either suffering irremediable disaster or—more frequently—just funking it and returning again to the Atlantic. After Magellan, the next successful, and the first English, passage was made nearly sixty years later, by Sir Francis Drake who went through it in 1579. The second Englishman to succeed was Thomas Cavendish who did it in 1586: and the third, who went through in 1593, was Richard Hawkins in the *Daintie*.

The Straits are some 300 miles long. The first half of the transit is comparatively easy, though still remarkably dangerous, with the navigator's skill constantly on stretch, and with no let-up from anxiety and vigilance. From the Atlantic entrance at Cape Virgins, the channel proceeds first in a south-westerly direction and then due south up the Broad Reach as far as Cape

Froward, through two narrows where one has to wait for a let-up from the prevailing westerly winds. But elsewhere in the Broad Reach the seaway is relatively wide, permitting tacks of a reasonable length: and the shores are not yet mountainous, so that the force of the wind and the down-draughts are not usually entirely unpredictable, though even here the tides are very strong, and the bottom very foul with jagged rocks. Anchoring is often necessary, and very hard on hempen cables. The ships of that day could carry only six anchors at most, and when they were lost the ship was helpless.

After Cape Froward conditions grew much worse, with a narrower, more tortuous passage, swifter currents and numerous projecting reefs. The shores became a tangle of cliffs and mountains which split up the wind into furious squalls from various and unpredictable directions. Yet the main force of the wind was always from the west, and therefore, for any east-bound passage, dead contrary. The available anchorages were so few and far between that it was often necessary to run for long distances in the wrong direction before it was possible to stop and drop anchor. In this part sails were torn, anchors dragged or lost, timbers shattered, and men's hearts broken by unremitting toil, on a diet at best of seal-flesh and penguin, and at worst on mussels and limpets.

Timing was all-important. One had to arrive during the brief southern summer—the only time when success was even possible. To reach Cape Virgins too late in that summer meant no hope for the slackening of the westerly gales. To wait for the next season meant wintering in a Patagonian harbour, with inevitable loss of morale to the crews, or beating back to Brazil with the virtual certainty of never facing the Straits at all—for wintering in Brazil was soon found tantamount to abandoning the attempt altogether. Exceptionally, both Magellan and Drake wintered near the eastern entrance to the Straits, but both had to quell a mutiny before they could proceed. Fenton and many others wintered in Brazil and then gave up.

Even with the best commanders the thing was really a matter of luck. John Davis, for example, was unsurpassed in leadership, courage and technical skill. He actually got right through, but then a prolonged gale drove him back into the straits, and

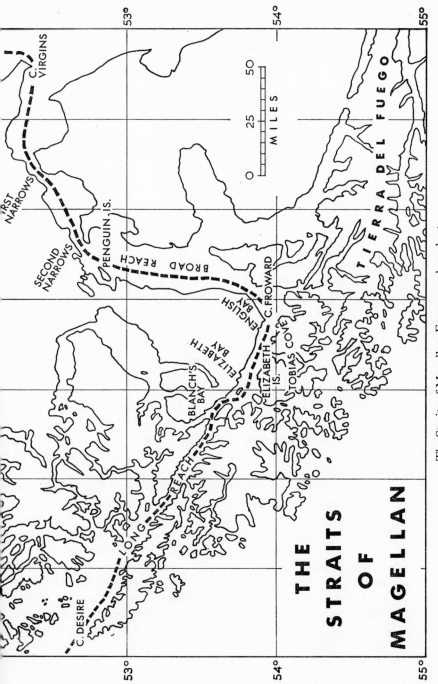

The Straits of Magellan. From a modern chart

persisted until his stores and anchors gave out. Cavendish was a callous slave-driver who thought nothing of marooning his men to conserve his victuals. He was lucky the first time, in 1586, but on his second attempt in 1591 with Davis as his second, he gave up before the greater humanity of his partner.

Magellan took thirty-seven days to get through. Drake was exceedingly lucky, and took only sixteen days; but, as soon as he got clear, he was driven back in a south-easterly direction—right over the ground which he *thought* was solid earth. He had in fact discovered—but it is doubtful whether he realized it at the time—the existence of Cape Horn: that, in fact, the Straits were not the only way through from Atlantic to Pacific, with South America to the north and the Great Southern Continent to the south. Cavendish took fifty-one days, and Richard, blown back several times when all but through, made it at last in forty-six days.

The mere fact of getting through at all entitles Richard to a very high place among sixteenth-century navigators.

d. THE LAST FIGHT OF THE 'DAINTIE'

Let us have done, then, with Richard the administrator, the navigator, the technician, the theorist, the scholar, the *authority*, and view him simply as a leader of men, in his supreme hour showing himself the equal of any Englishman of his day, or of any day: in courage certainly, but also probably in skill. Yet we must still help him because to the last he will not help himself. His ingrained honesty impels him to report his failures as well, and as fully, as his successes. Only so will he receive his due. Was Drake never guilty of mistakes of battle? Of course he was. But, since he was no author—nor, let us face it, either so modest or so relentless a truth-teller—we seldom learn what they were. But Richard omits nothing, excuses nothing, slurs over nothing. Everything is set down plainly for all to read who want to.

Fine reading it is too, though overlong to report fully. Nor perhaps is a close report so necessary as it would have been had so many of us moderns not been brought up on the story of the *Revenge*; for the two tales are in most respects so remarkably alike that it will often serve to dwell upon the differences, taking the similarities for granted.

VI. Sir Richard Hawkins. From a reproduction in Mary Hawkins's
Plymouth Armada Heroes

VII. Sir Francis Drake. By courtesy of the Plymouth Corporation

Richard was right again: the alarm of his coming outstripped him, and gave his enemy ample time to prepare an Armado to receive him. When he first met it—off Chincha in latitude 15° S. —it consisted of six ships, most of them superior to his own in every way. But at this first meeting the Spaniards sadly botched their business through defective seamanship. The admiral, Don Beltran de Castro, managed to snap his mainmast: the vice-admiral split his mainsail, the rear-admiral cracked his main-yard. Only one enemy reached a station from which he could attack; and he thought better of it, hauled off and rejoined the three lame ducks. The *Daintie* extricated herself with ease and proceeded northwards along the coast.

None the less, quite indecisive as this first round had been, it boded ill for Richard, and that for two reasons. First, had it come to close quarters, he would certainly have discovered his gunner's incompetence, or treachery, and he would have reme-died things before the real clash came. This, of course, he was not to know till later: but another circumstance he did discover, and, to such a seaman as he, it must have seemed sinister indeed. All the Spanish ships, he found, could sail more close-hauled than he could, so that, theoretically, they would always be able to dictate the tactics of any future fight.

Here we come upon the first great difference between his action and Grenville's. The *Revenge* had the legs of every single unit in the 'fifty-three'; so that, had Grenville desired it, he could have kept the wind at will, and so dictated the whole affair. But the *Daintie*, though to windward when the enemy was first sighted, soon found herself literally surrounded by the Spaniards, to windward, to leeward, ahead and astern. The *Revenge*, it is true, ultimately got into this position. But that hardly signifies. She need not have got into it: the *Daintie* could not avoid it. What this meant to Richard was that he must face the prospect of being boarded: and here indeed was reason to make the staunchest nerve quiver; for in the Armado there were 'well neere two thousand men', while for effective fighting the *Daintie* had—seventy-five!

For the moment, however, she was safely away, and Richard's narrative reveals but little sign of trepidation in either com-mander or ship's company. The crew probably exaggerated

the ineptitude of their foe, and Richard would be too wise a
leader to scare them. Yet—more unexpectedly—even he seemed
content to carry on as though no enemy were about. He simply
sailed northwards, looking into the ports as he passed them and
chasing any sail he met at sea—again with significant ill-success.
Even the local merchant shipping could out-weather him and
escape. He made no attempt to get out of it while he could: and
indeed his only alternative to accepting battle would have been to
turn south again, out of sight of the land, and to leave the Pacific
altogether. Evidently he was not prepared to do that; nor,
necessarily, would his people have allowed it. All the negative
evidence points to the fact that such a way out never crossed his
mind. In his very full disquisition he would certainly have mentioned it if it had. The more likely explanation is that he himself, though by now aware of his inability to fight his ship on his
own terms, thought, like his people, that the Spaniards had
neither the seamanship nor the will to tackle him seriously.

He was wrong. Don Beltran de Castro was in fact a very
determined man who after his initial fiasco, was more determined than ever to bring the English interloper to book. That
resolution, though Richard could not know it then, had been increased a hundredfold by the reception accorded to him and his
men when they limped empty-handed back to Callao, the port of
Lima.

> They were so mocked and scorned by the women as scarce anyone
> by day would show his face: they reviled them with the name of
> cowards and *golnias*, and craved licence of the vice-roy to bee admitted
> in their roomes, and to undertake the surrendry of the English shippe.

Such insults were not to be borne by Spanish pride, and
Viceroy and Admiral between them made a very wise decision.
They cut the Armado down to its two strongest ships and a pinnace, and into these they put all their best men, soldiers,
mariners, gunners: all the best stores, artillery, ammunition;
and Beltran led them out again to purge themselves of their
women's scorn. The Admiral, Richard tells his father in a letter
written to him from captivity[1] was of much the same size,
weight and armament as Sir John's own ship in the Armada
campaign—the *Victory* of 800 tons as against the *Daintie*'s 350—

[1] In an Appendix to *The Observations* (Argonaut Press edition).

while the Vice-Admiral was more or less the size of his own ship. Unquestionably the second Armado was much the more formidable of the two.

Let us consider for a moment this matter of odds. In contemplating the Azores fight, the mind is apt to be hypnotized by that famous 'fifty-three to one'. But a little reflection will show that they were quite uselessly long for the Spaniards' purposes. If it was to be an affair of boarding and 'hand-to-hand', as in the event both actions became, of what possible use were fifty-three? In fact, as Sir Walter Raleigh tells us, thirty-eight of them did not engage at all, while only two, or at the very most four, could conveniently board at any one time, And, if it was to be a question of broadsides, numbers were little if any more helpful, unless the enemy thought fit to fire indiscriminately upon friend and foe alike. In fact, when we come down to earth we find that by far the leading part in the destruction of Grenville's ship was taken by one man, Don Bernendona, who was the first to lay his ship aboard the English ship, clinging on with wonderful tenacity and shattering losses until the *Revenge* was enmeshed beyond hope. Anyway, in tackling the *Daintie*, Don Beltran must have felt that the odds were good enough. On his second sortie his numbers were reduced, it is true, from 2,000 to a mere 1,300, 'and those of the choise of Peru', but Richard still had only his seventy-five.

At length the day came; the Spaniards led on by almost hourly information of the *Daintie*'s whereabouts, the English making no attempt to avoid them. Battle was joined off the bay of San Mateo (or Atacames) on June 20, 1594.

At first sight it may well be wondered why Richard failed— indeed, hardly tried—to avoid a hand-to-hand encounter: for all our experience gleaned from the Armada action (in which, we recall, he had played quite a prominent part) seemed to favour a gun-duel. There, the English, with guns of lighter shot but of longer range, had deliberately kept their distance from the heavier, shorter-range fire of the Spaniards; and—with reservations—the policy had paid. Also, in 1588 the English had been seriously outnumbered in manpower: and they were even more seriously outnumbered now. This too, one would think, would have been a strong inducement to Richard to keep his distance.

In fact, however, the special conditions prevailing now gave him but little choice. Everything conspired to force him into 'push of pike', however much he might have preferred 'long-bowls'.

First, and foremost, he now knew that he *could* not keep the enemy at off-fighting distance, because of the superior weatherliness of their ships, where, in the Channel in 1588, the exact reverse had been the case. Second, though he was not outnumbered in guns to the same extent as in men, the enemy's artillery, he tells us, was still twice as numerous as his own. He also informs us, it is true, that it was not piece for piece so heavy. But this almost certainly means that it was of longer range. Thus, with the Spaniards' superior sailing, it was they, not he, who could choose the range: which would be—if they were wise enough to avail themselves of Armada experience—within their own longer range but outside his shorter range. In a gun-duel, therefore, there was very grave danger of his ship being battered to pieces with no real chance of retaliation. This is in fact what had happened to the only Spanish ships which succumbed in battle in 1588. In a word, the 'long-bowls' advantage had passed from England to Spain in Richard's battle.

Apart from all this, however, there was a third consideration, at the moment tragically cogent. Even as the enemy approached him, he discovered that, thanks to his precious gunner, he was in no position at all for off-fighting. It may well be, in fact, that this was the decisive factor in his mind. It remains possible that, up to this last terrifying discovery, he had intended to keep the fighting open. Yet probably not. There is one passage in the *Observations* which, though a little obscure, perhaps reveals his real intentions. If this be so, his object would seem to have been to encourage them to board, and to hope that he could blast them to pieces as they did so:

> Had our Gunner been the man he was reputed to be, and as the world sould him to me, she (Spain) had received great hurt by that manner of boarding. But contrary to all expectation, our stearne peeces were unprimed, and so were all those we had to leeward, save halfe one in the quarter; which discharged, wrought that effect in our contraries as that they had five or sixe foote water in hold before they suspected it.

His inference seems to be this: 'I did not mind Don Belfran

attempting to board me. I hoped he would; and I think I was right. For if those few guns of mine could so nearly do my business for me, what would have been the effect of my full battery—and a competent gunner? The Spaniards' rash way of boarding alone might have given me the victory.'

That, however, was not to be. They approached; were badly punished, but not stopped. They boarded.

Now Richard records another reason why he may have welcomed Don Beltran's attempt at a *coup-de-main*. It transpires that the *Daintie* was far better equipped than the enemy ships with 'close-fights'—that is, deliberately prepared anti-boarder defences within the ship itself. She was in fact a tight little fortress, with loop-holed 'cobridge-heads' (wooden bulkheads, defending if not both forecastle and poop, at least the poop.) Within this perimeter the whole English crew could assemble, invisible to the boarding enemy and immune from all the effects of his hand-gun fire, and while pouring out murderous vollies from point-blank range upon the completely exposed attackers. We learn also that the Spanish ships were not so fitted, but that, whenever they lay close alongside the *Daintie*, the English were able, in next to no time, to clear their decks of anyone rash enough to expose himself.

Certainly the Spaniards lost heavily in this phase. But they were determined, and well led. Moreover it was just on such occasions that they were at their best. Here of course it was the soldiers who were bearing the brunt, and throughout the whole of Spain's great days, her soldiers—the 'invincible' Spanish infantry—were by far her most formidable warriors.

None the less they failed. Twice they secured an entry: twice they were flung out. They retreated a little, cannonading their victim the while. But they soon returned for a third and even more determined assault. This time Don Beltran prepared to come in over the *Daintie*'s weather bow, having previously tried to enter her from the leeward side. (This, according to Richard, was at once unusual and inept.) In this new scheme, his Vice-Admiral, to avoid dispersal of force, was to board his superior's ship on its disengaged side, so that all the forces at the Spaniards' disposal could pour into the enemy in one irresistible wave. But the Vice-Admiral, no doubt seeking the glory

of conquering the foe all by himself, thrust in in front of his
senior and grappled the *Daintie* on her weather broadside. This
disobedience not only spoiled the whole plan: it proved quite
suicidal to the culprit, because his ship was

> utterly without fights or defences. What with our muskets, and what
> with our fire-workes, wee cleared her decks in a moment so that
> scarce any person appeared.

and all this without his 'brasse balls of artificial fire, his six
slur-bowes with their hundreth bals'!

Indeed just then, he says, as few as a dozen Englishmen
could have carried the Vice-Admiral. But he does not blame himself for not allowing it because, with the odds as they still were,
any such division of force would have been most unwise. He
was doubtless right. He would inevitably have lost that precious dozen in the counter-attack even then impending from the
infuriated Admiral. That sensible man, thwarted of his chance
to reach the *Daintie*'s weather bow by the great length of the
Vice-Admiral which overlapped the *Daintie*, still lay just to
windward. At this juncture, in fact, Don Beltran did the only
possible thing. He boarded his Vice-Admiral on her free windward side, and extricated her from her predicament. His scheme,
however, was ruined. His subordinate's casualties in both ship
and men were too crippling for further immediate action. He
ordered both his ships to haul off, and the great assault had
failed, with losses which would have been fatal had the odds
been more equal. At this moment, in fact, in his long uphill
climb to safety, Richard was at the highest point he ever reached.
The Spanish ships now stood off a little, and fell back upon gunfire for the rest of the battle. Don Beltran had had his lesson. He
would have been wiser to have relied on superior range and
sail-power from the start.

Here the first day ended, and the first phase. Let us return to
the similarities between the fights of the two Richards. At this
stage we may surely quote *A Ballad of the Fleet* verbatim, and
still report the *Daintie*'s action with complete accuracy:

> And the Spanish fleet with broken sides lay round us all
>   in a ring;
> But they dared not touch us again, for they feared that
>   we still could sting.

There were of course differences of detail. The ring surrounding Grenville was, for what that is worth, much the more substantial: but Grenville, with longer-ranging and better guns than the enemy, was in a better posture to answer back, at any rate so long as his ammunition lasted. Again, Grenville was in his predicament, one might almost say, from choice: Hawkins in his from necessity. Still, whatever the cause there they were, both untaken and, by boarding anyway, apparently untakable; but both so crippled aloft as to be virtually immobile. In both of them powder and shot were all but expended: in both the casualties were gradually reducing the survivors to impotence. At this point in the respective fights, in fact, the conclusion of the action was foregone: in both it was only a question of time.

Yet it is just here, *in* that question of time, that our Richard gains a clear lead over the other Richard. Let us take up his story and see.

All through the night the Spaniards kept up a desultory fire; which, from the prudent range of their choice, probably did no great damage; but meanwhile, of course, the shorter-carrying English guns did even less. Then Don Beltran began to grow impatient. He was perhaps thinking of those horrid rude women in Lima. Besides like all the Spanish sea commanders, he preferred hand-to-hand to long bowls, which seemed to him somehow ignoble. He was, however, sufficiently prudent not to persist in his first expensive policy, and he could hardly fail to see that he still held practically all the trumps. The English corsair was now too damaged to run; and even if she could, had really nowhere to run to. But still he chafed at the delay, and as soon as dawn came he sent in to parley, offering what under the circumstances were quite generous terms: what Richard calls 'a buena querra'; that is, *'en buena guerra'*, involving surrender, but promising quarter and a fixing of suitable ransoms by agreement.

Just before the offer was made, however, the English had suffered certain crippling losses. The *Daintie's* Master, Cornish, a very good man and in Richard's complete confidence, now 'had one of his eyes, his nose and halfe his face shot away'. At much the same moment Master Henry Courton, a volunteer and a firm friend of the General, had been slain; and, worst of all, the General himself, Richard Hawkins, had

> received six wounds; one of them in the neck very perillous; another through the arme, perishing the bone, and cutting the sinews close by the arme-pit; the rest not so dangerous.

True there remained the captain, in personal command of the ship; Richard, as general, commanded the whole expedition. John Ellis was a good enough man, as events were to prove, but not perhaps quite of the timbre of that trio so cruelly disposed of.

Richard himself nowhere says how he came by these hurts. But there survives a contemporary Spanish narrative by one Garcia Hurtado Mendoza, and his account of what happened is so typical of the spirit of the age that it is most likely true. As the second morning dawned, Don Beltran's flagship—presumably manoeuvring for a better position, not with any intention of further boarding—chanced to pass so near to the *Daintie* that to Richard, who was on her deck, there was suddenly presented an opportunity of being able to reach, and secure, the greatest prize of all, the Spanish admiral's royal standard. Calling therefore for a running bowline, he neatly lassoed it—and tugged. This, in those times, was just the kind of swaggering gesture expected of a dashing commander: and we can only suppose that to Richard, in spite of his constitutional good sense, the temptation was irresistible. (*Autre temps, autres moeurs!* Only imagine their Lordships' faces on learning of a like spree on the part of their Admiral Cunningham!) Yet, on the whole, the lapse is somehow gratifying. The danger hitherto has been to make Richard appear too perfect a paragon.

Yet it was a suicidal risk to take: like thrusting one's hand, ungloved, into a hornets' nest. The reaction was swift and inevitable. Out rushed the most redoubtable of the hornets:

> Diego di Avila, Juan Manrique, Pedro de Reinalte, Juan Velasquez, and others came to the rescue and defended it valorously. The Englishman paid for his audacity by two wounds, one in the neck and the other in the arm, both received from gunshots.[1]

[1] *The Hawkins Voyages* (Hakluyt Society, 1878), p. 345. This account, purely for Spanish consumption, differs so often and so widely from that in the *Observations* that no attempt has been made to reconcile them. Here in the main Richard's own account is used.

None the less, Don Beltran was Castilian enough to admire immensely the madcap gallantry of it. Doubtless it is exactly what he would have done himself; and, for ever afterwards, he held his erstwhile enemy in the highest esteem.

Yet the English had paid too dearly: there was only one Richard Hawkins. He was carried below in great pain and, though thereafter he seems to have been conscious all the time, never relinquishing the command, he came no more upon deck.

One of the first to visit him below was the captain, Ellis, bearing Don Beltran's message of parley. The poor man was clearly shaken, perhaps through lack of sleep and by his leader's fall; certainly by what his own eyes revealed to him, the ever-growing damage to the ship, the mounting casualties among his men. He therefore recommended accepting the offer, especially as (according to him) the gentlemanly Don Beltran had made one very important concession, well beyond the normal *'en buena guerra'* contract. He had promised to send all the Englishmen home, the better sort only to pay ransom.

No one needs to be reminded what the other Richard said when his story reached this point. It was simply (in effect), 'To Hell with the whole brood of Spaniards whom you can't trust anyway! Fight on! We'll never surrender!' And now *our* Richard said precisely the same thing—only, rather unfortunately, when he came to write it down twenty-eight years later, he allowed it to cover several pages. And indeed a very eloquent, well-composed plea it is, including a Latin tag or two and several most apposite historical parallels. It is a great pity that he should have let his literary talents run away with his pen at this solemn juncture; for nothing could be more absurdly unrealistic than the picture which he contrives to paint: himself in agony and barely conscious, the dead and dying lying around him; the anxious captain soliciting a prompt reply; the haughty Don above, importunately awaiting it; and Richard quoting parallels and precedents!

Yet, though the verbiage rings patently false, its gist is equally certainly true. The sequel abundantly proves it. Richard refused to consider any composition. We can only apply the acid test of results.

Here indeed the two stories which we have been following take very different turns: and they reveal with startling clarity the cardinal differences in the characters of the two Richards. With the headstrong Grenville, obviously, it is all or nothing. 'Fight on! Fight on!' he cries, so long as such a course is in any sense feasible. But then comes the moment when, transparently, it is not: and Grenville, as resolved as ever not to give in, switches right over in one move from 'Fight on' to 'Sink her! Split her in twain! If we can't keep her, by God Spain shall not have her either!' But—since most men are not Grenvilles, nor even pale replicas of him—this is altogether too strong meat for most people: for his own captain, for instance, and for his master. Then at once two parties are formed, a pro-surrender party and an 'anti'. They argue it out: but from the first the dice are loaded. The champion of the 'anti's', though undoubtedly much the strongest personality on board, lies below, immobile, in fact dying. His staunchest ally, the immortal gunner, does his best, but cannot prevail against his superiors, the captain and the master, who go round the ship's company canvassing for surrender. And inevitably they win. When invited to make the supreme sacrifice ordinary men, however brave, require a strong and, above all, an undivided lead. Possibly Grenville, had he been on deck, could have provided it. But he was not there: the 'pros' had a nearly clear run, and, as Raleigh puts it,

[of] the common sort . . . the men drew back from Sir Richard and the Master Gunner, [it] being no hard matter to dissuade men from death to life.

So, early in the morning of the day after the fight had started, they surrendered. They had been fifteen hours at it, and had sustained the individual assaults of fifteen ships for that period— with, of course, an unpleasant and unused reserve of thirty-eight looking on. No one can, or should be blamed; not even the captain and the master. In an age when 'fair composition' was quite honourable, the exception was not these men, but Grenville.

The *Daintie's* story, however, runs quite differently; or rather, perhaps, it includes at this point a phase which has no counterpart in the *Revenge's*. For, at this point, where Grenville failed Hawkins succeeded; not because his was the stronger character, but because he was the more reasonable, the more perceptive, the more in tune with his people: and probably the more persuasive. He did not dramatize the situation. His was no call to heroic extremes. He did not say, 'There's no other course but to die: so *die*!'—though very likely he thought there was no other way. He said, 'Carry on with the fight. That is your clear duty as Englishmen.' He held out no particular hope of salvation, but at the same time did not present them with no alternative but certain and violent death. He told the captain, and through him the whole ship's company, 'You have served me faithfully hitherto, and to the best of my ability I have served you. Don't spoil it all now, when you're in danger and I'm down and out. Go on serving me and your country.' Both of them say, 'Fight on!'

Here is the measure of his triumph. He carried the captain with him and, with the captain, the whole company. It does not really matter what words he used: it is what *happened* that counts, and this is certain. His conversation with Ellis must have taken place, roughly, in the early morning of the second day, when his fight had been in progress, like Grenville's, for some fifteen hours. The captain—and let us by no means underestimate him either—departed convinced, and somehow contrived to convince everyone else on board: to such tune that

> in accomplishment of this promise and determination, they persevered in sustaining the fight, all this night, with the day and night following and the third day after. In which time the enemy never left us, day nor night, beating continually upon us with his great and small shott . . . the enemie being ever to windward and wee to lee-ward, their shott much damnifying us, and ours little annoying them.

Here is indeed a profound difference between *Revenge* and *Daintie*. In the one, fatal division: in the other complete unity: no parties, no 'pro-surrenders'. From now until the end there is apparently no whisper of defection, no looking-over-the-shoulder. Nor, during the whole of that time, was Richard once upon deck to hearten his people. Here surely is the surest manifestation of leadership; lacking, no doubt, the heroic incandescence of Grenville's, yet not less, but definitely more, effective. From his bed of pain far below Hawkins retained control where, from his, Grenville lost it.

It must not be overlooked, however, that this two-days-and-a-night interlude is extra to the Hawkins story. After that, the similarities reappear. But it does speak volumes for both general and men: it certainly goes far towards obliterating Richard's regretable literary lapse (of 1622) and firmly establishes him as a great battle-leader (in 1594).

But the thing was a partnership. Richard stands vindicated. What of the other half—the men? He has enabled us to watch them closely for a full year, and certain characteristics stand out, clearly revealed. They were very typical of the English crews of their day, and, for all their obvious limitations, they were very good: entirely uneducated; apt, sheeplike, to get silly collective notions into their heads and, mule-like, to relinquish them most reluctantly; brave to the point of folly sometimes, full of superstitious fears at others; soaring to heights of confidence, quickly passing into abysses of despair: childlike in their simplicity sometimes, at others suspicious and grasping beyond belief: yet evidently leadable—by the right man—and, when so led, as invincible as does not matter. Richard had shown many times already that he was the right man, and this last fight is the supreme proof of it.

His people's strengths and weaknesses emerge as the fight proceeds. They begin in a spirit of bravado, hardly restrained from doing the stupidest of things: rushing upon the enemy without forethought or preparation of any kind; 'vaunting and bragging' of what they were going to do to him:

> One promised that he would cut downe their mayne yard; another that hee would take their flagge . . . others into wishings that they had never come out of their countrey if they should refuse to fight with two shippes whatever.

Once the show started, however, and there was no time for boasting, they acquitted themselves like what they really were, true-hearted men. Once their blood was up, they had no equals.

This was during the boardings and the close-work. But then came the pause, and the offer to parley. Blood cooled, odds were calculated and found to be (as in very truth they were) all but impossible—and they clamoured for the captain to go to the general and tell him so. Here it would be interesting to know more of Captain Ellis; for it was he who, once convinced by Richard, had to go back and face the people who sent him. We do not know what he said: we only know how nobly he succeeded; which in its turn can only mean that he too was a fine leader. Anyway, one somehow feels, he cut the quotations and the precepts to the bone: and anyway, the immediate loyalty and co-operation which he secured was complete. For the moment morale was very high.

Gradually, however, a crack of quite a different kind began to show in that morale. It was in no way due to any lack of loyalty towards their wounded leader: but it was due, almost certainly, to the existence of those wounds—and to the absence of the good master, Cornish, and the trusted volunteer, Courton. Evidently the ship was now under-officered, under-led. Somehow—and obviously he was in no position to know exactly why—the drink began to circulate unduly, and true courage to degenerate into Dutch courage. Richard thus quaintly reports what happened:

> For after I was wounded . . . the pott, continually walking, infused desperate and foolish hardinesse in many, who blinded by the fume of the liquor, considered not of any danger, but thus and thus would stand at hazard, some in vaine glory vaunting themselves, some other rayling upon the Spaniards, another inviting his companion to come and stand by him, and not to budge a foote from him; which indiscreetly they put in execution, and cost the lives of many a good man, slaine by our enemies muskettiers who suffered not a man to show himself but they presently overthrew him.

They meant well, poor souls. What they lacked was an officer who could be everywhere at once, controlling not their essential bravery but their senseless bravado.

As things stood, though, it was not good enough. Every single man who could keep his feet was now worth his weight in gold. A war of attrition could end in only one way. Yet still the dwindling band stuck it out. For twenty-three out of every twenty-four hours, Richard says, the unremitting cannonade went on; and, from his mention of the enemy's musketeers, it seems certain that as the English guns fell silent, either through damage or exhaustion of ammunition, so they could reduce their range, with guns of all sizes.

It could not last. Details may perhaps be omitted: indeed must be, because the general, in his physical and mental hell below, did not witness many of them, and so fails to report them fully. Yet once or twice, as Richard was to discover afterwards, the English were nearer to delivery than they knew. The Spaniard was having his crises too. Thus sometime before the end came, the enemy's flagship was all but dismasted. Two (in one place Richard claims three) of our round-shot lodged in his fore-mast, and

> had either of them entered but four inches further into the heart of the maste, without all doubt it had freed us, and perhaps put them in our hands.

But it was not to be. Maybe only four inches separated victory from defeat, but defeat at last it was.

> The third day, in the afternoone, which was the 22nd of June 1594[1] according to our computation, and which I follow in this my discourse, our sayles being torne, our mastes all perished, our pumpes rent and shot to peeces, and our shippe with fourteene shot under water and seven or eighte foote of water in hold; many of our men being slaine, and the most part of them which remayned sore hurt, and in a manner altogether fruiteles, and the enemie still offering to receive us *en buena querra*—

everybody on deck, officers and men alike, and still with no dissidents, at length, and altogether, gave up hope. When the sad truth had to be conveyed to the general, still lying below more dead than alive, it is significant, as it is certainly pathetic, that Captain Ellis, surviving yet, could not bring himself to the task, but sent down Richard's own trusty body-servant to break the news. When the truth was out, Richard, very low now and convinced of imminent death, still refused to give the word, but at last agreed to leave the final decision to the captain; not as evading his responsibility, but because, whatever benefit might accrue to the survivors, he was now convinced that he would not

[1] Markham (*The Hawkins Voyages*, p. 343) seems to challenge this date, deciding that it ought to be July 2nd. Actually, however, Richard is perfectly right; for he says, 'in our computation', which was, of course, that of the Julian Calendar still used in this country until the 1750s. It was then ten days ahead of the Gregorian Calendar already used in Spain. Thus Markham (though wrong in casting doubt upon Hawkins's date) was right about July 2nd—or would have been had he stated that he was using the Gregorian (or Spanish) Calendar, which we all use today.

be one of them, and therefore felt that he should not impose upon them sufferings which he himself would never share. Then of course the captain surrendered.

Yet even so there was at the last a faint echo about the *Daintie* of Grenville's robust 'Sink her! Split her in twain!': for on surrendering, the remnant of her people, reduced now from their original seventy-five by nineteen dead and nearly forty wounded, stationed one dauntless man in the hold determined, should the Spaniards depart one hair's breadth from Don Beltran's generous terms, to plunge a torch into the remaining powder, and blow the company, their conquerors and the *Daintie* herself sky-high. Fortunately, however, the enemy decided for once to play fair. Perfidy held no place in Beltran's nature. He sent a high-ranking officer of his own expressly to protect the English general, and to see that no one else was molested. Then Richard was carefully conveyed to the Spanish flagship where Don Beltran in person received him—'with great courtesy and compassion, even with tears in his eyes, and words of great consolation'.

Clearly Richard lacked the berserk streak which shot through his fiery namesake. So he never talked of wholesale immolation of ship and people together. Nor, of course, was his gunner of the calibre of Grenville's. Clearly ship-splitting was not his line at all! Yet when Captain Ellis 'made his composition', the *Daintie* was worse off than the *Revenge* at her corresponding moment, even by the computation of the *Revenge's* surrender-party. To Grenville's last appeal they had replied that 'the ship had six foot water in hold, three shot under water, which were so weakly stopped as with the first working of the sea she needs must sink'. This is to be set against the *Daintie's* 'seven or eight foote water in hold' and 'fourteene shott under water.'

Yet to the last the older Richard had the luck of the hero stakes. The *Revenge* did sink: the *Daintie* did not. But with neither of these results had either Richard anything to do. The *Revenge* went down because she was called upon, almost at once, to face a full Atlantic gale, and (had she managed that) to make a long ocean-trip to Spain: and she managed neither, having never been, as we have seen, noted for her sea-worthiness. But

the *Daintie*, an admirable sea-boat, had the much kindlier
Pacific to deal with, fair weather and a much easier and safer
voyage. Even so, we learn, she would not have done it but for
the superlative skill of one Miguel Anjel Filipon (Richard calls
him Michaell Angel), an expert ship-salvager by profession,
who for his outstanding services on this occasion was rewarded
by King Philip himself; and who had no counterpart at all in the
Revenge story. So it comes about that Grenville, fighting
gloriously, dies appositely—always the tactful thing for any
would-be English hero to do if he wants the full applause of his
countrymen (*vide* Moore and Nelson): and, though his ship is
surrendered, he does not have the ultimate stigma of the enemy
possessing her. But poor Hawkins, though he fights gloriously
too, lives, not only to become a prisoner but also to have it
recorded of him that Spain got, and kept, his ship.

In fine, let it be repeated, it is not that Grenville has received
too much credit: it is only that Hawkins received too little! It
should be clear by now that, in terms of endeavour and pure
gallantry, there was not much to choose between their epic
fights. If we give Grenville the palm on the grounds of numbers
of the enemy, and 'on paper', there are still two counter-weights
to weigh down the scales on Hawkins's side. First, the *Revenge*
was a Queen's Ship, a true warship, designed from birth for
fighting; bigger,[1] much more heavily gunned and (relative to
the opposition) a far better sailer than the *Daintie* which, though
a somewhat exceptional one, was after all only a merchantman.
Second, where the Queen's ship lasted fifteen hours, the
merchantman lasted at least four times as long.

In conclusion, it is perhaps worthwhile to ask why the sailing performance of the *Daintie* fell so far short of that of the
enemy in the fight. The Spaniards, we must remember were
always good shipbuilders and ship designers—once they learnt
what was required of them. And in this case the lessons of the
Armada fight six years earlier had been quickly and thoroughly
taken to heart by Philip of Spain. This probably explains why
the *Daintie*—a merchantman still, even if rather a superior one—
was so outsailed by the Spanish warships which she met: for the

[1] The question of Elizabethan tonnage is a vexed one. We shall probably not
be far out if we assess that of the *Revenge* at 500 tons, and of the *Daintie* at 350.

requirements of sea-commerce must always have detracted from the performance of any merchant ship when opposed by true warships. What is harder to explain is why the *Daintie's* sailing fell so far short, not only of the enemy's warships, but also of their everyday merchantmen too: for these also seemed capable of hugging the wind a good deal more closely than she could. To account for this is difficult. Probably the reason lies in the fact that the English ship had already sailed half round the world, and for that reason stood in need of a refit more than did the local merchantmen, which were all fresh from port. In fact she probably needed a thorough scraping of sea-growths from her bottom—the kind of service which could only be carried out by large repairs which were impossible to make off a hostile coast, where no careening facilities were available. Could Richard have achieved that, the results might have proved very different. Excuses, however, avail but little, and Richard was not the man to descend to them. The *fact* is inescapable: the *Daintie* was taken.

e. BEFORE AND AFTER THE FIGHT

It is curiously difficult to envisage a *young* Richard Hawkins. This is primarily because almost all our knowledge of him reaches us through the *Observations*, which is essentially the work of a greybeard. But of course, not only was he once young: he was still young when he made his famous voyage: thirty-three when he started, thirty-four when he fought Don Beltran. And already most, though not all, of his active service lay behind him; most of that remarkable store of experience on which he draws so lavishly in his book. Certainly the Elizabethan seamen matured early and, no doubt as a corollary, seldom reached ripe old age. Outside the *Observations* material for his life is quite exceptionally thin—a passing reference from other writers here, an extract from surviving public records there: a few—a very few—letters; virtually no *human* material. Even the present attempt at straight biography owes much to incidental passages in that book wherein from time to time he fortunately ranges beyond his immediate affairs.

Richard Hawkins, then (who of all the clan was destined to be the interpreter of his great father), was essentially a chip off the old block, though a more highly polished chip than the others. Still, he was the same type of man; and, like all the rest, almost certainly Plymouth-born, his mother having given him birth in 1560, just after the winding-up of the William–John partnership, but before the exigencies of John's life had brought him more or less permanently to London. So, unlike the others, though Plymouth-born he was not exactly Plymouth-bred, having passed the formative years of his youth with his parents in one of their new homes: mainly, probably, in the City house at St Dunstan's-in-the-East, but interspersed with periods passed on Thames-side at Deptford; and occasionally, after he had reached his seventeenth year, residing for a while in the dockyard at Chatham on the Medway.

We do not know the nature of his schooling, but we may be very sure that it equalled any which the London of that day could provide. Moreover, his after-life reveals him to have been a considerable scholar, reared (unlike grandfather and father) in the Classics, and a finished representative of the then comparatively new 'New Learning'. Of sheer learning, indeed, he possessed a much larger share not only than the rest of the family, but also than any of the great Elizabethan seamen, excepting only Raleigh, whose erudition exceeded Richard's. Yet with it all he *was* his father's son: his only son too, brought up by him with all that parent's love and interest in the sea, and the ships which use it. The only known portrait of him—and that an indifferent one—reveals a certain likeness to his father. But the face is rather more sensitive, perhaps more scholarly; and there is on it an expression of wonderment, almost of surprise, which does not appear at all in the portraits of Sir John. It is, in some odd way, rather a modern face, though that may be due only to the artist's treatment of it: and, of course, it may not represent Richard at all.

By 1582 he was twenty-two years old, and in that year took part in the expedition of his uncle William (see p. 66). So much is known, but only because he says so himself in his book, not because any other source thought fit to mention it. In that voyage he filled the post of vice-admiral to his uncle. This fact alone should make us chary of believing that it was his very first experience of ship life. In fact it almost certainly was not: he must already have learnt the ropes in one or more of his father's many ships. Indeed, on the analogy of his uncle and his father, he had very likely known the sea-life for as much as nine or ten years before turning up as second-in-command.

His conduct on one occasion during that voyage is surely not that of a newcomer on shipboard. He tells the story himself. One of the ships developed a leak, and her captain—half-heartedly, the young man thought—suggested the clearing of her cargo and the scuttling of her. This was about to be done when Richard piped up, and 'being more bold than experienced', offered to take the leaky vessel home himself, thus shaming her captain into vowing that nothing should induce him to desert his ship. So it was saved and brought safely home, to live afterwards to a ripe old age. For his conduct on that occasion his uncle commended him, evidently agreeing with his nephew about the pusillanimity of the captain.

Next, it is known that he went with Drake to the West Indies in 1585, having the command (though a very small one) of the *Duck Galliot*. That is all—save, ironically enough, a snippet of news about him as the expedition returned. His minute craft, a vessel of only 20 tons, and probably propelled by oar as well as sail, was driven by a gale into Mount's Bay, whence Richard, by a very swift journey overland to Exeter, contrived to be the first to announce the return of the expedition.

By 1588 he was considered worthy of the command of one of the Queen's Ships, the *Swallow*, of 360 tons. Here, though no surviving dispatch or letter mentions Richard by name, we can deduce a little. The *Swallow*, with her twenty-eight year-old captain, was in the thick of the fighting off Portland in the second big encounter; and in the culminating action off Gravelines (as perhaps we should expect) in his father's own division and in close support of him. Each of these allusions amounts to honourable mention, so that at least he did himself credit—as again we should expect.

Towards the end of this same year of 1588, that expedition which he deals with in the *Observations* was first mooted, as a joint enterprise between father and son and it was then that the *Daintie* was laid down. But for reasons of state the venture was held up, and in 1590 Richard was commanding the *Crane*, another small ship in his father's expedition to the coast of Portugal. Later that year, when his father went out to the Azores, he was with him as second-in-command, sailing in the Queen's Ship, the *Nonpareil*. No voyage is recorded between this one and his departure for the Southern Seas in June, 1593. But he may have been afloat again, for certainly the *Daintie* was serving off Portugal in 1590 and again in 1592 at the Azores. One thing, however, he certainly did do during the interval: he got married, to one Judith Hele, who came from a West Country merchant family. When he left for South America they already had one child, a daughter named Judith after her mother, born in November 1592 at Deptford where Richard was busy upon the *Daintie*. There were five other children of the marriage: but, for obvious reasons, there is a gap of more than eleven years between Judith and the next.

Doubtless Richard was rather sad at not being captain of the *Daintie* in 1592, because in that year she was in the very thick things—things too which ought to have been highly profitable to her owners, the Hawkinses. She was the protagonist in the taking of the most valuable prize of the whole war, the fabulous and vast *Madre de Dios*. But somehow, for all that the *Daintie* was still owned by Richard and his father, neither managed to make a penny out of her: for though she bore the brunt, her injuries prevented her from being in at the death.

When the moment for starting at length came in 1593, Sir John, for all his sixty-one years, would have loved to embark again, but could not secure the Queen's consent to quit his responsible office. So Richard went alone.

And what were his real plans? It is not at all easy now to discover them. The start of his book is very sudden, with none of that gradual easing into his subject which is so usual in the books of the period. There are, of course, reasons for this. When captured by the Spaniards, he freely admitted the fact that he came simply to raid them: and indeed, seeing that he was actually caught in the act, there could be no reason to hide the fact. He pretended, however, that Peruvian gold and merchandise were his sole objectives. But clearly there was more to it than that. In fact his very first sentence reveals as much. There he says his intention was a voyage to be made for the Ilands of Japan, of the Phillipines, and Molucas, the kingdomes of China, and East Indies, by the way of the Straites of Magelan, and the South Sea.

A very different and much more ambitious undertaking than a mere raid upon Spanish America.

But then he shuts up like a clam and reveals no more. Doubtless his reason for this is that, when he published his book twenty-nine years later, the political scene, as he then saw it, had totally changed. The Great Queen was no more, and her successor, King James, had ended hostilities with Spain, who was now a potential friend, being courted by England. But the original Hawkins object had been, in all probability, nothing less than a full-scale empire-building plan based upon discoveries much further south than Japan or the Philippines (though, under *very* favourable circumstances these might have been attempted). But the *real* motive was to be discoveries which he hoped to make in or around the Great Southern Land ('Terra Incognita Australis' of the theorists). Such rather wild dreams had long intrigued not only the Hawkins family but many other prominent 'colonists' like Sir Richard Grenville and Sir Walter Raleigh.

By 1622, however, these objectives would only have the effect of alarming Spain, and therefore of antagonizing the rather pawky Scot who now presided over the destinies of both England and the Northern Kingdom. And, so late in life, Richard had no intention whatever of stirring up any more formidable enemies. So he simply suppressed his real motives before sending his manuscript to the printer, thus banishing utterly from the pages of history the real blue-print of all Hawkins aspirations.

For the year June 1593 to June 1954 we know (by comparison) very nearly everything there is to know about Richard. But that will not happen again, because the *Observations* brings the story only to the moment when, a prisoner at Panama, he is in a fair way to recover. He intended another volume, but it was never written; or, if written, never published and now lost. The result is that, once more, our material becomes scanty: some of it, indeed, little better than hearsay.

Enough survives,[1] however, to make it apparent that Don

---

[1] e.g. in *Hawkins Voyages, op. cit.,* p. 348, and in *Sir R. Hawkins' Observations* (Argonaut Press, 1933) with Intro. by J. A. Williamson.

Beltran had nothing whatever to be ashamed of. He behaved throughout like the gentleman he was: in fact he probably saved both Richard and his people from a shocking fate by quickly taking the only possible step. Soon after their arrival at Panama was known, the Inquisition made formal application for the bodies of the prisoners. It was a dangerous moment. They were Lutheran and therefore, unless they would publicly recant, liable to the stake. Don Beltran, however, anticipating some such demand, lost no time in introducing Richard to the Viceroy of Peru whose favour he instantly won by his youth, and gallant bearing in adversity—it would certainly seem that he had something of his father's charm. The Marquis of Cañete was, on his own territory, nearly all-powerful. But not quite. Even he could not defy the Inquisition. But, fortunately for the captives, he too was a gentleman; in fact a very highly-placed nobleman. Further, being a Spaniard, he knew all about *mañana*. From the first he took the secular view of what constituted proper behaviour, and not that of the ecclesiastics. Richard's captor had included repatriation in the composition terms, and Cañete regarded that as conclusive. No one, not even the Inquisition, had the right to make a Spanish gentleman break his word and pledge. He therefore informed the Inquisition that, in this case of conflicting loyalties, his mind was not clear. He must write to the fount of all authority, His Most Catholic Majesty, and await his commands.

Here was a reprieve, and a long one. With the English and French corsairs about, one did not just send off a single courier with a dispatch. One waited for the sailing of the annual Flota: and the answer would come back by the same medium. In fact, all but two years had passed since the fight before the Viceroy received His Majesty's commands; and, when they did arrive, they were thoroughly vague: quite vague enough anyway for Cañete, now Richard's firm friend, to declare that the only thing he could do was to send the prisoner home to Spain.

The crucial passage in the King's letter is not without interest. He was growing old, steadily working himself to death, and it almost looks as though he was losing grip. He begged the question entirely. 'You understand,' he wrote, 'that he (Hawkins) is a person of quality. In this matter I desire that Justice may be done conformedly to the quality of the persons.' The Inquisition, of course, interpreted 'quality' to mean 'state of soul': which, being heretical was also damnable, and liable to the extreme ecclesiastical penalty. But the Viceroy said no. 'Quality' means 'social status'; and therefore, Hawkins, being a gentleman, must have gentleman's justice: that is, that any promise made to him is inviolable. Further, as a gentleman he is ransomable, and should be sent to Spain there to negotiate over this important matter. Further still, if we let the Inquisition reduce this gentleman to cinders, what about that other gentleman—a Spanish one too, the gallant Don Beltran de Castro who has been at such pains to capture the English gentleman? In short, burn Hawkins, and who is going to settle Don Beltran's legitimate bill—Richard's ransom?

The Inquisition protested; but against such relentless logic it protested in vain, and to Spain Richard was sent. On the way another battle nearly engulfed him. As the Flota approached the Azores, it all but ran into the Earl of Essex, then conducting what, in our books, we call 'the Islands' Voyage'. Shots were exchanged, but the Spanish ships, carrying fabulous wealth on board, ran for it and got safely into Terceira, where the defences proved too strong for the English to break them. Richard's luck was out again. All his captors had to do was to sit tight until lack of provisions drove the English home. Then they sailed unmolested to Seville.

Up till now Richard's captivity had been quite mild. But there can be little doubt that, once in Spain, his treatment was thoroughly dishonourable. He was now, of course, beyond the protection of Cañete; but there seems to have been no further squabble with the Inquisition, so that, on the secular point, there was no reason for any delay in implementing the surrender terms. Indeed it seems that Don Beltran, now on excellent terms with Richard, had most handsomely remitted the ransom, requiring only a token one of 'a couple of greyhounds for me, and other two for my brother the Conde de Lemos'. Yet Spanish red tape, and greed, seems to have insisted on that ransom being paid. Though its rightful recipient may have been fool enough to say he did not want it, the Government had no such reservations! So poor Richard was (to quote old John Hortop's striking words) 'cast into the everlasting prison remedilesse': not at first, probably, herded into the common gaol at Seville like any male-factor, yet certainly closely locked up. Now Don Beltran re-appears. Hearing what had happened, he protested furiously and often; altruistically too. But, great man as he was when walking his quarter-deck in the Pacific, in Spain he carried no guns to speak of, and the protestations were all ignored.

What follows is far from clear. Probably, Richard grew weary of his confinement and, in September 1598, succeeded in escaping from the castle of Seville. But he was retaken and, presumably to punish him for such a crime, he was loaded with chains and thrown into a dungeon. Here he might have languished for ever: but, somehow, in August 1599 he got a letter smuggled through to England, and in 1600 another to France. In the first he wrote a pathetic appeal to Elizabeth, describing his plight, restating the services of himself and his late father, and imploring her to do something to help him. She certainly received this letter, but seems to have done nothing about it—perhaps indeed there was not much that she *could* do. His letter of 1600 got through to the English Ambassador in Paris. In it he begs him to try and move the Queen, giving the news, incidentally, that all his people but himself have now been released according to the composition. But still nothing came of it, though his letters from Spain, carried probably by renegade Englishmen, continued to arrive fairly regularly—there are no less than nine of them among the State Papers.

When 1602 dawned he was in Madrid, having been moved from Seville in 1599. He was still a close prisoner, though not, probably, housed in a dungeon. At last, however, a much more powerful advocate made his appearance. Someone—possibly the Paris Ambassador, but more likely the still-persisting Don Beltran—succeeded in catching the eye of a really important personage. Count Miranda, Viceroy of Naples and President of the Council, was one of the foremost grandees of Spain; and as soon as he thought fit to declare that the injustice perpetrated upon Richard was a blot upon Spanish honour, things began to move. Even so, however, there was some delay, due this time (if we may credit a further letter from the prisoner to the younger Cecil) to even dirtier work on the English side: so dirty that we can only hope the poor captive was misinformed or else, distraught in his misery, exaggerating. What he alleged was that Dame Margaret, his stepmother, was refusing to produce the sum of £3,000, left by his father for no other purpose but to pay his ransom. On receiving this letter, Cecil intervened at once; the ransom was paid, and Richard was allowed to come home.

The man who returned, late in 1602, was by no means broken in either body or spirit. He was still only forty-two, and he must have been greatly heartened by his reception. He was knighted in 1603 by the new sovereign and, next year, became Member of Parliament for Plymouth. In 1604, also, he received a further token of the King's belief in him. He was appointed Vice-Admiral of Devon, an office which was then by no means a sinecure.

In that post, however, he was far from happy. In fact he was already beginning to suffer from the malaise which was now over-taking all the surviving Elizabethans. Like them, not knowing it at first, he had left his Age behind him, and with it its standards and ideals. In Sir Richard's eyes the pacifist King was no sort of substitute for that Queen whom he and his father had so long and faithfully served. Indeed the Fates were unkind to all surviving Elizabethans, but particularly to Richard. His captivity had deprived him of almost everything which he deemed worth while: not only of nine of the best years of his life, but also of all that was left of the Great Queen's reign, the last decade of the Anglo-Spanish War, and his greatest opportunity. For he was now become essentially a man of war, unlikely to shine in a world of peace. Moreover, when he set out in high hopes in 1593, that world may well have looked to be at his feet. He was something like very the 'coming man'. The older generation who had hitherto made the running was patently wearing out—in fact, as we can see now, dying out: Grenville in 1591, Frobisher in 1594, Drake and John Hawkins in 1595. They would need replacing: and why should not Richard be their heir?

Well, what we, wise in our knowledge of history, know now could not be known then—that successors of the calibre of Francis Drake and John Hawkins never did quite emerge from the ruck to take their places. The new generation never quite 'made the grade'. Raleigh was too many-sided, and perhaps too self-centred: Essex altogether too mercurial, unpredictable: Lord Thomas Howard hardly had his whole heart in it, and soon gave up the sea for politics. Mansell, Monson and Leveson were lesser men.

But Richard did seem to have all the essentials—youth, courage, skill, judgement, common sense. With the experience in high command which would almost certainly have come his way if he had been available, would not he have made the highest grade? Who shall say?

And yet—but this of course is only one man's opinion—and yet, the more one looks at him, and admires what one sees, the more convinced one becomes that Richard would *not* have made it: not quite. There is always a gap, definable even when narrow, between talent and genius.

His sun, in fact, was past meridian even when he came home. We need not dwell overlong upon its setting. The times were changing, and they caught him napping even in his vice-admiraltyship. That strange and lawless union of Channel trade and privateering, which his grandfather had helped to start, was dying: indeed *had* died, though perhaps few realized it yet. Trade languished, privateering was already branded by law as Piracy. Richard seems to have been slow in tumbling to the new conditions. In his job he was charged with the duty of scotching the law-breakers, but certain suits in which he became involved indicate that he may have had a foot in both camps. There is no hint, as there was with Grandfather William, of his being piratical himself. Rather, perhaps, he was not being quite so zealous in bowling out malefactors as the Law thought he should be. After all, some of these new 'criminals' were his own life-long friends. Matters came to a head in 1609, when he was tried before an Admiralty court, sentenced to pay a heavy fine, and to be imprisoned until he paid it. But he still had friends, notably the old Lord Admiral Howard. He was soon released from prison, and very likely from the fine too.

After a time there came what looks like a pointer. He left the old Hawkins home in Plymouth, and went out to live at Slapton, 22 miles to the east in the rural depths of the South Hams. Thus a significant link was severed. His father's death abroad and his own long absence had left the family fortunes stewardless, and they never fully recovered. At Slapton he passed most of his remaining years quietly but happily enough, fathering his five younger children. The eldest boy, a younger John, did go to sea, but made no signal mark there.

Richard, however, was never entirely 'on the beach'. There was talk, as late as 1614, of his leading another expedition through the Straits of Magellan under the flag of the East India Company, who had ideas about exploiting the Solomon Islands. This sounds like a sort of recrudescence of the Hawkins plan, ruined by Sir Richard's capture in 1594. But it came to nothing. Again in 1617 his name crops up in the court minutes of the E.I.C., as being nominated to command the next fleet to the East; but he was passed over, mainly on account of age: or, just possibly, because he was not available. For there is some sort of hint that, in 1616, he may have made a voyage to Newfoundland. Seven of the returning ships, all merchant, were on this occasion taken by Barbary pirates, and it was thought at the time that Richard was in one of them. If so, the luckless man must have been once more loaded with chains. But this is very far from being a certainty: and, anyway, he was back in England by the end of 1617.

At last, however, he did land a job in 1620, and a rather important one too. He was appointed Vice-Admiral of a royal fleet under Sir Robert Mansell, sent out to the Mediterranean to punish the Algerians for their piracies. The expedition, like most of those which sailed in James I's day, was ill-equipped and, in many respects, shockingly mismanaged: and it failed miserably, though the Admiral was only partly to blame and the Vice-Admiral even less so. They returned to a sorry scene of cross-accusations and face-savings. There was no money for paying either officers or men, and everybody was busy shifting the blame upon someone else.

Evidently Richard, turned sixty now, ageing, weary, disillusioned, had had enough. He was summoned to London to attend one of the many privy councils where they were wrangling over these unsavoury topics. On April 16, 1622, he reached Town and, in his will, executed that day, described himself as 'sick and weak in body but of perfect mind and memory'. Next day, in the Council Chamber itself, he had a stroke of apoplexy and died almost at once—of sheer vexation, they said at the time.

Two months later the *Observations of Sir Richard Hawkins, Knight,* appeared: and now for the first time his countrymen could read the full story of the *Daintie*'s last fight, and see for themselves how very complete, whether in peace or in war, their Compleat Seaman was. To the last Fate had its sport of him, because Richard, for all that he was as modest a man as one could wish for, would surely have liked to know what his contemporaries thought of him as a seaman. Well, if we have but half the faith that he had, we shall believe that he *does* know; knows too what his grandchildren's great-grandchildren have come to think of his hero-father, whom he loved and so consistently honoured. And that must indeed delight old Richard's heart!

CHAPTER VI

William Hawkins III

༄༅༄

a. A KNAVE, VILLEYN AND A BOY

T H E last Hawkins of Plymouth to come up for review is John's nephew and William II's first-born son—the eldest of his large quiverful which he had by his two wives.

At once, however, we are faced by a novel difficulty. William Hawkins III of Plymouth is an established historical character about whom, up till Armada Year, much is known. Again, in 1607 a William Hawkins appears on the scene as a leading and important character in the story of the East India Company. This man too is an established historical character with a detailed and well-authenticated story to tell. The only doubt is whether these two William Hawkinses are the same man. Or are they separate men?

The weight of the evidence is that they are the same man. Indeed there is only one authority who declares that they were different men. But he is rather passionately convinced that he is right. The authority in question is Sir John Knox Laughton, a historian of the late nineteenth century whose views cannot lightly be set aside, if only because he wrote all but 1,000 articles on naval and maritime personalities for the *Dictionary of National Biography*. This was, of course, an immense feat, but it means that the resulting biographies are inevitably unequal in merit and in accuracy. That is only to be expected because, learned man and scholar as he undoubtedly was, he can hardly have put profound historical research into every article : and indeed his work does abound in errors. Other things being equal, the safest expert to follow would probably be the late Dr J. A. Williamson. But unfortunately he is not going to help greatly here because he deliberately hedges, dismissing the moot point in the words, 'but the identification of the two Williams is not strictly proven'. One gains the impression that he thought the two Williams were the same man, but, having read Laughton, he thought it expedient to be a little prudent about his own judgement. On the other hand, Clements Markham, the Hakluyt Society's editor of *The Hawkins Voyages*, accepts the men as being identical without even discussing the point. So does Mary Hawkins in her *Plymouth Armada Heroes*. Here, having mentioned the difficulty, this author will tell the stories of both men, which never overlap.

Mary Hawkins records, in her genealogical table, that William III was born 'about 1565'. But this is probably too late, perhaps by as much as five years. If his birth-date were 1560, he would have been of the same age as his cousin Richard, which seems about right. Unquestionably he had been one of the 'circumnavigators' who went round the world with Drake. If he were not born until 1565 this would mean that he embarked on that long voyage when only twelve years old: which (as was shown in the case of William II) is perfectly possible. It is his next known voyage, however, in which we should like to find him older, because he certainly sailed with Edward Fenton in 1582, and his position in that expedition was Lieutenant-General and second-in-command. In those days, where influence counted for so much, the paternal interest might well have served to secure the place at the age of twenty-two, which he would have been had he been born in 1560. But to have been Lieutenant-General and second-in-command of a big expedition at the age of seventeen is perhaps a little too much to believe. But that he *was* young at the time is clear enough because Fenton himself calls him a boy.

The whole voyage was botched from the beginning. The idea in its original form was to sail under Martin Frobisher, with Fenton as his Second. Frobisher was rather a quarrelsome person, and Fenton, though very well backed by, among others, the Muscovy Company, was a fussy and rather incompetent soldier, despised in the other Service. In the end Frobisher refused to go with Fenton, who was appointed in his place to the chief command. But there were dangerous undercurrents militating against success. There was Drake money invested in the undertaking, and Drake, just home from his trip round the globe, not unnaturally favoured another irruption into the Pacific, and plundering the Spaniards on the coast of Peru. The Hawkinses, though they did not subscribe, were all for a Pacific–Peruvian adventure too. But the Earl of Leicester, who provided the flagship—his own ship, the *Galleon Leicester*—and most of the cash, as well as appointing the leader, wanted, this time, a peaceful trading voyage, and issued the instructions to Fenton. He was to look, first, for a north-west passage leading from the Atlantic to the Pacific: but he was to proceed in his search only as far as lat. 40°N. Then, if he had failed to find it, he was to sail for the Moluccas in the East Indies by way of the Cape of Good Hope: and he was to *trade* all the way. He was further told, however, that he might finally go and discover the passage between Asia and North America. This then hypothetical passage was known as the Strait of Anian and is now, of course, called the Behring Strait.

At this point Drake (and the Hawkinses) succeeded in securing representation on the higher command of the expedition. They probably intended from the first to force it to go where they wanted. They succeeded in getting John Drake, the nephew of Francis, made captain of one of the ships; and the youngest William, William II's son, was wished upon Fenton, and installed in the flagship as second-in-command. Here were seeds of inevitable disaster: for from the start the two halves of the command were pulling in entirely different directions!

Fenton's masters—Leicester, Burghley and the Muscovy Company—were of course the most powerful people in the land. But they were not afloat in the expedition. Young Drake and young Hawkins, on the other hand, were on the spot; and both, though very young, were very forceful, forming around them an anti-Fenton party with their confident talk of halcyon days in the *Golden Hind*, of *Acapulcos* and other treasure ships, only awaiting the bold men who would dare the Straits of Magellan to win them. And poor old Fenton, only a soldier at best, and far from sure of himself, was not very clever at resisting. In fact he failed completely and finally had to return home with nothing accomplished. He made one somewhat futile attempt to leave William Hawkins behind, sailing off without him. But John Drake, in his little ship the *Francis* picked him up and brought him back to the *Leicester*.

Fenton of course had one huge advantage which, had he used it properly, should have been decisive. He was the General— the accredited leader—and anyone who went to the length of disobeying him was in theory simply a rebel and a traitor. So William could not openly oppose him, any more than Doughty could *openly* have opposed Drake.

Things, then, went from bad to worse. Fenton failed to find his north-west passage—naturally, because it is not there. He then went south as far as Brazil, where was the parting of the ways—south-east for Good Hope, south-west for the Magellan Straits.

But here the thing developed into an unseemly wrangle. Fenton, like all weak men, blustered and lost his temper: William III (who has left a record) kept his—largely no doubt because, not being the boss, he could not afford to lose it.

There followed, according to William, an unpleasantness which lasted for months, boiling up into a good old Elizabethan slanging match. William's account of it is overlong: all that is given here is the final row when they reached the Downs. (The dashes, by the way, are not an attempt of a prudish editor to protect the ears of the modest modern reader from crude Elizabethan expletives. They merely mark the fact that the surviving manuscript[1] has been badly damaged by fire.)

> The XXVII of Juyn we ankered in the downes wheare I was re-served with [put back into] Irons from the shore lest I sholde go to my lorde . . . The letter which I had wrytten to my lorde was opened and I was kept from sending it by the Generall. And two dayes before that the Generall, coming from the poope, commanded me in his anger to the Bilbowes wythout any cause whye: at wch manyfest wrong . . ., perceiving hym to have no reason in hys dealynge, kneeling uppon my knees I appealed to the Queenes matie, praying hym also to follow her mats Comyssion, or ells I said unto hym that he must looke to aunswere this wronge: at wch appeale I called the whole ship to wytnes: whereat he made but a tushe, neyther putting of [f] his cap or using any other reverence at all:

---

[1] B.M. MS. Otho E. VIII. Where the sense is clear blanks have been filled in in square brackets.

but wyth vile speches towardes me sayed that if I spoke one worde
more he woulde dashe me in the teeth, and called me villeyn sclave
and errant knave with many more vile wourdes, the wytnessing
whearof I refere to the whole companye . . .

Poor William is at a sad disadvantage, seeing that, after
all, Fenton as C.-in-C., can certainly get him hanged for
mutiny!

He now goes on with his story. The same day, it appears, the
General went into William's cabin and confiscated his pistols.
William protested, saying that he was only doing his duty, being
more interested in the success of the voyage than people like
Fenton!—which was, at best, a thoroughly cheeky thing for a
youngster to say to his superior. Anyway, it enraged Fenton
who replied, 'I know your kind well enough. You and your
precious pals, if you had had your way, wouldn't have gone
either by the Good Hope or the Straits. But', he added, 'I have
three strings to my bow that you know nothing of.' 'I only know
of one string', retorted William, 'and it's different from all
yours, which are *rotten*!'[1] 'Pah!' quoth Fenton, 'I know *your*
string, and it's an impossible one. Sir Francis Drake and his
cronies know full well that they'll never be able to repeat it. He
played the thief and pirate! Do you suppose *I'll* stoop to that?
No, I know how to make my voyage without any of your blasted
advice!' Then he called William a thief in so many words, to
which the young man replied, 'You may say such things now
when I can't answer back, but when we get home we shall see
how you justify it. When we set out, we were both gentlemen—'
'Gentlemen, forsooth!' cried Fenton, 'I'm a better gentleman
than you'll ever be!'

> *Hawkins.* What make you of me, then?
> *General.* A knave, villeyn and a Boye!
> *Hawkins.* If I weare at home, I woulde not be afearde to follow you
> in anny grounde in Englande: but heare in this place for quyetness
> sake I let it passe and will beare every wronge, be it never so
> great.
> *Gen.* Wilt thoe so?
> *Haw.* Yea, truelye!

[1] Fenton's 'three strings' were (a) to reach the Pacific by the (non-existent)
Passage at 40°N. (b) To try further north still. (c) To go *via* the Cape of Good
Hope. William's 'string' was to go *via* the Magellan Strait.

> Then the General woulde have drawen his longe knife and have
> stabbed Mr Hawkins, and, intercepted of that, he tooke up his longe
> staffe and therewith was ronnyng at Hawkins, but the Master, Mr.
> Bannester, Mr. Cotton and Symon Fernandez stayed his ffurie . . .
> *Haw.* Truelye, General, in this place yo're a justice [the law is on
>   your side]. But . . . he that cannot hold his handes heare is not
>   worthie of the place. . . . So let it go!

Au fond probably William was in the wrong. He was skating
on very thin ice: in fact, playing the Doughty (in reverse) to
Fenton's Drake (see pp. 102–3 above). For where Doughty had
been trying to prevent Drake from entering the Pacific for
plunder, William was trying to force Fenton to do just that
thing. Fortunately for William, Fenton was no Drake: for had
he been, in all probability William would have been a Doughty!

Incidentally John Drake did not come home with Fenton.
Instead, he actually rebelled, and made for the Straits. But he
got no further than the River Plate, where he was captured, and
never came home.

Thereafter William III's name appears in no more records
before Armada Year. Perhaps his share in Fenton's débâcle had
not endeared him to the authorities. He does not appear among
the officers said in a list of 1586 to be serving in that year. Nor
is his name mentioned in any list of 1587. Yet he may have been
employed in the latter year. It was then, we recall, that Drake
slipped out of Plymouth and made his famous 'singeing' raid on
the Iberian coast: and after he had got safely away, a ship was
dispatched to find him, and to tell him not to proceed against the
Spaniards. That ship never made contact with him. Instead it
picked up a rich prize and brought it safely home. It was clearly
a Hawkins ship, but only one authority mentions her commander's name. This authority is one of John's more scurrilous
detractors, and he says that the ship's captain was 'a base son of
Hawkins'—meaning from the context John Hawkins. Now nowhere else is there any trace of John's having had a base son at
all. Indeed, from what we know of him it is highly improbable
that he ever had one. He was happily married, and infidelity
was quite foreign to his known nature. Yet John's vilifier evidently meant to assert that the man in charge of that ship was *a*

Hawkins: and there was such a ship, which did do what he asserts. Who then was this Hawkins? It was almost certainly not John's only *legitimate* son Richard, for had it been, someone would almost certainly have connected him with the incident. In fact he would probably have mentioned it himself in *The Observations*. The chances are, then, that it was not John's son, but his nephew, William III, who already had among certain of the Hawkinses' enemies the reputation of being 'base' in quite another sense of that word—not illegitimate but just unworthy. This would be, admittedly, an unkind thing to say of William, but it was just the kind of thing that a Hawkins ill-wisher *might* have said. Incidentally the prize in question was credited to the Hawkins family.

If, then, this argument is sound, *something* which William III did during this crucial year is known, though there is nothing particularly glorious, or even creditable, about it; unless we suppose, as we well may, that the captain of that Hawkins ship did not try very hard to find Drake. In that case William, if it *was* William, may be said to have made a real contribution to his country's good, because the expedition which he *failed* to stop was an immense contribution to England's safety!

So we come to Armada Year: and here William III certainly reappears. In that year every true Englishman rallied to the great cause: nor did the Government think fit to exclude from service any English seaman. (The slightly egregious Edward Fenton himself was given a ship, and quite an important one too —the Queen's Ship *Mary Rose*, of 600 tons.) He was attached, like Richard Hawkins, to John's own squadron, and he twice receives honourable mention in the mêlée at Gravelines. The ship assigned to William was the *Griffin*, of 200 tons, one of the larger merchantmen assigned to Drake's Western Squadron. So he certainly saw service during the whole action. When the fleet was divided into four squadrons, he probably sailed with John's division (though we are not expressly told so), and therefore followed him into the close fighting at Gravelines. These bigger merchant ships of the original Western Squadron were specially picked ships, armed on the scale of Queen's Ships. So the *Griffin* was sufficiently heavily gunned to make her presence felt, though no exploits of hers have survived.

b. E.I.C. CAPTAIN

Now comes the long gap in our knowledge of the youngest William. Indeed, possibly, we may never come up with him again, as has already been hinted. After the great fight of 1588 there is no more mention of him at all in all the annals of the Anglo-Spanish war. He falls clean out of it. Of course he may have died, either from drowning, from violent or from natural death; or he may just have done nothing more to bring him again on to the page of history. On the other hand, though, he may have had before him a very distinguished career in another milieu altogether. And the present writer, for one, believes that he had. He believes, in short, that the captain of the *Hector*, a unit of the third fleet which sailed under the aegis of the East India Company in 1607, was that same William III who had had a row with Fenton in 1582 and had commanded the *Griffin* in the Channel in 1588.

And why not? Because Sir John Laughton thought, towards the end of the nineteenth century, that this man was another William Hawkins altogether? Well, coincidences do happen in history no less than in everyday life. But it does seem to this author a mistake to insist upon coincidence when such is entirely unproven. There is no earthly reason why the young seaman-leader of 1588 should not have become, in 1607, a middle-aged captain in the East Indian Company. In the matter of age, it fits well enough. Supposing that, in 1588, he was twenty-eight years old—and he was then, if anything, less— he would, by 1607 be only forty-seven: and the Company was not particularly fond of appointing youngsters to the responsible posts of captain in their ships. Again, Laughton's William Hawkins is known to have departed this life in 1613; even then only fifty-three years old if he was Fenton's Hawkins. After all, the name of Hawkins, still less of William Hawkins, is not so common as all that. If the name had been Smith or Jones, perhaps coincidence would be admissible because not so very curious after all. In this author's view, in fact, it is not the historian's task to prove that the two were the same man: it is rather his task, if he can, to prove that they were different men!

By the same token, this author has never been impressed by the school of criticism which maintains that the well-known Stratford actor did not write the plays: but that another and otherwise unknown man named William Shakespeare did!

The assumption here, therefore, is that the two men are identical. And at once there occurs some kind of explanation as to why we have that blank in our knowledge stretching from 1588 to 1607, or rather from 1595 to 1607, because we know from Sir John's will that he was still alive in the former year. One thing which is certain about the captain of the *Hector* is that he must have spent some time, probably some years, out of England and very likely in the Levant. For when we pick him up again he is an Englishman possessed of a very rare qualification. He can speak Turkish fluently—so fluently that he has been entrusted by his Sovereign, now James I, with a letter of introduction to the Grand Khan, or Great Mogul, in India. To attain such fluency, a long sojourn in the East is indicated, far away from England, and therefore far away from the Anglo-Spanish War. Nor is there anything strange in the fact that he is now a servant of the East India Company. It is true that none of the other Hawkinses had been that, though a little later (as we saw) Richard was to be in the running for an E. I. C. appointment. But then, for as long as the war with Spain lasted, the other Hawkinses had their hands very full. Besides, there *was* no E. I. C. until after William II and John were dead, while Richard was still a prisoner in Spanish hands. In fact, in 1600, when the Company was formed, there *was* no Hawkins of Plymouth available to take an interest in it, except of course William III, if (as we are assuming) he was still alive and available. Indeed— if he were—it is just the kind of undertaking in which we should expect a Hawkins to interest himself, not having much left to do at home.

There survive three writings from the pen of Hawkins of the *Hector*. The first is the captain's log-book, written as he accompanied the Third Fleet of the E. I. C. to sail for India. The second continues straight on from the first. It is William's report to his directors of his adventures *in* India, and it carries on his story after he leaves India and up to a few days before his death. The third and last document is a discourse, also penned for the benefit of the Company, on what contemporary life at the Court of the Great Mogul was like.

These papers reveal in no uncertain way several distinctive Hawkins characteristics; reminiscent particularly of John. Both are men of supreme courage, and of a very ready kind of courage too: quick to see and to grasp, and quick to act when action is necessary. Like John too, William has developed in a very high degree what we may call the Art of Diplomacy, which made him—again like John—a most successful negotiator in difficult circumstances. There is also something of the John Hawkins charm: he can win, and keep, friends in the most unlikely places. Finally, there is something of the John Nicholson, the Livingstone, the Lawrence of Arabia about him: he can get on famously with people rather less civilized than himself—or should one say *differently* civilized? Here he is very like his grandfather, old William. And this is as it should be, because where William I was among the first of England's overseas traders, William III was among the very first of England's Ambassadors and Empire-builders.

It was on March 28, 1607 that William joined his ship the *Hector* in the Downs, and on April 1st, with the Admiral, the *Dragon* (Captain Keelinge) in company, they left that anchorage. In those far-off days there seemed to be all the time in the world, and they did not reach the Cape until nearly the end of the following December, when they dropped anchor in Saldanha Bay. On the first day of the New Year they got away and sailed along the coast of Africa. By February 19th they were in the Bay of St Augustine, on the south-west coast of Madagascar. Incidents happened almost daily, but William's log is, on the whole, strictly factual. That of the General, Keelinge, is somewhat less so. Thus, on the 20th, when William has nothing to record, we learn from Keelinge that 'George Evans (one of the *Hector*'s company) was shrewdly bitten with an Alegarta.'[1] but neither mentions poor George's ultimate fate. All the way along both men collect water and flesh—the *Hector* secured '5 calves, 2 sterres, 3 cows, 3 sheep and 1 lambe at Augustine,' and, when they can procure them, 'limons' (at one place they bought 200 of them for a penny knife!). In that same bay, how-

[1] *Purchas His Pilgrimes*, vol. II., p. 511 (Maclehose Edition).

ever, Keelinge suffered the material loss of two anchors. Yet William at least always played the game. He went ashore on the day that the alligator got George and, finding an empty native boat, left in it 'some beades and trifles . . . to allure the naturalle'.

At another place they had some pretty good fishing, taking 'within one houre and a halfe 6,000 small and good fish—Cavallos'. Another day they went ashore and tried to bag an elephant, putting seven or eight musket balls into him,

> but being near night we were constrayned aboord, without effecting our purposes on him.

A few days later there is entered in Keelinge's log the mysterious words, 'Here we found the beautiful beast'—in a paragraph all by itself. And soon afterwards, 'I found certain Spiders whose webb was perfect good, and strong as silke.'

After a time they came to a Portuguese town whose Governor appears to have been a bit of a humorist,

> Afternoone, I saluted the Towne with five Pieces of Ordnance. The Governor sent me a Goate. I presented the Governor with three yards of Stemmel-cloath, one blue Calico, one piece (stocked), one Barrell and two sword blades. The Governor sent me a Goate.

But if we pause to chronicle such matters whenever they occur, we shall never arrive in India: for both accounts are full of them. We must then regard them as the merest samples of things important enough to them at the time, but simply incidental to a voyage through virtually unknown seas, and of but small relevance compared with what happened when, on August 27th, they at length reached Surat, on the west coast, some 200 miles north of Bombay. On the 28th, William came ashore in the *Hector*'s pinnace.

c. THE AMBASSADOR

Once landed, his troubles began: for he found himself in a new world where everything was strange to him. One thing he very soon discovered was that no business whatever could be done with anyone, from the lowliest customs-house officer to the Great Mogul himself, until one had contrived to press a present upon him—great or small according to the status of the person one dealt with.

He found the local native merchants very kind and affable, as were the ordinary people whom he met in the streets. Yet from the first he discovered that he had enemies: ruthless men who would murder him as soon as look at him. There were two classes of these 'natural foes' whom he ran up against at once. They were, first, the Portuguese, who were madly jealous of all Europeans other than themselves, and especially those who were attempting to trade in the country. Second, were the Jesuit priests who always aided and abetted the Portuguese. They had long since secured a foothold, which they were assiduously enlarging all the time. His other principal opponents, as he was gradually to discover, were the nobility of the land; and mostly the Mohammedan nobility who, once he reached his goal at the Great Mogul's court, were also insanely jealous of him, fearing that he would get the ear of the potentate and upset their own nefarious schemes.

It was uphill work all the way. Once his ship had departed he was left with no fellow-Englishmen except for one merchant named William Finch: who, however, for a long time was of no use to him because he was sick, nigh unto death. He also had a personal servant, a staunch lad named Nicholas Ufflett, who stayed with him throughout, and one boy. When William at length left Surat on his long, difficult and dangerous journey to Agra, he left Finch behind, now completely recovered, as his representative in charge of the factory which he had set up there.

From the first, however, the local representatives of the Great Mogul robbed him unmercifully, always with fair words but with foul deeds, causing his stock-in-trade to be removed, 'for safe keeping', into the Custom House at Surat. And most of this he never saw again in spite of his most desperate endeavours. The Portuguese merchants were a good deal worse, constantly seeking to poison him, and, failing in that, making deliberate attempts to murder him in cold blood. The Jesuit fathers invariably stood four-square behind them, giving them spiritual countenance, and often active assistance too.

But William survived, partly from a never-ceasing vigilance, partly by sheer guts. There were two principal plots against his life, both Jesuit-inspired, with Portuguese personnel. On the first occasion he was invited by an apparently innocent and friendly Indian merchant to witness the freighting of a ship of his. These freightings were common excuses for a party: so William accepted the invitation. But there were two Portuguese frigates moored in the harbour, and from these, unknown to him at first, there came

> three gallant fellowes to the tent where I was, and some fourtie followers Portugals. The three gallants . . . armed with coats of Buffe downe to the knees, their Rapiers and Pistols by their sides, demanded for the English Captaine, upon the hearing of which I arose and told them that I was the man.

Then, quietly drawing his sword, he faced them—as we may be very sure all our other Hawkinses would have done—and, as ever, cool courage told. Moreover, in any tight corner William always seemed able to find a friend:

> The Captain Mogol [the ship's owner] perceiving treason towards me, both he and his followers drew their weapons and, if the Portugals had not been the swifter, both they and their scattered crew (in returning to their frigate) had come short home.

The natives themselves were never hostile or treacherous: for William knew how to deal with them, and they, knowing William, liked what they knew.

The second time the same combination attacked him, they did so at his house near the Customs, 'some 30 or 40 of them', bringing with them their Jesuit allies, 'to animate the soldiers and to give them absolution.' But William had converted his house into a miniature fortress, and they did not dare to attack it with its faithful four defenders. Then William got his own back. He complained to the Governor of the town, an official with whom he had been careful to establish good relations. This Governor was not one of the nobility, but very likely an ex-merchant himself: and he 'presently sent out word to the Portugals that, if they came into the Citie armed againe, at their own peril be it'. So, by dint of forethought and diplomatic dealings with potential admirers, he escaped again.

But now at last, after he had been waiting for several months in Surat, there came to him a much more important personage, who was, throughout, to prove his worst and most persistent ill-wisher. The man was Mocreb Chan, and he was Viceroy of the whole district of Cambaya in which Surat was situated. This fellow was evidently a most disreputable character, who invariably fawned upon William when in his company, taking from him all the presents he could afford to offer, yet hanging like grim death on to his goods in the Customs House. On William stating his business, Mocreb Chan answered in honeyed terms that it was not in his power to give the Englishman trading-rights in the territory of his Viceroyalty. But if he would care to undertake the dangerous journey to Agra—about the same distance from Surat as Inverness is from London—he could put his request to the fount of all power, the Great Mogul himself: imagining, it would seem, that it would be a simple matter to intercept and murder him on the road. But this, of course, was just the journey that William had come all these thousands of miles to make. So, not revealing that he had any suspicion of the man's good faith, he accepted the idea with alacrity.

Again, however, he took all possible precautions. Taking advantage of Mocreb Chan's saying one day that he could not furnish an armed guard for the road, he remarked that he would be quite happy to provide his own. One of the endless local wars was raging in the Deccan, and this country lay right on his route. Fortunately, however, the e.i.c. never kept him short of money, so that he could always hire a sufficient bodyguard: and, beginning by now to know the country, he was prudent enough to engage a strong force of roving Pathans, then as now a warlike people, among the best fighters in all India, and notoriously trustworthy—if they approved of him—to the man who was hiring them. This too stood him in good stead because he discovered on the way another of Mocreb Chan's agreeable little plots to destroy him. The Viceroy suborned (as he thought) two of William's personal servants to set upon him one morning and slay him. But one of the two—William's coachman, who was daily exposed to his master's habitual charm—gave the plot away the evening before: indeed had, it seems, taken Mocreb's money with no intention whatever of hurting a hair of William's head. Later, he exchanged his Pathans for a new party of the same race whose captain, having been imprisoned by the

Portuguese, was their deadly enemy: and he proved a firm and trusted admirer of William. So at length, on April 16, 1609, having already been in the country for eight months, he reached Agra in safety. His courage, forethought and adroitness had brought him through in triumph.

Now, faced with altogether bigger game, he still needed all these qualities. The Great King at that time was Jehángir, son of the formidable Akbar Khan who had died in 1605. But he, it would seem, was not nearly so formidable, being, as a rule, quite pleasant to talk to—if he took to a man—and naturally of weak will-power, being—as William was soon to discover, only too prone to listen to the person or persons who for the moment had his ear.

William got off to a good start. His masters, the Directors of the Company, were far-sighted men who knew enough about the East to realize the importance to their representative of the outer man. They had therefore supplied him with a gorgeous set of robes, to be worn on the occasion of the first interview. It was 'scarlet and violet in colour, with a cloak lined with taffeta, pointed with silver laces'.[1] Nothing like a portrait of William III has survived, but one imagines a man of good physique with, surely, a good presence about him. No doubt, in that Oriental Court where the men on the whole were not of great stature, he made that presence felt: and the Great King seems to have fallen for him at once, though William was not the man to boast about such things, and does not do so here.

> After salutation done, with a most kind and smiling countenance he bade me most heartily welcome, upon which speech I did my obeysance and dutie again. Having His Majestie's Letter[2] in my hand, he called me to come neare unto him, stretching downe his hand from the Seat-Royall where he sate in great Majestie something high, for to be seen of the people: receiving very kindly the Letter of me, viewing the Letter a prettie while, both the Seale, and the manner of making it up, he called for an old Jesuite that was there present to read it, who discommended the stile, saying it was basely penned, writing Vestra without Maiestie.

Ubiquitous Order of Jesus!—even here seeking to minimize the effect of the letter. But the potentate was under the eye and the

---

[1] *The Gateway to India*, by A. R. Ingram (O.U.P., 1938, p. xviii).
[2] i.e. King James I's.

charm of the Englishman, and did not heed the criticism. Instead, having discovered that this handsome stranger spoke Turkish—a language with which he was very familiar himself— he there and then carried him off to his more private apartments, where they had a chat which lasted for two whole hours.

Thereafter William grew in favour, being sent for daily by the King, who loved to hear him speak of his travels. But there were inconveniences as well as advantages in this intimacy. For one thing, the other courtiers and the nobility grew wildly jealous at the notice taken of a mere foreigner, while his old foes, the Portuguese and the Jesuits, fairly ground their teeth. Another thing was that the Great Mogul evidently grew so fond of William's company that he wanted him to stay at the Court for keeps! To this William made the tactful reply that His Majesty King James, whose Ambassador he was, would be expecting him home to report the success of his mission, and especially an answer in the affirmative to King James' request for trading facilities. To that Jehángir replied, 'You will do your King much better service—and me too—if you will stay here *as* Ambassador until your King shall send out a successor to you. If you will do that, I will grant him his request—and yours— and allow you to set up your permanent factory at Surat!'

He followed this up with promises of a much more personal nature. First, he was most insistent that William 'should choose a woman from among his ladies, and marry her, if I would'. He replied diplomatically, refusing because, as a Christian, he ought to marry a Christian. But here Jehángir was one too much for him. From his harem he produced a fair Armenian belonging to the ancient Church of Armenia, whose father Mabarique Sha (or Mabarik Khan) had been in great favour with Akbar, Jehángir's father. At the same time William was offered what amounted to a starting salary of £3,200 a year, with generous yearly rises. This was of course tempting, being the kind of transaction which his masters of the Company expected and encouraged— that their employees should (as William himself wrote to them) 'feather my neast' in lieu of salary. He *was* feathering it too: for, in modern terms, he was to receive the equivalent of not less than £64,000 the first year, with progressively more in subsequent years!

At the same time the Grand Khan showed his partiality to William in another way. Finding (as all foreigners invariably did) a difficulty in pronouncing 'Hawkins', he changed it to 'English Chan', or in his own tongue, 'Inglis Khan', which means English Lord, and which bore with it in Persia the rank of Duke. All these marks of favour were due, of course, to the personal impression which William made upon the Great Mogul. All this time he had been at the grave disadvantage of being unable to *buy* favour by the normal Indian method of presenting gifts. He was, for instance quite unable to keep up with Mocreb Chan in this curious competition. For that worthy still held William's goods in the Custom House at Surat, and still, from time to time, selected the most intriguing of them and sent them to the King—with his love and loyalty naturally! But still William succeeded in holding his own by virtue of the attraction he inspired whenever he was with Jehángir. He could not, however, *always* be 'in the Presence'.

Meanwhile, William got married. But, being a moral, God-fearing man like all his kin, he was quite set on doing the thing properly, using Christian rites too, and not those of Mahomet: Protestant ones too, and not Catholic ones. And there were no Protestant ministers in India! He had been informed, however, that failing an ordained priest, *any* English Protestant could tie the knot. So he was solemnly married by his faithful Nicholas Ufflett, the only Englishman now remaining with him, his boy, Steven Gravenor, having just died. He thought this was lawful,

> till I met with a preacher that came with Sir Henry Middleton, and, he showing me the error, I was new marryed againe: for ever after I lived content and without feare, she being willing to goe where I went, and live as I lived.

It was always, however, *Gulielmus contra Mundum*, with his enemies constantly plotting his overthrow, using any means that came their way, however discreditable. The struggle indeed was ding-dong, especially as his king of trumps was so utterly unreliable. So William was sometimes right up, and at other times right down. Once at least he succeeded in getting Mocreb Chan sent for to Agra, dismissed from his offices and imprisoned: and, no less than twice, he succeeded in getting Jehángir to confirm the establishment of the Surat factory. But then

Mocreb Chan bought his way out of gaol and regained the King's ear. So it all was to do again.

His Majesty was indeed a broken reed, all too ready to follow the counsel (as well as accept the gifts) of the latest comer. He made William endless promises—and meant them until the next man came along, when he broke them without any compunction at all. At last, after nearly three years fraught with endless anxieties and vicissitudes, William found that he had had enough, and gave up in despair. It now became a question of getting out of the country with any of his possessions at all: for, once he left the Court and the shadow of the Great Mogul's protection, he was fair game to any of his would-be murderers. But then it occurred to him, ingenious fellow, that, though the Portuguese were for ever plotting to assassinate him while he stayed, they would probably go to great lengths to see him go! And so it proved. They arranged for him and his wife to proceed to Goa, their territory and their principal mart, thence to take one of their ships to Lisbon, and so to England.

So William, with his faithful Ufflett, departed unostentatiously from Agra. But before he could reach Goa he received news which made him materially alter his plans. Having got as far as Cambaya, he heard that Sir Henry Middleton, out from England on the 1610 voyage of the Company, was lying off Surat. He therefore sent Ufflett ahead, to get in touch with Sir Henry and arrange a meeting-place. On the January 26, 1612, he reached Middleton's fleet with his wife and much of his recently-acquired wealth. Sir Henry received him with joy.

d. JEHANGIR KHAN

William's third and last memorandum, addressed to his Directors, is entitled 'A brief Discourse of the Strength, Wealth and Government, with some Customes of the Great Mogul: which I have both seen and gathered by his Chief Officers and Overseers of all his Estate'. It appears in *Purchas His Pilgrimes*. Its interest is great and lasting, especially to historians of the Indian sub-continent. But already it is somewhat far removed from the story of our first Ambassador, and still further removed from that of the Hawkins family. So here we must be content with only one facet of it—with that portion which deals with Jehángir Khan's character, since that at least had some influence upon both our first Empire-Builder and our last Hawkins of Plymouth.

The Great Mogul was fantastically wealthy. In terms of modern spending-power his annual income, according to William's reckoning, was around five hundred million pounds. William breaks up this total into things like 'treasure', 'beasts, wild and domesticated', and 'wives' (all told, 500 of them): but here we shall not follow him. The reason for all this wealth lay in the fact that he was in effect the heir of all his nobility. Upon the death of each one of them he had first claim on all his possessions, though normally he took only such articles as attracted his eye, handing the rest back to the man's heirs. Even so, however, he accumulated so much that it had become the custom to divide his treasure up into 365 parts and, every day, to bring one part before him for his inspection.

But clearly it was not good for any man's soul to own riches in such vast quantities, and in Jehángir's case it led him on to abysmal cruelties, many of which were scarcely human, let alone humane. As a courtier for three years, William had every opportunity for observing some of them. He was feared by all his subjects because his power of life and death over them was absolute: but he was not loved by any of them.

At one time, for instance, he developed a passion for elephant-fights, holding them as often as four times a week. In these both men and beasts were often slain. If a man was hurt in such a fight, the King commanded him to be cast alive into the river, saying, with sinister logic, 'as long as he lives he will do little else but curse me.'

He also doted upon seeing men executed, especially by being torn in pieces by elephants. In William's time he lost his temper with his secretary one day, gave him a mortal wound with his sword and then delivered him to be torn in pieces by the huge beasts. Another time, the keeper of the King's china, a great friend of William's, had the misfortune to break a dish for which the King had a great attachment. When he discovered it, he had the wretched man thrashed by his fifty official executioners until he was all but dead, and then thrown into perpetual imprisonment.

Then he had a craze for lions. One day a noble Pathan made the mistake of bragging of his prowess in the King's presence. It chanced that just then the King was inspecting 'a wylde lyon, a very great one', held on a chain by twelve men. 'Go,' said Jehángir, 'wrastle and buffet with this lyon!' The Pathan replied that to go unarmed against so strong a beast was no trial of his manhood. But the King would not be moved, and the man had to do as he was bid. He stood up to the great beast, without weapons, for a creditable time, but was at last knocked down and devoured. This gave the bloodthirsty tyrant an idea—unarmed man *v.* lion! So he sent for ten of his horsemen who happened to be on guard that night, and sent them in, one by one, to 'buffet the lyon'. All were grievously mauled, and three of them died. But then the King's whimsy took a happier turn. Instead of having fierce, full-grown animals, he conceived the idea of taking the baby lions as they were born, and having them house-trained,

> so ever after, untill my coming away, some 15 young lyons . . . played one with another before the King, frisking between men's legs, and no man hurt in a long time.

He was no more tender to his family than he was to his subjects. One day he caused all his brothers' children to embrace Christianity—not on account of any zeal for that faith, as the Jesuits at first fondly thought, but because he feared they would oust his own family: and 'every Moslem so loathed every Christian that [he thought] his rivals would thereby lose all chance of having any subjects'—a subtle piece of wickedness!

But his crowning iniquity was what he did to one of his own children. He had a little son called Sultan Sheriar, a child of phenomenal pluck. One day the King asked him to go somewhere with him. The boy agreed, but the King got it into his head that the child was a little unwilling. Thereupon the King set upon him and knocked him about so mercilessly that any other lad in the world would have blubbered, or at least wept. But not Sultan Sheriar: he took the blows without a sound. Then his father asked him why he did not cry, to which the little fellow replied, 'My Nana told me that princes *don't* cry when they are beaten: so, since then, I have never cried; and nothing, not even death, shall make me.' This strange (and to us pathetic) answer so enraged the brutal father that he sent for a bodkin and thrust it right through Sheriar's cheeks. But still, though he lost much blood, he refused to weep. 'There is,' William concludes, 'great hope of this child to exceed all the rest.' But the boy never came to the throne.

Evidently William was profoundly impressed by the power and the wealth of the Great Mogul whom he knew: but evidently too he regarded him as being at once a difficult, dangerous and unpredictable acquaintance. He was personally fortunate in his dealings with him, because from the first the spoilt monster yielded to his charm and he never suffered any unpleasantness at his hands. Yet he was highly conscious of the danger all the time. Round the King's seat in the Throne-Room there was stretched a cord of crimson; and to the area inside it were summoned all who enjoyed the King's favour. William had secured the entrée there on his first visit, and had kept it throughout—until, one day, his enemies had prevailed with the King, perhaps only temporarily, and he had found himself left outside. And then he concluded that the moment had come to make himself scarce. Until such time as the prestige of the King of England was sufficient to protect his own Ambassador, Agra was no place for him!

But now he was safe. He remained for some time in the Indian Ocean, first joining Captain John Saris, in command of the 1611 fleet. He finally left for home in the *Thomas*, arriving in Saldanha Bay on April 21, 1613. On that day he received letters from the Directors, and thereafter kept his own report to them up to date until May 20 of the same year. Then, quite suddenly, his journal ends abruptly. He was dead: but the ship was so near home that his wife brought the body back.

The poor little lady, disconsolate, was now stranded in a foreign land. But she was not without friends, because not without funds. She had with her some very fine diamonds, valued at £4,000. So she had no difficulty in finding another husband in the person of one Gabriel Towerson, a servant of the Company.

With him she went out East again in 1617, when she and her new husband revisited Agra—the Great Mogul still being Jehángir. There, fortunately for herself, she resolved to stay awhile with her own people. But Towerson returned home, to be sent out once more as Principal Factor in the Moluccas. And here he was judicially murdered by the Dutch in the dastardly Massacre of Amboyna, in February 1623.

Though the tide had turned against William during his last days in India, he certainly had not failed. He had, all alone, succeeded in establishing diplomatic relations with the high overlord of the whole country: and the trading-station at Surat remained thereafter inviolate, a memorial to the fact. For already the writ of Jehángir ran sluggishly as one neared the coast and the sea-ports, whose real rulers were well aware that William had dwelt for nearly three years in the Court at Agra, and had left it a richer man than he was when he went there: and that, for the moment, was enough for them. For England's sea-power was even now beginning to make itself felt in the Indian Ocean. In 1611 Captain Thomas Best had utterly defeated the Portuguese in battle near Surat, and all else quickly followed that victory. In fact, before ever William left the Indian Ocean for the last time, the British Raj had already been born; and William Hawkins—our William III—was the man largely responsible for its birth.

Some Hawkins Descendants

ໜໜໜ

THE main male line of William II, it seems, died out after two generations, though one of his daughters, who married John Newton of Crabaton, had children, descendants of whom probably survive. This author, however, knows nothing of them.

Of the other branch of the family—John's and Richard's—there is a much longer story to tell. Mary Hawkins, in her *Plymouth Armada Heroes* (1888) has a table which is carried down almost to the present day. But it is by no means complete even where descendants named Hawkins are concerned: and she omitted almost all those with other surnames, i.e. those descended from female Hawkinses.

The intention here is to pick out just a few of the more distinguished descendants who happen to be known to this author. He makes no claim to omniscience here, and there may well be more—and more distinguished ones—which are left out.

I. 'Serjeant' William Hawkins (*1673–1746*)

This man was probably great-grandson of Sir Richard. He was admitted a member of the Inner Temple in 1700, and became a serjeant-at-law in 1723. His main call to fame is his great work *The Treatise of the Pleas of the Crown*, which was *the* textbook on the subject all through the eighteenth century, during which it ran through five reprints. Another book of his which passed through many editions was an abridgement of *Coke's Institutes*.

II. 'Professor' William Hawkins (*1722–1801*)

Son of the last-named, he was educated at Pembroke College, Oxford, of which college he was Founder's Kin, being descended through his maternal grandmother from Thomas Tesdale. Boswell mentions him as 'one of the most distinguished *alumni* of Oxford', where in 1757 he was appointed to the Chair of Poetry. He was already ordained, and in 1764 was appointed to the lucrative Rectory of Whitchurch Canonicorum in Dorsetshire. In 1767 he was given a prebendal stall at Wells.

Throughout a long life he was a prolific writer of sermons and tracts, of poetry and even of drama. He had some reputation in his day, but is now completely forgotten by all but students of eighteenth-century literature. And that may be as well, because he was one of those somewhat presumptuous writers who thought that they could improve upon William Shakespeare. The latter's *Cymbeline* with his alterations, was played at Covent Garden Theatre in 1759 where it flopped badly. He did, however get a good notice from Oliver Goldsmith in the *Critical Review* on one play of his called *Aleppo*. He was still writing cheerfully up to 1801, when he had a fit while in Oxford, and died there.

John and Richard would have had no particular sympathy with these two descendants. But they would have had a good deal more for the two now to be mentioned.

III. Rear-Admiral Abraham Mills Hawkins (*1784–1857*)

His naval career fell within the period of the Napoleonic War. He had no very powerful influence, but he gradually worked his way up by merit. He was made a Lieutenant in 1807, but it was only in August 1812 that he had any real chance to distinguish himself. But when he had, he took it. While in the frigate *Horatio* he was sent, in command of four ship's boats, up a deep Norwegian fiord. Here, after a very hard fight, he captured a Danish schooner and a cutter, and brought them back to his ship. In the course of the action he received a severe wound in the right hand and another in the left arm. For this service he received a wound pension of £150 and was promoted to Commander's rank. He never recovered the full use of his right hand, and after 1814 active employment in the peacetime navy became very uncertain. He was, however, promoted Captain in 1835, and lived long enough to become Rear-Admiral on the Retired List in 1851. It was not exactly a great naval career, but it was well above the average, and both John and Richard, we may be sure, would have been proud of their descendant's prowess in the Norwegian fiord.

IV. Commodore John Croft Hawkins (*1798–1851*)

Only a distant cousin to the last-named, yet certainly a true decendant of the Hawkinses of Plymouth, this officer was just too young to make his mark in the Napoleonic War. So after it was over, and while still only a midshipman, he turned over in 1816 to the Bombay Marine, later to become the Royal Indian Navy. Here he saw a tremendous amount of service, in the Persian Gulf and elsewhere. He rose rapidly: in 1824 to Lieutenant, in 1831 to Commander. In 1832 he made a remarkable overland journey through Persia to India, receiving the special thanks of the Board of Control. In 1838 he surveyed much of the Euphrates, for which, in 1839, he was promoted Captain. As Commodore in the Persian Gulf he performed several feats of great personal daring, as when he tackled a noted pirate and brought him to book. Then, by a risky piece of diving he saved H.M.S. *Fox* from destruction. Nelson's old officer, Sir Henry Blackwood, spoke in glowing terms of his skill and energy which, he declared, had never been surpassed. Seven times he received the thanks of the Indian Government and three times that of the Home Government. He died at Bombay, comparatively young, esteemed as the most distinguished officer of his day in the Indian Service. He had many of the qualities of all the Plymouth Hawkinses: all of whom would in fact have been proud of him.

These four are all the Hawkinses that we shall name. But there are two others with different surnames who were none the less direct descendants of William I, John and Richard. And they deserve a mention.

V. Sir William Ellias Taunton, K.C. (*1774–1835*)

'Serjeant' William Hawkins had a sister named Catherine, whose great-grandson—six generations down from Sir Richard—was Sir William Elias Taunton, in his day a very distinguished legal figure. The son of a Clerk of the Peace for Oxford, he was a Scholar of Westminster and then of Christ Church, Oxford In 1793 he won the Chancellor's prize for the English Essay, after which, in 1799, he was called to the Bar, and joined the Oxford Circuit. In 1801 he was appointed a Commissioner of Bankrupts, and in 1806 became Recorder of Oxford. Made a K.C. in 1821, he was appointed a judge of the King's Bench in 1830 and knighted a few days later. He was a solid and valuable rather than a brilliant pleader, but on the Bench he scarcely had time to make his mark, since he died suddenly in 1835.

He wrote one widely-read pamphlet, *On the conduct of the respective Governments of France and Great Britain in the late negotiations for Peace*, and he did good work on the Records Commission for twelve years, from 1820 to 1832.

VI. Major-General Harold Victor Lewis, C.B., C.I.E., D.S.O., M.C. and Bar (*1887–1945*)

But the man whose career would have enthralled his Hawkins ancestors was a modern soldier of the great twentieth-century wars. He was the Judge's great grandson, and his name was Harold Victor Lewis. After an unsurpassed record at Sandhurst, from which he passed out first, gaining more awards than, up to that time, any other cadet had ever won, he joined the Indian Army on his twenty-first birthday in 1908. During the First World War he saw service on almost all the main fronts, gaining many distinctions and medals. He was in the first Indian battalion that went into action in Western Europe, where he was among the very few surviving officers. During the operations against the Germans in East Africa, he performed the remarkable feat of marching on foot all the way from the borders of Ethiopia in the northern hemisphere to the frontiers of Mozambique at 15°S.—not less than 1,000 miles through tropical Africa as the crow flies—and more than twice that distance as General von Lettow Vorbeck jinked. And before the war ended, though still a substantive Lieutenant, he had risen by brevet to the rank of Lieutenant-Colonel.

But his greatest achievements were performed before and during the first war and in the inter-war years following, on the North-West Frontier of India. 'Louisa'—as he was known throughout the Indian Army—had wonderful linguistic gifts, and could speak an unprecedented number of Indian dialects. He also had a unique love for, and understanding of, all the tribes on that remote frontier of Empire. To him they were almost his children: and to them he was almost their father. So, whenever any trouble, small or great, blew up along that remote border, the authorities, instead of sending out a punitive force to deal with it, gradually contracted the habit of saying to themselves, 'Ah! This is the moment to send for Louisa.' So he would go out into the wilds, with only one or two orderlies under him—or even with none at all—seeking out the trouble-makers (most of whom he already knew, personally and intimately), and holding quite informal conferences with them. Again and again he went to hidden areas where no other white man could venture to go and yet remain alive: and again and again he returned, not only unscathed but also with his mission fully done, and without a drop of blood shed. There was somewhere a most human link between Louisa and those wild Pathans, Mahsuds, Afridis and Mohmands. They loved him and trusted him, as of course he loved and trusted them. Here surely, was John Nicholson born anew. It would perhaps be unwise to stretch heredity too far: it was such a long way from Louisa to his ten-great-grandsire, William I. Yet were not old Hakluyt's words still true, still ringing down the centuries—*exact*!

> He used there such discretion, and behaved himself so wisely with those people that he grew into great familiarity and friendship with them.

When the second war came, Louisa had reached the rank of Major-

General. He was given a division, but those old legs which had once carried him all the way from Ethiopia to Mozambique were at last letting him down, and he had to forgo active service. Instead, they put him in charge of the Welfare of the whole sub-continent and of all the soldiers in it, British and Indian alike, so that, to the last, he could 'use discretion and behave himself wisely.' He died suddenly in September 1945—on the very day he went on to the Retired List.

God rest his gallant soul! He was this author's elder brother.

Index